Honduras

Richard Arghiris

Credits

Footprint credits

Editor: Felicity Laughton
Production and layout: Emma Bryers
Maps: Kevin Feeney

Managing Director: Andy Riddle
Commercial Director: Patrick Dawson
Publisher: Alan Murphy
Publishing Managers: Felicity Laughton, Nicola Gibbs
Digital Editors: Jo Williams, Tom Mellors
Marketing and PR: Liz Harper
Sales: Diane McEntee
Advertising: Renu Sibal
Finance and Administration: Elizabeth Taylor

Photography credits

Front cover: Stephen Wray / Shutterstock
Back cover: Dennis Sabo / Shutterstock

Printed in Great Britain by CPI Antony Rowe, Chippenham, Wiltshire

MIX
Paper from responsible sources
FSC® C013604
www.fsc.org

Every effort has been made to ensure that the facts in this guidebook are accurate. However, travellers should still obtain advice from consulates, airlines, etc, about travel and visa requirements before travelling. The authors and publishers cannot accept responsibility for any loss, injury or inconvenience however caused.

Publishing information

Footprint *Focus Honduras*
1st edition
© Footprint Handbooks Ltd
November 2011

ISBN: 978 1 908206 43 5
CIP DATA: A catalogue record for this book is available from the British Library

® Footprint Handbooks and the Footprint mark are a registered trademark of Footprint Handbooks Ltd

Published by Footprint
6 Riverside Court
Lower Bristol Road
Bath BA2 3DZ, UK
T +44 (0)1225 469141
F +44 (0)1225 469461
footprinttravelguides.com

Distributed in the USA by Globe Pequot Press, Guilford, Connecticut

The content of Footprint *Focus Honduras* has been taken directly from Footprint's *Central America Handbook* which was researched and written by Richard Arghiris and Peter Hutchison.

Contents

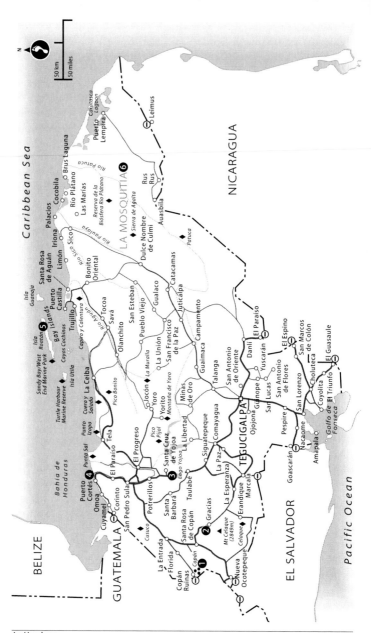

Sliced, spliced and spread across a mountainous interior, Honduras is a pleasantly challenging surprise that has developed in curiously disconnected zones. In the heart of the mountains Tegucigalpa epitomizes the Latin city – a chaotic celebration of colonial architecture divided by steeply sloping cobbled streets. By contrast, the republic's second and more modern city, San Pedro Sula, on the coastal lowland plain, has a neat matrix of calles and avenidas that seem rather dull by comparison.

A world away, the Bay Islands bask under sunny skies. Utila thrives on a throw-it-together-and-see-if-it-works existence. It's easily the cheapest place to learn to dive in the western hemisphere.

Honduras is the second largest Central American republic after Nicaragua, but its population is smaller than that of neighbouring El Salvador, the smallest country. Bordered by Nicaragua, Guatemala, El Salvador and a narrow coastal Pacific strip, it is the northern Caribbean coast and beautiful Bay Islands that are a natural focus and a prime destination for visitors.

Inland, the mountainous terrain creates natural obstacles to easy, direct travel around the country. It also means that, for trekking and hiking, there are great swathes of beautiful hillside, much of which is dotted with small communities, largely disinterested in the comings and goings of the few travellers who venture so far off the beaten track.

In October 1998 Hurricane Mitch deluged Honduras with torrential rain leaving an estimated 10,000 people dead and damage to almost all parts of the country. While the physical damage has been cleaned up, 13 years on the economic and social impact continues to ripple through the country.

Planning your trip

Where to go

With the popularity of the Bay Islands as a diving destination, mainland Honduras is often missed in the frenzied rush towards the sea. And, while the beauty of the islands cannot be overstated, picking a route that takes in some of the smaller towns of Honduras gives a far better understanding of the country as a whole.

The capital, **Tegucigalpa**, has an old, colonial sector and a new section with modern hotels, shopping malls and businesses. Across the Río Choluteca is Tegucigalpa's twin city, **Comayagüela**, the working heart of the city with the markets and bus terminals. Around the capital, there are colonial villages, old mining towns, handicraft centres and good hiking areas, including **Parque Nacional La Tigra**, which will make ideal trips for a day or two.

West of Tegucigalpa, near the border with Guatemala, is Honduras' premier Maya archaeological site **Copán**, where new discoveries continue to be made, and some fine Maya art can be seen. A short distance from the site, the well-restored town of **Copán Ruinas** is a colonial gem and, nearby, the site of **El Puente** is beginning to reveal treasures hidden for centuries. Closer to the capital, quiet colonial towns such as **Gracias** and graceful **Santa Bárbara** are the site of opal mines, Lenca indigenous communities and the **national park** of **Mount Celaque**. There is lots of good hiking in the vicinity of the popular colonial city of **Santa Rosa de Copán**. A good way to explore this more traditional part of the country is to pick a route, travel in short distances and soak up the calm and tranquillity.

From Tegucigalpa a paved highway runs north to **San Pedro Sula**, the second city of the republic and the country's main business centre. The road passes the old colonial capital of Comayagua and beautiful Lago Yojoa. Northwest of San Pedro Sula, the **north coast** has a number of centres of interest to the visitor. The main port is **Puerto Cortés**, to the west of which is **Omoa**, an increasingly popular beach and fishing village with an old fort, from which an overland route enters Guatemala. East of San Pedro Sula are **Tela**, a more established resort, and **La Ceiba**, a good base for visiting the nearby national parks of Pico Bonito and Cuero y Salado, whitewater rafting trips on the Río Cangrejal and departure point for the Bay Islands and La Mosquitia. Further east, **Trujillo**, sitting at the southern end of a palm-fringed bay, was once the country capital.

Curving in an arc off the cost near La Ceiba, the **Bay Islands** of **Utila**, **Roatán** and **Guanaja**, plus the smaller **Hog Islands**, are some of Honduras' main tourist destinations. Travellers visiting just one part of Honduras often pick the islands. The diving is excellent and Utila is currently the cheapest dive centre in the Caribbean. The islands also have good beaches.

Northeast of Tegucigalpa is the province of Olancho, an agricultural and cattle-raising area that leads eventually to the Caribbean coast at Trujillo. Juticalpa and Catacamas are the main towns, and the mountains of the district have cloud forest, hiking trails and beautiful conservation areas. Beyond Olancho is **La Mosquitia**, most easily reached from La Ceiba, which is forested, swampy and very sparsely populated. Efforts are being made to promote sustainable development among the Miskito and the Pech. Small-scale ecotourism initiatives have been set up in some coastal communities and inland, making for adventurous and rewarding travel where the main ways of getting around are by boat, small plane or on foot.

Don't miss ...

Honduras' short **Pacific coast** on the Gulf of Fonseca is little visited, other than en route to Nicaragua and El Salvador. The main towns in the region are **Choluteca** and, in the gulf, **Amapala**, on the extinct volcanic Isla del Tigre. Another route to Nicaragua is that east of the capital through the town of **Danlí**, which passes the Panamerican Agricultural School at Zamorano and the old mining town of **Yuscarán**.

When to go

Climate depends largely on altitude. In Tegucigalpa, at 1000 m, temperatures range from 4°C (January-March) up to 33°C (April-May). In the lowlands to the north, temperatures in San Pedro Sula range from 20°C to 37°C with the coolest months being from November to February. On the Caribbean the dry season stretches from February to June, while the heaviest rains fall between August and December. Inland, rain falls throughout the year, with the drier months being from November to April. Some of the central highland areas enjoy a delightful climate, with a freshness that makes a pleasant contrast to the humidity and heat of the lowland zones.

What to do

Adventure tourism
Mountain biking is increasingly popular as is horse riding around Copán. Hardcore adventure can be found in the swamp wetlands and tropical forests of Mosquitia, usually by taking an organized tour.

Scuba-diving
Diving off the Bay Islands has long been the number one attraction, with some of the best and most varied diving in Central America. PADI courses are among the cheapest in the world. Snorkelling is also excellent.

Nature tourism
Nature trips take advantage of the wide variety of national parks. Birders have known about the treasures of the country for years, but hikers and trekkers are beginning to venture out through the valleys and across the hills that are often shrouded in cloud forest.

Whitewater rafting
Rafting is growing steadily in Honduras with the hotspot being the River Cangrejal, close to La Ceiba, where Grade II, III and IV rapids test both the novice and experienced paddler. The sport is relatively new to Honduras and more sites are sure to be found in the coming years.

National parks

The extensive system of national parks and protected areas provides the chance to enjoy some of the best scenery Honduras has to offer, much of it unspoilt and rarely visited. The National Parks' Office, **Conama** ① *next to the Instituto Nacional Agrario, 4 Av, Colonia Alameda, in Tegucigalpa*, is chaotic but friendly and a good source of information. **Cohdefor** ① *10 Av 4 Calle NO, San Pedro Sula, T2253-4959*, the national forestry agency, is also much involved with the parks. Parks have different levels of services – see individual parks for details. Natural reserves continue to be established and all support and interest is most welcome. Parks currently in existence are **La Tigra**, outside Tegucigalpa (page 22), and the **Río Plátano** (page 108). Underdevelopment since 1987 are **Monte Celaque** (page 40), **Cusuco** (page 58), **Punta Sal** (page 68), **Capiro y Calentura** (page 73), **Montaña Cerro Azul-Meámbar** (page 55), **Montaña de Yoro** (page 74) and **Pico Bonito** (page 70). These parks have visitor centres, hiking trails and primitive camping. The following have been designated national parks by the government: **Montecristo-Trifinio** (page 43), **Santa Bárbara** (page 56), **Pico Pijol** (page 74), **Sierra de Agalta** (page 107) and **Montaña de Comayagua** (page 54). Wildlife refuges covered in the text are **Cuero y Salado** (page 71), **Las Trancas** (page 42) and **La Muralla-Los Higuerales** (page 105). For information on protected areas in the **Bay Islands**, see page 86.

Getting there

Air

Tegucigalpa, La Ceiba, San Pedro Sula and Roatán all have international airports. There are no direct flights to Tegucigalpa from Europe, but connecting flights can be made via Miami, then with **American Airlines** or **Taca**. There are flights to Tegucigalpa, San Pedro Sula and Roatán from Houston with **Continental** and services to Tegucigalpa from New York. **Taca** flies daily from Guatemala City and San Salvador, with connections throughout the region via El Salvador.

American Airlines fly daily from Miami, as do **Taca** and **Iberia**. There are also frequent services from San Pedro Sula. Services are also available with **Spirit Air** and **Delta**.

Road

There are numerous border crossings. With **Guatemala** to the west you can cross near Copán Ruinas at El Florido, on the Caribbean coast at Corinto or to the south at Agua Caliente. For **El Salvador** there are crossings at El Poy, leading to Suchitoto in the west, and Perquín leading to San Miguel and the east. For **Nicaragua**, the border post town of Guasale in the south leads 116 km on a very bad road to the Nicaraguan town of León, while the inland routes at Las Manos and El Espino guide you to Estelí and Matagalpa, in the northern hills. Crossing to Nicaragua through the Mosquitia coast is not possible – officially at least.

Taxes are charged on entry and exit at land borders, but the amount varies, despite notices asking you to denounce corruption. Entry is 60 lempiras and exit is 30 lempiras. Double is charged on Sunday. If officials make an excess charge for entry or exit, ask for a receipt. Do not attempt to enter Honduras at an unstaffed border. When it is discovered that you have no entry stamp you will either be fined US$60 or escorted to the border, and you will have to pay the guard's food and lodging; or you can spend a night in jail.

Sea

A regular weekly service departing Mondays at 1100 links Puerto Cortés with Mango Creek and Placencia, in Belize – see page 82 for details.

Getting around

Air

There are airstrips in all large towns and many of the cut-off smaller ones. Internal airlines include Isleña, www.flyislena.com (part of the Taca airlines group), Sosa and **Atlantic Air**. **Atlantic Air** serves La Ceiba, San Pedro Sula, Tegucigalpa, Roatán and Utila. **Sosa**, the largest domestic carrier, serves Roatán, Utila, Guanaja, San Pedro Sula, Tegucigalpa and other destinations in Honduras. La Ceiba is the main hub for domestic flights, especially for **Sosa** and **Atlantic**, and most flights to and from the islands stop there. Airport **departure tax** is US$37 (not charged if in transit less than nine hours). There is a 10% tax on all tickets sold for domestic and international journeys.

Road

Until recently, Honduras had some of the best roads in Central America. However, since the political crisis in 2009 many sections have become neglected and pitted with huge potholes, particularly between San Pedro Sula and Copán. Traffic tends to travel fast on the main roads and accidents are second only to Costa Rica in Latin America. If driving, take care and look out for speed bumps – *túmulos*, which are usually unmarked. Avoid driving at night; farm animals grazing along the verges often wander across the road. Total road length is now 15,100 km, of which 3020 km are paved, 10,000 km are all-weather roads and the remainder are passable in the dry season.

Bus There are essentially three types of service: local (*servicio a escala*), direct (*servicio directo*) and luxury (*servicio de lujo*). Using school buses, a *servicio a escala* is very slow, with frequent stops and detours and is uncomfortable for long periods. *Servicio directo* is faster, slightly more expensive and more comfortable. *Servicio de lujo* has air-conditioned European and Brazilian buses with videos.

Buses set out early in the day, with a few night buses running between major urban centres. Try to avoid bus journeys after dark as there are many more accidents and even occasional robberies.

If you suffer from motion sickness, the twisty roads can become unbearable. Avoid sitting at the back of the bus, take some water and sit by a window that will open. Minibuses are faster than buses, so the journey can be quite hair-raising. Pickups that serve out-of-the-way communities will leave you covered in dust (or soaked) – sit in or near the cab if possible.

Car Regular **gasoline/petrol** costs around US$3.60 per US gallon and US$3.25 for diesel. The **Pan-American Highway** in Honduras is in bad condition in parts. One reader warns to "beware of potholes that can take a car. They suddenly appear after 20 km of good road without warning." If hiring a car, make sure it has all the correct papers and emergency triangles, which are required by law.

Cycling Bicycles are regarded as vehicles but are not officially subject to entrance taxes. Bicycle repair shops are difficult to find, and parts for anything other than mountain bikes may be very hard to come by. Some buses and most local flights will take bicycles. Most main roads have hard shoulders and most drivers respect cyclists. It is common for cars to blow their horn to signal their approach.

Hitchhiking Relatively easy. Travel is still on foot and by mule in many rural areas.

Taxi Widely available. Tuk-tuks have become very popular in Honduras, and are a quick and cheap way to move around in towns and cities.

Maps
The **Instituto Geográfico Nacional** produces two 1:1,000,000 maps (1995) of the country: one is a tourist map which includes city maps of Tegucigalpa, San Pedro Sula and La Ceiba, and the other is a good road map although it does not show all the roads. Both maps are widely available in bookshops in major cities and some hotels. **International Travel Maps (ITM)** has a 1:750,000 map of Honduras.

Sleeping

Accommodation in Honduras varies greatly. In Tegucigalpa and San Pedro Sula you will find the mix ranges from business-style hotels of international standards down to simple, but generally clean rooms. In popular tourist spots the focus is more on comfort and costs rise accordingly. Get off the beaten track and you'll find some of the cheapest and most basic accommodation in Central America – complete with accompanying insect life, it can be unbearable or a mind-broadening experience depending on your mood. There is a 4% extra tax on rooms in the better hotels.

Eating and drinking

The cheapest meals are the *comida corriente*, or the sometimes better prepared and more expensive *comida típica*, which usually contain some of the following: beans, rice, meat, avocado, egg, cabbage salad, cheese, bananas, potatoes or yucca, and always tortillas. *Carne asada* is charcoal-roasted meat and served with grated cabbage between tortillas; it is good, although rarely prepared hygienically. Make sure that pork is properly cooked. *Tajadas* are crisp, fried *plátano* chips topped with grated cabbage and sometimes meat; *nacatamales* are ground, dry maize mixed with meat and seasoning, boiled in banana leaves. *Baleadas* are soft flour tortillas filled with beans and various combinations of butter, egg, cheese and cabbage. *Pupusas* are thick corn tortillas filled with *chicharrón* (pork scratchings), or cheese, served as snacks with beer. *Tapado* is a stew with meat or fish, plantain, yucca and coconut milk. *Pinchos* are meat, poultry, or shrimp kebabs. *Sopa de mondongo* (tripe soup) is very common.

Fish is sold on the beaches at Trujillo and Cedeño; also freshly fried at the roadside by the shore of Lago Yojoa. While on the north coast, look out for *pan de coco* (coconut bread) made by Garífuna (Black Carib) women, and *sopa de camarones* (prawn soup) prepared with coconut milk and lemon juice. Honduras is now a major producer of tilapia with exports to the US and fresh tilapia available in many restaurants.

Sleeping and eating price codes

Sleeping

$$$$	over US$150	**$$$**	US$66-150
$$	US$30-65	**$**	under US$30

Price codes refer to a standard double/twin room in high season.

Eating

$$$	over US$15	**$$**	US$8-15	**$**	under US$8

Price codes refer to the cost of a two-course meal, not including drinks.

Drink

Soft drinks are called *refrescos*, or *frescos* (the name also given to fresh fruit blended with water, make sure you check that bottled water is used as tap water is unsafe); *licuados* are fruit blended with milk. Bottled drinking water is available in most places. *Horchata* is morro seeds, rice water and cinnamon. Coffee is thick and sweet. The main brands of **beer** are Port Royal Export, Imperial, Nacional, Barena and Salva Vida (more malty than the others). Local **rum** is cheap, try Flor de Caña white, or seven-year-old amber. Twelve-year-old Flor de Caña Centenario is regarded as the best.

Festivals and events

Most Roman Catholic feast days are celebrated.
1 Jan New Year's Day.
14 Apr Day of the Americas.
Mar/Apr Semana Santa (Thu, Fri and Sat before Easter Sun).

1 May Labour Day.
15 Sep Independence Day.
3 Oct Francisco Morazán.
12 Oct Columbus' arrival in America.
21 Oct Army Day.

Shopping

The best articles are those made of wood. Straw items, including woven ornaments, are also highly recommended. Leather is cheaper than in El Salvador and Nicaragua. As a single stopping point, the region around Santa Bárbara is one of the best places, with outlets selling handicrafts from nearby villages. In Copán Ruinas you can also get a wide range of products, including cigars and high-quality jewellery, as well as many Guatemalan handicrafts at similar prices. Alternatively you can explore the villages yourself and see the goods being made. Coffee is OK, but not great. Sales tax is 12%; 15% on alcohol and tobacco.

Essentials A-Z

Customs and duty free
There are no customs duties on personal effects. You are allowed to bring in 200 cigarettes or 100 cigars, or 500 g of tobacco, and 2 quarts of spirit.

Electricity
Generally 110 volts but, increasingly, 220 volts is being installed. US-style plugs.

Embassies and consulates
For a full list visit
http://hn.embassyinformation.com.
Belize, 114 Bella Vista,
Belize City, T02-245-889.
Canada, 151 Slater St, Suite 805-A,
Ottawa, Ontario K1P 5H3, T613-233-8900.
El Salvador, 89 Av Norte between
7 and 9 Calle Pte 561, Col Escalón,
San Salvador, T2263-2808.
France, 8 rue Crevaux,
75116 Paris, T4755-8645.
Germany, Cuxhavener Str 14,
D-10555 Berlín, T30397497-10.
Guatemala, 19 Av "A", 20-19, Zona 10,
Guatemala City, T2363-5495.
Israel, 60, Medinat Hayehudim St,
Entrance "A", 2nd floor, Herzlya Pituach
46766, Tel Aviv, T9957-7686.
Japan, 38 Kowa Bldg, 8F No 802,
12-24 Nishi Azabu 4, Chome Minato Ku,
Tokyo 106-0031, T03-3409-1150.
Mexico, Alfonso Reyes 220, Col Condesa,
México DF, T55-211-5747.
Netherlands, Nassauplein 17,
2585 EB, La Haya, T70-364-1684.
Nicaragua, Reparto San Juan del
Gimnasio Hércules, Calle San Juan 312,
Managua, T270-4133.
Spain, Paseo de la Castellana 164,
28046 Madrid, T91-579-0251.
UK, 115 Gloucester Place,
London W1H 3PJ, T020-7486-4880.

USA, 3007 Tilden St NW, Suite 4-M,
Washington, DC 20008, T202-966-7702.

Health
Inoculate against typhoid and tetanus. There is cholera, so eating on the street or at market stalls is not recommended. There are hospitals and private clinics in Tegucigalpa, San Pedro Sula and larger towns.

Identification
It is advisable to carry some form of identification at all times, because spot checks have increased, especially when entering or leaving major towns and near to international borders.

Internet
Internet cafés are widely available in the capital and in popular locations. Prices and connections vary greatly; in cities good speeds are at about US$1 per hr. On the islands, prices are a bit higher.

Language
Spanish is the main language, but English is often spoken in the north, in the Bay Islands, by West Indian settlers on the Caribbean coast, and in business communities.
See also page 120.

Media
The principal newspapers in Tegucigalpa are *El Heraldo* and *La Tribuna*. In San Pedro Sula they are *El Tiempo* and *La Prensa*. Links on the net at www.honduras.com. The English weekly paper *Honduras This Week*, is now mainly online at www.hondurasthis week.com. They're frequently looking for student interns.

There are 6 television channels and 167 broadcasting stations. Cable TV is available in large towns and cities.

Money ➔ *US$1=18.90 lempiras (Sep 2011).*
The unit of currency is the **lempira** (written
Lps and referred to as lemps) named after
a famous indigenous chief who lost his life
while fighting the invasion of the Spanish.
It is reasonably stable against the US dollar.
Divided into 100 centavos, there are nickel
coins of 5, 10, 20 and 50 centavos. Bank
notes are for 1, 2, 5, 10, 20, 50, 100 and 500
lempiras. No one has change for larger
notes, especially the 500. Any amount of
any currency can be taken in or out of
the country.

Credit cards and traveller's cheques
Acceptance of credit cards in Honduras is
widespread but commissions can be as high
as 6%. Some businesses may try to tack on
a service charge to credit card purchases,
which is illegal. Ask the manager to call
BAC and check if the charge is permitted.
It is advisable to have US$ cash, in smaller
denominations, US$10-50.

MasterCard and Visa are accepted in
major hotels and most restaurants in cities
and larger towns. Amex is accepted in more
expensive establishments. Cash advances
are available from **BAC**, **Banco Atlántida**,
Aval Card and **Honducard** throughout
the country. BAC represents Amex and
issues and services Amex credit cards.

TCs can be a hassle as most banks
and business don't accept them.

Cost of living and travelling
Honduras is not expensive: 2 people can
travel together in reasonable comfort for
US$25 per person per day (less if on a tight
budget), but prices for tourists fluctuate
greatly. Transport, including domestic
flights, is still the cheapest in Central
America. Diving will set you back a bit,
but at US$280 or so for a PADI course,
it is still the cheapest in Central America.

Opening hours
Banks In Tegucigalpa Mon-Fri 0900-1500;
on the north coast Sat 0800-1100.
Post offices Mon-Fri 0700-2000;
Sat 0800-1200.
Shops Mon-Fri 0900-1200, 1400-1800;
Sat 0800-1200.

Post
Airmail takes 4-7 days to Europe and the same
for the USA. Expensive for parcels. Probably
worth using a courier. 20 g letter to USA
US$0.80, Europe US$1.30, rest of the world
US$1.75. Parcel up to 1 kg to the USA US$18,
Europe US$29, rest of the world US$35.

Safety
There are serious domestic social problems
in Tegucigalpa and San Pedro Sula, including
muggings and theft, but there is a Tourist
Police service in place – in Copán Ruinas,
Roatán, La Ceiba, Tela and San Pedro Sula –
that has reduced the problem. Take local
advice and be cautious when travelling alone
or off the beaten track. The vast majority of
Hondurans are honest, friendly, warm and
welcoming, and the general perception is
that tourists are not targeted by criminals.

Telephone ➔ *Country code T+504.*
Local operator T192; General information
T193; International operator T197.
Hondutel provides international telephone
services from stations throughout the
country. The system has improved
dramatically in recent years due to
competition, with an increasing majority
of Hondurans owning a cell phone.
You can buy a cell phone for about
US$10 from Tigo, Claro and Digicel,
with phone cards from US$2 upwards.

Time
-6 hrs GMT.

Tipping
Normally 10% of the bill but more expensive places add a service charge.

Tourist information
Instituto Hondureño de Turismo, main office is at Edificio Europa, Av Ramón E Cruz and Calle República de México, Col San Carlos, Tegucigalpa, T2222-2124. Also an office at Toncontín Airport and several regional offices.

Useful websites
www.hondurastips.hn/ A reliable favourite with lots of information about Honduras and hotel, restaurant and transport listings (Spanish only). The biannual publication, *HONDURAS Tips*, edited by John Dupuis in La Ceiba, Edif Gómez, Local No 2, 4 Calle, T2440-3383, is full of interesting and useful tourist information, in English and Spanish, free (available in Tegucigalpa from Instituto Hondureño de Turismo, and widely distributed around the country in major hotels).
www.hondurasweekly.com News, cultural features, travel tips, listings and links.
www.letsgohonduras.com The official Tourist Office (IHT) guide on the internet, with basic highlights.
www.netsys.hn Good business directory and useful links (in English).

Several regional guides are being developed – these are mentioned within the text.

Visas and immigration
Neither a visa nor tourist card is required for nationals of Western European countries, USA, Canada, Australia, New Zealand, Japan, Argentina, Chile, Guatemala, Costa Rica, Nicaragua, El Salvador, Panama and Uruguay. Citizens of other countries need either a tourist card, which can be bought from Honduran consulates for US$2-3, or a visa, and they should enquire at a Honduran consulate in advance to see which they need. The price of a visa seems to vary depending on nationality and where it is bought. Extensions of 30 days are easy to obtain (up to a maximum of 6 months' stay, cost US$5). There are immigration offices for extensions at Tela, La Ceiba, San Pedro Sula, Santa Rosa de Copán, Siguatepeque, La Paz and Comayagua, and all are more helpful than the Tegucigalpa office.

You will have to visit a country outside of Guatemala, Honduras and Nicaragua to re-enter and gain 90 days.

Weights and measures
The metric system is official.

Contents

Honduras

Footprint features

At a glance

⊕ **Getting around** Buses, flights to cut out long journeys. Boats to the Bay Islands from La Ceiba, and to Belize from Puerto Cortés.

⟳ **Time required** You could easily spend 3 weeks exploring.

◈ **Weather** Wettest Aug-Dec. From Jan-Mar it's chilly in the central highlands at night, hot on the coast.

✕ **When not to go** Rainy season if you don't like getting wet.

Tegucigalpa and around

*Genuinely chaotic, Tegucigalpa – or Tegus as it is called by locals –
is cramped and crowded, but still somehow retains a degree of
charm in what remains of the colonial centre. If you can bear to
stay away from the Caribbean for a few days, it has much more
history and charisma than its rival San Pedro Sula, to the north.
Surrounded by sharp, high peaks on three sides, the city is built on
the lower slopes of El Picacho. The commercial centre is around
Boulevard Morazán, an area known as 'zona viva', full of cafés,
restaurants and shops. For contrast to the modern functional city,
you can visit some of the centuries-old mining settlements set in
forested valleys among the nearby mountains that are ideal for hiking.*

Getting there

Toncontín international airport is 6.5 km south of the centre, US$4-5 in a taxi to the centre.
The airport is in a narrow valley creating difficult landing conditions: morning fog or bad
weather can cause it to close. The Carretera del Sur (Southern Highway), which brings in
travellers from the south and from Toncontín Airport, runs through Comayagüela into
Tegucigalpa. There is no central bus station and bus companies have offices throughout
Comayagüela. On arrival it is very much easier – and recommended – to take a taxi to your
hotel until you get to know the city.

Getting around

The winding of streets in the city means that moving around in the first few days is
as much about instinct as following any map. There are cheap buses and taxis for
city transport. The Tegucigalpa section of the city uses both names and numbers for
streets, but names are used more commonly. In Comayagüela, streets designated by
number are the norm. Addresses tend not to be very precise, especially in the colonias
around Boulevard Morazán east and south of the centre of Tegucigalpa.

Tourist information

Instituto Hondureño de Turismo ① *Edif Europa, Av Ramón E Cruz and Calle República de
México, 3rd floor, Col San Carlos, T2238-3974, also at Toncontín Airport, open 0830-1530*,
provides lists of hotels and sells posters and postcards. Information on cultural events
around the country from **Teatro Nacional Manuel Bonilla** is better than at regional tourist
offices. **El Mundo Maya** ① *behind the cathedral next to the Parque Central, T2222-2946*, is a
private tourist information centre.

Best time to visit

The city's altitude gives it a reliable climate: temperate during the rainy season from May to November; warm, with cool nights in March and April; and cool and dry with very cool nights from December to February. The annual mean temperature is about 23°C (74°F).

Safety

Generally speaking, Tegucigalpa is cleaner and safer (especially at night) than Comayagüela. If you have anything stolen, report it to **Dirección de Investigación Criminal (DGIC)** ① *5 Av, 7-8 Calle (next to Edificio Palermo), T2237-4799.*

Background

Founded as a silver and gold mining camp in 1578, Tegucigalpa means silver hill in the original indigenous tongue; miners first discovered gold at the north end of the current Soberanía bridge. The present city is comprised of the two former towns of Comayagüela and Tegucigalpa which, although divided by the steeply banked Río Choluteca, became the capital in 1880 and are now united administratively as the Distrito Central.

Being off the main earthquake fault line, Tegucigalpa has not been subjected to disasters by fire or earthquake, unlike many of its Central American neighbours, so it has retained many traditional features. The stuccoed houses, with a single, heavily barred entrance leading to a central patio, are often attractively coloured. However, the old low skyline of the city has been punctuated by several modern tall buildings, and much of the old landscape changed with the arrival of Hurricane Mitch.

The rains of **Hurricane Mitch** in October 1998 had a devastating effect on the Distrito Central. But the damage caused by the Choluteca bursting its banks is hard to see these days, with the exception of the first avenue of Comayagüela, where abandoned homes and buildings remain empty. Bridges washed away by the floodwaters have now been replaced, power supplies are back and, in some respects, traffic is actually better now, since many routes were diverted from the heart of downtown. Today, Hurricane Mitch lives on as painful memory.

Sights → *Altitude: 1000 m. Population: 1.1 million.*

Crossing the river from Comayagüela by the colonial Mallol bridge, on the left is the old **Casa Presidencial** (1919), home to the National Archive. When this was a museum, visitors could see the President's office and the Salón Azul state room. Try asking – you may be lucky. (The new Palacio Presidencial is a modern building on Boulevard Juan Pablo II in Colonia Lomas del Mayab.)

Calle Bolívar leads to the Congress building and the former site of the University, founded in 1847. The site adjoining the church in Plaza La Merced is now the **Galería Nacional de Arte** ① *Tue-Fri 0900-1600, Sat 0900-1200, US$1.50,* a beautifully restored 17th-century building, housing a very fine collection of Honduran modern and colonial art, prehistoric rock carvings and some remarkable pre-Colombian ceramic pieces. There are useful descriptions of exhibits, and explanations of the mythology embodied in the prehistoric and pre-Colombian art.

Calle Bolívar leads to the main square, Plaza Morazán (commonly known as Parque Central). On the eastern side of the square are the **Palacio del Distrito Central**, and the domed and double-towered **cathedral**, built in the late 18th century but which have had a complete facelift. See the gilt colonial altarpiece, the fine examples of Spanish colonial art, the cloisters and, in Holy Week, the ceremony of the Descent from the Cross.

Avenida Miguel Paz Barahona, running through the north side of the square, is a key venue. To the east is the church of **San Francisco**, with its clangorous bells, and (on 3 Calle, called Avenida Cervantes) the old **Spanish Mint** (1770), now the national printing works.

Tegucigalpa

N	Sleeping 🛏	Granada 2 **8**	Iberia **12**
200 metres	Colonial **3**	Granada 3 **9**	Leslie's Place **6**
200 yards	Condesa Inn **4**	Honduras Maya **10**	MacArthur **13**
	Crystal **5**	Hotelito West **11**	Nuevo Boston **15**
	Granada 1 **7**	Humuya Inn **1**	Plaza **16**

From Plaza Morazán, heading west towards the river to Avenida Miguel Paz Barahona, opposite the post office is the **Museo Para La Identidad Nacional** ① *Tue-Sat 0900-1700, Sun 1000-1600, US$3.30*, a museum that is unashamedly about Honduras for Hondurans. Good multimedia presentation (with audio-guide, in Spanish only), and a well-thought-out trip through Honduran history, from plate tectonics to the present day. Its star attraction is 'Virtual Copán' – wide-screen CGI recreation of the Maya ruins; also occasional temporary exhibitions. Just enough detail without getting heavy. Every capital city in Central America should have a museum like this.

Head east a block, then left (north) along 5 Calle (Calle Los Dolores), is the 18th-century church of **Iglesia de Nuestra Señora de los Dolores**. Two blocks north and three blocks west of the church is the beautiful Parque Concordia with good copies of Maya sculpture and temples. On a hilltop one block above Parque Concordia, on Calle Morelos 3A, is **Museo de la Historia Republicana Villa Roy** ① *Mon-Sat 0800-16, US$1.10, www.ihah.hn*, the former site of the Museo Nacional and, in 1936, home of the former president, Julio Lozano. The building was restored, reconstructed and reopened in 1997. There are seven main rooms presenting Honduras' history from Independence in 1821 up to 1963, as well as cultural and temporary exhibits and a collection of graceful old cars.

Back on Avenida Miguel Paz Barahona, and further west, are the **Teatro Nacional Manuel Bonilla**, with a rather grand interior (1915) inspired by the Athenée Theatre in Paris and, across the square, the beautiful old church of **El Calvario**. Built in elegant colonial style, El Calvario's roof is supported by 14 pillars.

In Colonia Palmira, to the southeast of the city, is Boulevard Morazán, with shopping and business complexes, embassies, banks, restaurants, *cafeterías* and bars. You can get a fine view of the city from the **Monumento a La Paz** ① *open until 1700*, on Juana Laínez hill, near the Estadio Nacional (National Stadium), but don't walk up alone.

The backdrop to Tegucigalpa is the summit of **El Picacho**, with the Cristo del Picacho statue looming up to the north

To El Picacho & Parque las Naciones Unidas

San Pablo 🚇

COLONIA VIERA

4 C

COLONIA REFORMA

3 C

COLONIA MATAMOROS

2 C

Gutemberg

1 C

Spanish Embassy

Av La Paz

Plaza San Martín

4 AV

2 AV

US Embassy

Av Juan Lindo

To Valle de Angeles

3 C

6

COLONIA PALMIRA

1 Av B

Lloyds 💲

ℹ️

Centro Comercial Los Castaños

Boulevard Morazán

San Pedro **18**

Eating 🍴
Duncan Maya **3**
Taiwan **6**

(see Valle de Angeles, below), although this can be hard to see at times. From Plaza Morazán go up 7 Calle and the Calle de la Leona to **Parque La Leona**, a small handsome park with a railed walk overlooking the city and safer than Monumento a La Paz. Higher still is the reservoir in El Picacho, also known as the **United Nations Park**, which can be reached by a special bus from the No 9 bus stop, behind Los Dolores church (in front of Farmacia Santa Bárbara, Sunday only, US$0.15); alternatively, take a bus to El Piligüin or Corralitos (daily at 0600) from the north side of Parque Herrera in front of the Teatro Nacional Manuel Bonilla.

Comayagüela

Crossing the bridge of 12 de Julio (quite near the Teatro Nacional Manuel Bonilla, see above) you can visit Comayagüela's market of San Isidro. In the Edificio del Banco Central, is the **Pinacoteca Arturo H Medrano** ① *12 Calle entre 5 y 6 Av*, which houses approximately 500 works by five Honduran artists and the **Museo Numismático** ① *Mon-Fri 0900-1200, 1300-1600*, which has a collection of coins and banknotes. Funds have been set aside to restore the older parts of Comayagüela, which should make the place more enjoyable to explore.

Around Tegucigalpa → *For listings, see pages 23-30.*

Heading north out of Tegucigalpa on the Olancho road, you come to **Talanga**, with a post office and Hondutel near the market on the main road. From Talanga it is a short trip to the historic and beautiful settlements of Cedros and Minas de Oro. From the Parque Central an unpaved road leads south to the Tegucigalpa–Danlí road making a triangular route possible back to the capital.

Cedros is one of Honduras' earliest settlements, dating from Pedro de Alvarado's mining operations of 1536. It is an outstanding colonial mining town with cobbled streets, perched high on an eminence amid forests. The festival of El Señor del Buen Fin takes place in the first two weeks of January. Buses to Talanga, Cedros and nearby San Ignacio leave from Reynita de San Ignacio in Mercado Zonal Belén, Comayagüela, T224-0066.

Santa Lucía → *Altitude: 1400-1600 m.*

About 14 km northeast of Tegucigalpa, on the way to Valle de Angeles, a right turn goes to the quaint old mining village of Santa Lucía which is perched precariously on a steep, pine forested mountainside overlooking the valley with Tegucigalpa below. The town has a colonial church with a Christ statue given by King Felipe II of Spain in 1592. There is a charming legend of the Black Christ, which the authorities ordered to be taken down to Tegucigalpa when Santa Lucía lost its former importance as a mining centre. Every step it was carried away from Santa Lucía it became heavier. When it was impossible to carry it any further they turned round, and by the time they were back in Santa Lucía, it was as light as a feather.

The town is lively with parties on Saturday night, and there is a festival in the second and third weeks of January, celebrating the 15 January Día de Cristo de las Mercedes. There are souvenir shops in the town, including **Cerámicas Ucles** just past the lagoon, second street on left, and another ceramics shop at the entrance on your right. On the way into the town from the capital the road is lined with many nurseries, selling flowers and plants for which the region is famous. There are good walks up the mountain on various trails, with fine views of Tegucigalpa.

A good circuit is to descend east from the mountain towards **San Juan del Rancho** through lovely landscapes on a good dirt road, then connect with the paved road to **El Zamorano**. From there continue either to El Zamorano, or return to Tegucigalpa (see below for opposite direction).

Valle de Angeles → *Altitude: 1310 m.*

About 30 minutes' drive from Tegucigalpa, Valle de Angeles is on a plain below **Monte San Juan**, with **Cerro El Picacho** (2270m) and **Cerro La Tigra** nearby. It is a popular spot for trips from the city, with a cool climate year round and is surrounded by pine forests. The town's shady little main plaza is decorated with brightly painted benches and bandstand, a pretty little twin-domed church and fringed by several restaurants with outdoor tables. The **tourist office** ① *Sat, Sun 0900-1200, 1330-1800*, is helpful but with limited information. There are tracks going through the forests, old mines to explore, a picnic area and a swimming pool; consequently it is crowded on Sundays. At the top of Cerro El Picacho there is a stunning view of the city and, if so inclined, you can visit the **zoo** ① *daily, 0800-1500, US$0.20*, of mostly indigenous animals including jaguar, spider monkeys and other animals and birds.

Around Tegucigalpa

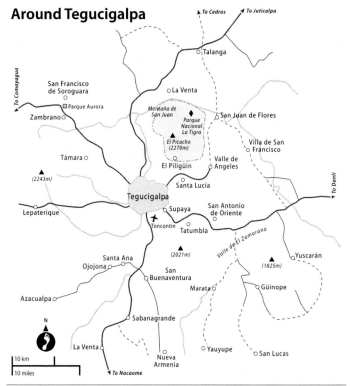

Parque Nacional La Tigra

ⓘ *US$10 entry. Go first to the Amitigra office, Edif Italia, 6th floor, about 3 blocks southwest of Amex office on Av República de Panamá, Tegucigalpa, T2232-2660, www.amitigra.org; helpful. Book a visit here in advance.*

Continue to San Juan de Flores (also called Cantarranas) and San Juancito, an old mining town. From here you can climb in the La Tigra cloud forest and even walk along the top before descending to El Hatillo and then to Tegucigalpa.

There are good climbs to the heights of Picacho and excellent hikes in the Parque Nacional La Tigra cloud forest. Only 11 km from Tegucigalpa, this cloud forest covers 238 sq km and is considered one of the richest habitats in the world with a great diversity of flora and fauna – bromeliads, orchids, arborescent ferns and over 200 species of bird. Single hikers must have a guide. There are two approach routes: go to **El Piligüin** (see below) for the Jutiapa entrance, from where you can start hiking, or to Gloriales Inn in El Hatillo. You can also walk 24 km from Tegucigalpa to the Jutiapa entrance. Then hike to the visitor centre of La Tigra at El Rosario (10 km, three hours, easy hiking, superb scenery). Alternatively, go to **San Juancito**, above which is the national park (well worth a visit, a stiff, one-hour uphill walk to El Rosario visitor centre, housed in the old mine hospital, with **park offices** ⓘ *daily 0800-1700*, friendly and helpful, with free park map/leaflet, dorms (**$** per person in basic but clean bunk rooms, with hot showers, breakfast available, extra) and starting point for six trails ranging from 30 minutes to eight hours, from 1800-2400 m above sea level (bring insect repellent).

Crumbling remains of the old mine buildings are dotted around the hillsides, some abandoned, others inhabited. Local resident Miguel Angel Sierra (T9648334) has some fascinating remnants, including an original gold mould and old photographs, all of which he is happy to show to visitors. The former US embassy at the Rosario mine has been renovated and turned into a museum and information centre, due to open soon, weekends only. The small **Pulpería-Cafetería El Rosario** sells snacks, coffee and groceries, useful if hiking in the park, and with lovely views from its tiny terrace and balcony.

A recommended hike is the **Sendero La Esperanza**, which leads to the road; turn right then take the **Sendero Bosque Nublado** on your left. The whole circuit takes about one hour 20 minutes. A few quetzal birds survive here, but you will need a good eye. In the rainy season (June, July, October and November) there is a spectacular 100-m waterfall (**Cascada de la Gloria**), which falls on a vast igneous rock. Do not leave paths when walking as there are steep drops. Also get advice about personal safety, as robberies have occurred.

From Parque Herrera in Tegucigalpa, buses throughout the day go to the village of **El Piligüin**, north of Santa Lucía. A delightful 40-minute walk down the pine-clad mountainside leads to **El Chimbo** (meals at *pulpería* or shop, ask anyone the way), then take bus either to Valle de Angeles or Tegucigalpa.

At Km 24 on the road to Danlí, there are climbs to the highest peak through the Uyuca rainforest. Information is available from the Escuela Agrícola Panamericana in the breathtaking **Valle del Zamorano**, or from the **Amitigra** office in Tegucigalpa (see above). The school has rooms for visitors. Visits to the school are organized by some tour operators. On the northwest flank of Uyuca is the picturesque village of **Tatumbla**.

Suyapa

Southeast of Tegucigalpa, the village of Suyapa attracts pilgrims to its big church, home to a tiny wooden image of the Virgin, about 8 cm high, set into the altar. A fiesta is held 1-4 February, see page 26. Take a bus to the University or to Suyapa from 'La Isla', one block northwest of the city stadium.

Sabanagrande

Further south (40 km) is Sabanagrande, just off the main highway. This typical colonial town, complete with cobbled streets, is a good day trip from Tegucigalpa. There is an interesting colonial church (1809), Nuestra Señora del Rosario 'Apa Kun Ka' (the place of water for washing), with the fiesta of La Virgen de Candelaria from 1-11 February. At 1000 m, it has a mild climate, beautiful scenery with pleasant walks, including views to the Pacific and the Gulf of Fonseca. The town is famous for its *rosquillas* (a type of biscuit).

Ojojona → Altitude: 1400 m.

Ojojona is another quaint, completely unspoiled, old village about 30 minutes (24 km) south of Tegucigalpa; turn right off the Southern Highway. The village pottery is interesting but make your selection carefully as some of it is reported to be of poor quality. La Casona del Pueblo offers the best handicrafts in town, including fine rustic ceramics. The local fiesta is 18-20 January. There are two well-preserved colonial churches in Ojojona, with fine paintings, plus two more in nearby **Santa Ana**, which is passed on the way from Tegucigalpa.

Tegucigalpa and around listings

For Sleeping and Eating price codes and other relevant information, see pages 10-11.

🛏 Sleeping

Tegucigalpa *p16, map p18*
There is a 4% tax on hotel bills, plus 12% sales tax: check if it is included in the price.
$$$ Honduras Maya, Av República de Chile, Col Palmira, T2280-5000, www.hotelhondurasmaya.hn. Spacious rooms and apartments, dated decor, casino, swimming pool, **Bar Mirador** with nightly happy hour 1700-1900, *cafeterías* (**Black Jack's Snack Bar**, **Cafetería 2000**), restaurant (**Rosalila**), very good buffet breakfast, conference hall and convention facilities for 1300, view over the city from upper rooms. Excellent travel agency in the basement. Expensive internet access.
$$$ Humuya Inn, Col Humuya 1150, 5 mins from airport, T2239-2206,

www.humuyainn.com. Rooms and service apartments, US owner. Recommended.
$$ Crystal, 2nd floor, Máximo Jerez y S Mendieta, T2237-8980. TV, a/c, OK rooms.
$$ Leslie's Place, Plaza San Martín, Col Palmira, T2220-5325. Close to good restaurants and bars in safe part of the city, a friendly little B&B with homely rooms and cosy lounge areas and garden, quiet and secure. Recommended.
$$ MacArthur, Av Lempira 454 and Telégrafo, T2237-9839, www.hotelmacarthur.com. A/c, TV, private bath, cheaper without a/c, small pool. Recommended.
$$ Nuevo Boston, Av Máximo Jerez 321, T2237-9411. Good beds, spotless, hot water, central. Good value, no credit cards, rooms on street side noisy, free coffee, mineral water and cookies in lounge, stores luggage, well run. Simple and recommended.

$$ Plaza, on Av Paz Barahona, in front of post office, T2237-2111, hotelplaza_centro@yahoo.com. good location, friendly staff, hot water, cable TV, free internet in the lobby and breakfast included.

$ Granada 1, Av Gutemberg 1401, Barrio Guanacaste, T2237-2381. Hot water on 2nd floor only, good, clean, safe, TV lounge. Internet café next door.

$ Granada 2, T238-4438 and **Granada 3**, T2237-0843, on the street leading uphill (to Barrio Casamate) from northeast corner of Parque Finlay. Good beds, hot water, safe parking, can be noisy from passing traffic so try to get a room at the back. Recommended.

$ Iberia, Peatonal Los Dolores, T2237-9267. Hot showers, clean, friendly and helpful owner happy to help guests get to know Tegus, refurbished, stores luggage, cheaper without fan.

Comayagüela *p20*

Convenient for buses to the north and west and there are many cheap *pensiones* and rooms. It is noisier and dirtier than Tegucigalpa, many places are unsuitable for travellers. If you are carrying luggage, take a taxi.

$ Centenario, 6 Av, 9-10 Calle, T2222-1050. Safe parking. Recommended.

$ Condesa Inn, 7 Av, 12 Calle. Clean, hot shower, a/c, TV, *cafetería*, very friendly, a bargain.

$ Hotelito West, 10 Calle, 6-7 Av. Towels and soap, hot water all day, very friendly, changes TCs. Recommended.

$ San Pedro, 9 Calle, 6 Av. With bath (cheaper without), or with private cold shower. Popular, restaurant.

Santa Lucía *p20*

$$ Hotel Santa Lucía Resort, 1.2 km before Santa Lucía, set among pine trees dripping with moss (*rigil*), T2779-0540, www.hotelsanta luciaresort.com. Spacious and comfy log cabins, with cable TV, lounge area, and balcony; pleasant grounds and ample parking space.

$$ La Posada de Dona Estefana, overlooking the church in the heart of the well preserved colonial town, T2779-0441, meeb@yahoo.com. Very pretty rooms, with cable TV and great views from balcony; lounge and pool; breakfast included.

Valle de Angeles *p21*

$$ Hotel y Restaurante Posada del Angel, northeast of centre, T2766-2233, hotelposada delangel@yahoo.com. Swimming pool, indifferent service, moderate prices.

$$-$ Villas del Valle, 500 m north of town, T766-2534, www.villasdelvalle.com. Selection of rooms, cabins and suites. Honduran and European food in the restaurant.

Parque Nacional La Tigra *p22*

$ Eco Albergue La Tigra, in the old hospital of the mining company. Price per person. Rooms named after local birds, capacity for 50.

$ Hotelito San Juan, San Juancito. 6 rooms with shared bathroom.

❶ Eating

Tegucigalpa *p16, map p18*

Take a walk down the pedestrianized stretch of Av Paz Barahona. In the evening, take a taxi to Blv Morazón. Most places close on Sun. There are good Chinese restaurants on Calle del Telégrafo in centre; huge servings at reasonable prices.

$$$ El Corral, 4a Av, opposite Hotel Clarión, Col Alameda, T2232-5066. Big, brash steakhouse, with excellent grilled meats and decent wine list. Lively at weekends, with live music, karaoke and dancing.

$$$ El Trapiche, Blv Suyapa, opposite National University. Colonial ranch atmosphere, good steaks and national dishes. Recommended.

$$$ Roma, Av Santa Sede, Calle Las Acacias 1601, 1 block off Av República de Chile. The oldest Italian restaurant in the city, good pizzas.

$$ Casa María, Av Ramón E Cruz, Col Los Castaños, 1 block off Blv Morazán. Colonial building, good food.

$$ Duncan Maya, Av Colón 618, opposite central **Pizza Hut**. Lively place, popular with locals, occasionally has live music. Good and reasonably priced.

$$ El Crustáceo, Plaza San Martín y 3 Calle, Col Palmira. Seafood specialists in vaguely *cabaña*-style building with open-air terrace, popular with local rich kids.

$$ El Gachupín, off Blv Morazán, Col El Castaño Sur. Superb, Mediterranean-style food, garden.

$$ El Pórtico, near Blv Morazán, T2236-7099. Good food but don't be in a hurry.

$$ Mei-Mei, Pasaje Midence Soto, central. Chinese. Recommended.

$$ Rojo, Verde y Ajo, 1 Av B, Col Palmira. Good food, reasonable price, closed Sun.

$$ Tony's Mar, Blv Juan Pablo II y Av Uruguay, Col Tepeyac, T2239-9379. Seafood, good, simple, New Orleans style.

$ El Patio 2, easternmost end of Blv Morazán. Traditional food, good service and atmosphere, and generous portions. Recommended.

$ Taiwan, round corner from **Hotels Granada 2** and **3**, on Av Máximo Jerez. Chinese food, huge portions, good value.

Bakeries

Antojitos, next door to **Hotel Granada 3**. Convenient for breakfast, closes at 1100, easiest place to eat in the area.

Basilio's Repostería y Panadería, Calle Peatonal between Los Dolores and S Mendieta. Good cakes, bread and pastries.

Salman's. Several outlets. Good bread/pastries.

Cafeterías

Al Natural, Calle Hipólito Matute y Av Miguel Cervantes. Some vegetarian, some meat dishes, huge fresh fruit juices, antiques, caged birds, nice garden atmosphere.

Café y Librería Paradiso, Av Paz Barahona 1351. Excellent coffee and snacks, good library, paintings and photos to enjoy, newspapers and magazines on sale, good meeting place.

Don Pepe's Terraza, Av Colón 530, upstairs, T2222-1084. Central, cheap, live music, but typical Honduran atmosphere. Recommended.

Comayagüela *p20*
Cafeterías

Bienvenidos a Golosinas, 6 Av, round corner from **Hotel Colonial**. Friendly, basic meals, beer.

Cafetería Nueva Macao, 4 Av No 437. Large portions, Chinese.

Comedor Tulin, 4 Av between 4 and 5 Calle. Good breakfasts.

Santa Lucía *p20*

$$ Miluska. A Czech restaurant serving Czech and Honduran food. Recommended.

$ Comedor, next to the plaza/terrace of the municipality. On Sun food is available on the streets.

Valle de Angeles *p21*

$$ Epocas, Calle Mineral, opposite the Town Hall on the main plaza, T9636-1235. A wonderful ramshackle place, full of antiques and bric-a-brac, from old French horns to vintage cash registers (some items for sale); mixed menu of steak, chicken and fish as well as *típicos*; cheerfully talkative parrots in the backyard.

$$ La Casa de las Abuelas, 1 block north of Parque Central, T2766-2626. Pleasant courtyard with wine bar, café, library, satellite TV, email, phone, information and art gallery.

$$ Las Tejas, opposite the **Centro Turístico La Florida**. A Dutch-owned restaurant, serving traditional mix of meat and *típico* dishes.

$ Restaurante Papagaio, Calle Peatonal, 1 block down from plaza, T9920-0714. Tue-Sun 0900-1800. Simple but friendly little place with large garden and kids' play area, serving breakfasts, steaks, pasta and *típicos*.

$ Restaurante Turístico de Valle de Angeles, T2766-2148, on top of hill overlooking town, with rustic decor, cartwheel table tops and lovely views over forested valley Good meat and fish dishes but slow service.

Parque Nacional La Tigra *p22*

$ Grocery store, next door to **Hotelito San Juan**, San Juancito. Sells fuel, drinks and can prepare *comida corriente*; same owners as hotel, T2766-2237.

$ Señora Amalia Elvir, before El Rosario. Meals are available at Señora Amalia's house.

⚙ Entertainment

Tegucigalpa *p16, map p18*
Bars and clubs

In front of the Universidad Nacional on Blv Suyapa is **La Peña**, where every Fri at 2100 there is live music, singing and dancing, entrance US$1.40. Blv Morazán has plenty of choice in nightlife including **Taco Taco**, a good bar, sometimes with live mariachi music; next door **Tequila**, a popular drinking place only open at weekends. **Tobacco Road Tavern**, a popular gringo hang-out, in the downtown area on Calle Matute. **Iguana Rana Bar** is very popular with locals and visitors, similarly **La Puerta del Alcalá**, 3½ blocks down from Taca office on Blv Morazán, Col Castaño Sur. Pleasant open setting. Tierra Libre, Calle Casa de las Naciones Unidas 2118, 5 mins' walk from Plaza San Martín in Col Palmira, T3232-8923. Arty cinephile café/bar, with occasional screenings, small and friendly, with good cocktails and snacks (Mon-Sat, 1700-2400).

Cinemas

Plazas 1 to 5, in Centro Comercial Plaza Mira- flores on Blv Miraflores. **Regis**, **Real**, **Opera**, and **Sagitario** at Centro Comercial Centroamérica, Blv Miraflores (for good US films). **Multiplaza**, Col Lomas del Mayab, 6-screens. In the city centre, **Lido Palace**, **Variedades** and **Aries**, 200 m up Av Gutemberg leading from Parque Finlay to Col Reforma.

⚙ Festivals and events

Suyapa *p23*

1-4 Feb Fiesta, with a televised *alborada* with singers, music and fireworks, from 2000-2400 on the 2nd evening.

Sabanagrande *p23*

1-11 Feb Fiesta of La Virgen de Candelaria.

Ojojona *p23*

18-20 Jan Fiesta.

⚙ Shopping

Tegucigalpa *p16, map p18*
Bookshops

Metromedia, Edif Casa Real, Av San Carlos, behind Centro Comercial Los Castaños, Blv Morazán, English books, new and second-hand, for sale or exchange. **Librería Paradiso** (see under Cafeterías, above). Books in Spanish. **Editorial Guaymuras**, Av Miguel Cervantes 1055. Second-hand bookstalls in **Mercado San Isidro** (6 Av y 2 Calle, Comayagüela), cheap.

Markets

Mercado San Isidro, 6 Av at 1 Calle, Comayagüela. Many fascinating things, but filthy; do not buy food here. Sat is busiest day.
Mercado de Artesanías, 3 Av, 15 Calle, next to Parque El Soldado. Good value.

Good supermarkets: **La Colonia**, in Blv Morazán; **Más y Menos**, in Av de la Paz. Also on Calle Salvador, 1 block south of Peatonal.

Photography

Kodak on Parque Central and Blv Morazán; **Fuji** by the cathedral and on Blv Morazán.

▲ Activities and tours

Tegucigalpa *p16 map p18*
Columbia, Calle Principal between
11 y 12 Av, Blv Morazán, T2232-3532,
columbiatours@sigmanet.hn. Excellent
for national parks, including Cusuco,
Pico Bonito and Cuero y Salado, as
well as Punta Sal and Bay Islands.
Explore Honduras Tour Service, Col
Zerón 21-23 Av, 10 Calle NO, San Pedro Sula,
T2552-6242, www.explorehonduras.com.
Copán and Bay Islands tours.
Gloria Tours across from north side of
Parque Central in Casa Colonial, T2238-2232.
Information centre and tour operator.
Trek Honduras, Av Julio Lozano 1311,
T2239-9827. Tours of the city, Bay Islands,
Copán, San Pedro Sula, Valle de Angeles
and Santa Lucía.

⊖ Transport

Tegucigalpa *p16, map p18*
Air
Toncontín Airport opens at 0530. Check in at
least 2 hrs before departure; snacks, souvenir
shops, several duty-free stores and internet.
Buses to airport from Comayagüela, on 4 Av
between 6 and 7 Calle, or from Av Máximo
Jerez in downtown Tegucigalpa; into town
US$0.19, every 20 mins from left-hand side
outside the airport; yellow cabs, US$9-10,
smaller *colectivo* taxis, US$6 or more.

    Airline offices Atlantic Airline, T2220-
5231; **Air France**, Centro Comercial Galería,
Av de la Paz, T2237-0229; **Alitalia**, Col
Alameda, 5 Av, 9 Calle No 821, T2239-4246;
American, Ed Palmira, opposite Honduras
Maya, 1st floor, T2232-1414; **British Airways**,
Edif Sempe, Blv Comunidad Económica
Europea, T2225-5101; **Continental**,
Av República de Chile, Col Palmira,
T2220-0999; **Grupo Taca**, Blv Morazán y
Av Ramón E Cruz, T2239-0148 or airport
T2233-5756; **Iberia**, Ed Palmira, opposite
Honduras Maya, T2232-7760; **Isleña**

Airlines, T236-8778, also at Toncontín
Airport, T2233-2192, www.flyislena.com;
Japan Airlines, Edif Galería La Paz, 3rd floor,
Local 312, 116 Av La Paz, T2237-0229;
KLM, Ed Ciicsa, Av República de Chile y
Av República de Panamá, Col Palmira,
T2232-6410; **Lufthansa**, Edif Plaza del Sol,
No 2326, Av de la Paz, T2236-7560. **Sol Air**
in Tegucigalpa on T2235-3737; **Sosa Airline**,
at the airport, T2233-7351.

Bus
Local Fares are US$0.08-0.12; stops are
official but unmarked.

Long distance To **San Pedro Sula**
on Northern Hwy, 3¼-4 hrs depending
on service. Several companies, including:
Sáenz, Centro Comercial Perisur, Blv Unión
Europea, T2233-4229, and **Hedman Alas**,
11 Av, 13-14 Calle, Comayagüela, T2237-
7143, www.hedmanalas.com, US$18;
both recommended; **El Rey**, 6 Av,
9 Calle, Comayagüela, T2237-6609; **Viajes
Nacionales** (Viana), terminal on Blv de Las
Fuerzas Armadas, T2235-8185. To **Tela** and
La Ceiba, Viana Clase Oro, and **Etrusca**, 8 Av,
12 y 13 Calle, T2222-6881. To **Choluteca**, Mi
Esperanza, 6 Av, 23-24 Calle, Comayagüela,
T2225-1502. To **Trujillo**, Cotraibal, 7 Av,
10-11 Calle, Comayagüela, T2237-1666.
To **La Esperanza**, Empresa Joelito, 4 Calle,
No 834, Comayagüela. To **Comayagua**, most
going to San Pedro Sula and **Transportes
Catrachos**, Col Torocagua, Blv del Norte,
Comayagüela. To **Valle de Angeles** and
Santa Lucía, from stop on Av La Paz (near
filling station opposite hospital). To **Juticalpa**
and **Catacamas**, Empresa Aurora, 8 Calle,
6-7 Av, Comayagüela, T2237-3647.

    For travellers leaving Tegucigalpa, take
the Tiloarque bus on Av Máximo Jerez, by
Calle Palace, and get off in Comayagüela at
Cine Centenario (Av 6) for nearby **Empresa
Aurora** buses (for **Olancho**) and El Rey
buses (for **San Pedro Sula**). 3 blocks

northwest is Cine Lux, near which are **Empresas Unidas** and **Maribel** (8 Av, 11-12 Calle, T2237-3032) for **Siguatepeque**. Tiloarque bus continues to Mi Esperanza bus terminal (for **Choluteca** and **Nicaraguan border**). Take a 'Carrizal' or 'Santa Fe' bus ascending Belén (9 Calle) for **Hedman Alas** buses to **San Pedro Sula** and for Comayagua buses. The **Norteño** bus line to San Pedro Sula is alongside Mamachepa market, from where there are also buses for **Nacaome** and **El Amatillo** border with El Salvador.

International Ticabus, 16 Calle, 5-6 Av, Comayagüela, T2222-0590, www.ticabus. com, to **Managua** (US$32, 8 hrs), **San José** (US$52), **San Salvador** (US$20), **Guatemala City** (US$40, 12 hrs) and **Panama** (US$87) daily. Make sure you reserve several days ahead. **Hedman Alas** have a service to **Guatemala City** and **Antigua** that leaves Tegucigalpa for San Pedro Sula, 0545, 12 hrs, US$52. Alternatively to **Nicaragua**, take **Mi Esperanza** bus to San Marcos de Colón, then taxi or local bus to El Espino on border. To **San Marcos**, 4 daily from 0730, direct to border at 0400, US$2.50, 5 hrs (0730 is the latest one that will get you into Nicaragua the same day). Or **Mi Esperanza** bus to Río Guasaule border, several daily, 4 hrs, US$2. To **San Salvador**, Cruceros del Golfo, Barrio Guacerique, Blv Comunidad Económica Europea, Comayagüela, T2233-7415, US$18, at 0600 and 1300, 6 hrs travelling, 1 hr or more at border. Connections to **Guatemala** and **Mexico**; direct bus to border at El Amatillo, US$2.50, 3 hrs, several daily; alternatively from San Pedro Sula via Nueva Ocotepeque and El Poy. To **San Salvador** and **Guatemala**, with King Quality from Tegucigalpa (T2225-5415) from **Cruceros del Golfo** terminal, 0600 and 1300 and San Pedro Sula (T2553-4547) at 0630. Alternatively, to Guatemala go to San Pedro Sula and take **Escobar**, **Impala** or **Congolón** to Nueva

Ocotepeque and the border at **Agua Caliente**, or via **Copán**.

Car

Car hire Avis, Edif Palmira and airport, T2232-0088. **Budget**, Blv Suyapa and airport, T2235-9531. **Hertz**, Centro Comercial Villa Real, Col Palmira, T2239-0772. **Maya**, Av República de Chile 202, Col Palmira, T2232-0992. **Molinari**, 1 Av, 2 Calle, Comayagüela and airport, T2237-5335. **Thrifty**, Col Prados Universitarios, T2235-6077. **Toyota**, T2235-6694.

Car repairs Metal Mecánica, 1 block south of Av de los Próceres, Col Lara. Volkswagen dealer near Parque Concordia, good.

Taxi

About US$4-6 per person, but you can often bargain down to around US$3 for short distances within the city. More after 2200, cheaper on designated routes, eg Miraflores to centre.

Santa Lucía *p20*
Bus
To Santa Lucía from Mercado San Pablo, **Tegucigalpa**, Bus 101, every 45 mins, US$0.50, past the statue of Simón Bolívar by the Esso station, Av de los Próceres.

Valle de Angeles *p21*
Bus
To Valle de Angeles every 45 mins, US$0.50, 1 hr, leaves from San Felipe, near the hospital. To **San Juan de Flores** 1000, 1230, 1530.

Parque Nacional La Tigra *p22*
Bus
Buses leave from Mercado San Pablo, **Tegucigalpa**, for **San Juancito** from 1000, 1½ hrs, on Sat and Sun bus at 0800 packed with people visiting their families, US$1; passes turn-off to Santa Lucía and goes through Valle de Angeles. Return bus from

San Juancito at 1500 from across the river and up the hill, opposite the park. On Sat, buses return at 0600 and 1200 from church, board early. For return journey double check local information. Alternatively, from behind Los Dolores church in Tegucigalpa you can take a bus to **El Piligüín/Jutiapa** at 0600; it passes through beautiful scenery by El Hatillo and other communities. From El Piligüín, it is a long, hot walk up to the park entrance.

Ojojona *p23*
Bus
Buses leave **Comayagüela** every 15-30 mins from Calle 4, Av 6, near San Isidro market, US$0.50, 1 hr. From same location, buses go west to **Lepaterique** ('place of the jaguar'), another colonial village, over 1-hr drive through rugged, forested terrain. Distant view of Pacific on fine days from heights above village.

Directory

Tegucigalpa *p16 map p18*
Banks
There are many ATMs in the city centre. All banks have several branches throughout the city; we list the main offices. Branch offices are allowed to change TCs, only US$ cash. **HSBC**, 5 Calle (Av Colón) in the centre and at 5 Calle in front of Plaza Morazán. **Banco Atlántida**, 5 Calle in front of Plaza Morazán (may agree to change money on Sat up to 1200). **Banco de Honduras** (Citibank), Blv Suyapa. **Banco del País**, Calle Peotonal in the centre, changes TCs. **Banco de Occidente**, 3 Calle (Cervantes) y 6 Av (S Mendieta) in the centre.

Visa, MasterCard and Amex cash advances (no commission) and TCs at **BAC**, Blv Morazán, and at **Honducard**, Av de la Paz y Ramón E Cruz, and at **Aval Card**, Blv Morazán. Banks are allowed to trade at the current market rate, but there is a street market along the Calle Peatonal off the Parque Central, opposite the post office and

elsewhere. Exchange can be difficult on Sat, try **Coin**, a *casa de cambio* on Av de la Paz, inside **Supermercado Más y Menos**, same rates as banks, no commission, Mon-Fri 0830-1730, Sat 0900-1200, changes TCs but will photocopy cheques and passport; another branch of **Coin** on Calle Peatonal, good rates. Recommended.

Cultural centres
Alianza Francesa, Col Lomas del Guijarro, T2239-6163, cultural events Fri afternoon, French films Tue 1930. **Centro Cultural Alemán**, 8 Av, Calle La Fuente, T2237-1555, German newspapers, cultural events. **Instituto Hondureño de Cultura Interamericana** (IHCI), Calle Real de Comayagüela, T2237-7539, has an English library and cultural events.

Embassies and consulates
Belize, T2220-5000, Ext 7770. **Canada**, Ed Financiero Banexpo, Local 3, Col Payaqui, Blv Juan Bosco II, T232-4551. **Costa Rica**, Col El Triángulo, 1a Calle, opposite No 3451, T2232-1768, bus to Lomas del Guijarro to last stop, then walk up on your left for 300 m. **Ecuador**, Av Juan Lindo 122, Col Palmira, T2236-5980. **El Salvador**, 2 Av Calzada República de Uruguay, Casa 219, Col San Carlos T2236-8045. **France**, Col Palmira, 3 Calle, Av Juan Lindo, T2236-6432. **Germany**, Ed Paysen, 3rd floor, Blv Morazán, T2232-3161. **Guatemala**, Col Las Minitas 4 Calle, Casa 2421, T2232-9704, Mon-Fri 0900-1300, take photo, visa given on the spot, US$10. **Italy**, Av Principal 2602, Col Reforma, T236-6391. **Japan**, Col San Carlos, between 4 and 5 Calle, 2 blocks off Blv Morazán and Av de la Paz, T2236-6828, behind Los Castaños Shopping Mall. **Mexico**, Av República de México, Paseo República de Brasil 2402, Col Palmira, T2232-6471, opens 0900, visa takes 24 hrs. **Netherlands** (Consulate), Edif Barahona, Col Alameda, next to INA, T2231-5007.

Nicaragua, Av Choluteca 1130, bloque M-1, Col Lomas del Tepeyac, T2232-9025 daily, 0800-1200, US$25, visa can take up to 2 days. **Norway**, consular services in front of Residencial el Limonar, T2557-0856. **Panama**, Ed Palmira No 200, opposite Honduras Maya, 2nd floor, T2239-5508. **Spain**, Col Matamoros 801, T2236-6589, near Av de la Paz and US Embassy. **Sweden** (Consulate), Av Altiplano, Retorno Borneo 2758, Col Miramontes, T2232-4935. **UK**, Edif Banexpo, 3rd floor, Col Payaqu, T2232-0612. **USA**, Av La Paz, Mon-Fri 0800-1700, take any bus from north side of Parque Central in direction 'San Felipe', T2236-9320.

Emergencies
Police 199; Red Cross 195; Fire 198.

Immigration
Dirección General de Migración, Av Máximo Jerez, next to Hotel Ronda, Tegucigalpa.

Internet
Café Don Harry, Av República de Chile 525, Edif Galerías TCB, T2220-6174. **@ccess Cyber Coffee**, Centro Commercial La Ronda, Av Máximo Jerez next to Super Donuts, Mon-Sat 0800-1900, US$1.50 for 30 mins. **Cyberplace Center**, Av Máximo Jerez and Las Damas, Mon-Sat 0900-1900, US$1 per hr. **Cyberiada Internet Café**, Plaza Brezani, Av Máximo Jerez, Calle H Matute, open 24 hrs, US$1.80 per hr with free coffee. **Multinet**, on Barahona, also in Blv Morazán and Centro Comercial. Lots of machines with full services, 0830-1900, Sun 0900-1700. US$1.50 per hr. **Office Comp**, Av Cervantes, next to Hotel Excelsior, Mon-Sat 0830-1900. US$1 per hr. Small, but with high-speed connection. **PC Cyber**, Edif Paz Barahona, Calle Peatonal, Mon-Fri 0830-1700, Sat 0830-1400.

Laundry
La Cisne, 1602 Calle La Fuente/Av Las Delicias, US$2.50 up to 5 kg, same-day service. **Lavandería Italiana**, Barrio Guadalupe, 4 blocks west of Av República de Chile 300 block. **Lavandería Super Jet**, Av Gutemberg, 300 m east of Hotel Granada, US$0.20 per kg. **Mi Lavandería**, opposite Repostería Calle Real, 3 Calle, 2 Av, Comayagüela, T2237-6573, Mon-Sat 0700-1800, Sun and holidays 0800-1700.

Medical services
Dentist Dra Rosa María Cardillo de **Boquín**, Ed Los Jarros, Sala 206, Blv Morazán, T2231-0583. Recommended. **Dr Roberto Ayala**, DDS, C Alfonso XIII 3644, Col Lomas de Guijarro, T2232-2407. **Hospitals** Hospital y Clínica Viera, 11 y 12 Av, 5 Calle, Tegucigalpa, T2237-1365. **Hospital la Policlínica** SA 3 Av, 7 y 8 Calle, Comayagüela, T2237-3260. **Centro Médico Hondureño**, 3 Av, 3 Calle, Barrio La Granja, Comayagüela, T2233-6028. **Pharmacies** Farmacia Rosna, pedestrian mall off Parque Central, T2237-0605, English spoken. Recommended. **Regis Palmira**, Ed Ciicsa, Av República de Panamá, Col Palmira.

Post
Av Paz Barahona/C del Telégrafo, Lista de Correos (Poste Restante) mail held for 1 month, 20 g letter to US (US$0.80), Europe (US$1.30), rest of the world (US$1.75).

Telephone
Hondutel, Calle del Telégrafo y Av Colón, has several direct AT&T lines to USA, no waiting. Phone, fax and telegrams; open 24 hrs for phone services only. Also at 6 Av, 7-8 Calle, Comayagüela, with post office.

Work
Peace Corps, opposite Edif Ciicsa, on Av República de Chile, uphill past Hotel Honduras Maya.

Western Honduras

*Close to the Guatemalan border, the serene ruins of Copán are
Honduras' major Maya attraction. Treasured for its exceptional
artistry when compared to other Maya sites, the ruins enjoy a calm
and pleasant setting. The quiet town of Copán Ruinas nestles among
hills nearby. In fact, the whole area is sprinkled with interesting towns
and villages, mostly in delightful hilly surroundings; some with a
colourful colonial history, others with their foundations in the Lenca
communities, and many producing handicrafts. The ruins of Copán
aside, one of the enjoyable aspects of western Honduras is that there
are no 'must-sees' – just pick a route, take your time and enjoy the
scenery and whatever else you may find.*

San Pedro Sula to Copán → *For listings, see pages 43-52.*

The Western Highway runs parallel to the border from San Pedro Sula southwest along
the Río Chamelecón to Canoa (58 km), from where there is a paved road south to Santa
Bárbara (a further 53 km). Continuing along the Western Highway, the road from Canoa
towards Guatemala runs southwest to La Entrada (115 km from San Pedro), where it forks
again left for Santa Rosa (see below) and right for an attractive 60-km road through deep
green scenery to Copán Ruinas.

The regular bus is recommended rather than the dangerous minibus service, which
can be a bit hair-raising. The road is paved throughout and in good condition.

La Entrada is a hot, dusty town and the place to change buses. Going south takes you
to Santa Rosa and towards El Salvador, west to Copán and Guatemala.

El Puente ① *daily 0800-1600, US$5*, is a national archaeological park reached by taking
a turn-off, 4.5 km west from La Entrada on the Copán road, then turning right on a
well-signposted, paved road 6 km to the visitor centre. It is near the confluence of the
Chamelecón and Chinamito rivers and is thought to have been a regional centre between
AD 600 and 900.

Copán Ruinas → *For listings, see pages 43-52.*

① *www.copanhonduras.org.*

A charming town set in the hills just to the east of the border with Guatemala, Copán
Ruinas – to give the town its full name – thrives and survives on visitors passing through
to visit the nearby ruins. Nevertheless, it is arguably the best-preserved and one of the
most pleasant towns in Honduras. Close to the border with Guatemala, it's a good place
to stop for a few days before heading straight to San Pedro Sula (172 km) and the Bay
Islands or Tegucigalpa (395 km), with the impressive ruins of Copán, good hotels and

restaurants, coffee plantation tours, hiking, caving, hot springs, horse riding, language schools and volunteer opportunities.

The **Museo Copán** ⓘ *Mon-Sat 0800-1600, US$2*, on the town square has explanations in Spanish of the Maya empire and stelae. There is an interesting selection of artefacts, a burial site and a tomb that was unearthed during a road-building project. It is a good idea to visit the museum before the ruins. The completely restored Old Cuartel now houses the **Casa K'inich Interactive Children's Museum** ⓘ *up the hill from Hotel Marina Copán, US$1.10, Tue-Sun 0800-1200,1300-1700*, an interesting museum for everyone, not just for kids, and in a nice spot with great views of the town from towers in the perimeter wall. The **Enchanted Wings Butterfly House** ⓘ *2 blocks west of the cemetery on the road to Guatemala, T2651-4133, daily 0800-1700, US$5.50*, is run by Bob 'The Butterfly Guy' Gallardo, specialist in Honduran butterflies. The garden, complete with restaurant, is beautiful and has exhibits of rare butterflies, an orchid garden and birdwatching tours can be arranged. Recommended. An excellent permanent **photography exhibition** ⓘ *Mon-Fri, 0800-1600, free*, has opened at the Municipalidad on the main plaza. There are rare period photos and documentation from the first archaeological expedition to Copán at the turn of the 20th century, donated by Harvard University's Peabody Museum and archaeologists Barbara and Bill Fash.

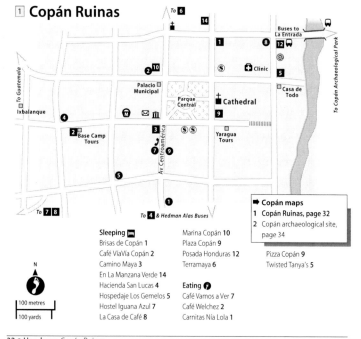

① Copán Ruinas

Sleeping 🛏
Brisas de Copán **1**
Café VíáVía Copán **2**
Camino Maya **3**
En La Manzana Verde **14**
Hacienda San Lucas **4**
Hospedaje Los Gemelos **5**
Hostel Iguana Azul **7**
La Casa de Café **8**

Marina Copán **10**
Plaza Copán **9**
Posada Honduras **12**
Terramaya **6**

Eating 🍴
Café Vamos a Ver **7**
Café Welchez **2**
Carnitas Nía Lola **1**

Pizza Copán **9**
Twisted Tanya's **5**

➡ **Copán maps**
1 Copán Ruinas, page 32
2 Copán archaeological site, page 34

Copán archaeological site

ⓘ *Daily, 0800-1600, US$15 entry to ruins and Las Sepulturas, admission valid for 1 day; US$7 to enter the museum with entrance to the tunnels an additional pricey US$15. Bilingual guided tours available (US$25, 2 hrs), recommended. The Copán Guide Association has a kiosk in the parking area where qualified bilingual guides can be hired at a fixed rate.*

Photographs of the excavation work and a maquette of the site are located in a small exhibition room at the visitor centre. There is a *cafetería* by the entrance to the ruins, and also a handicrafts shop, in the Parque Arqueológico, next to the bookshop, with local and country maps, and a Spanish/English guide book for the ruins, which is rather generalized. Useful books are: *Scribes, Warriors and Kings: City of Copán*, by William and Barbara Fash, and *History Carved in Stone*, a guide to Copán, by William Fash and Ricardo Argucía (3rd edition, 1998, US$3), published locally and available at the site. Luggage can be left for free.

The magnificent ruins of Copán are one of Central America's major Maya sites, certainly the most significant in Honduras, and they mark the southeastern limit of Maya dominance. Just 1 km from the village, there is a path beside the road from Copán to the ruins which passes two stelae en route. Get to the ruins as early as possible, or stay late in the day so you have a chance to be there without hordes of people.

Museo de Escultura Maya

ⓘ *US$10, ticket from main ticket office not at the museum.*

It is essential to visit the museum before the ruins. The impressive and huge two-storey Museum of Maya Sculpture and sculpture park houses the recently excavated carvings. In the middle of the museum is an open-air courtyard with a full-size reproduction of the Rosalila temple, found intact buried under Temple 16 with its original paint and carvings (see below). A reproduction of the doorway to Temple 16 is on the upper floor. The museum houses the original stelae to prevent weather damage, while copies will be placed on site. More than 2000 other objects found at Copán are also in the museum which has good explanations in Spanish and English. The exit leads to the ruins via the nature trail.

Archaeological site

When John Lloyd Stephens and Frederick Catherwood examined the ruins in 1839, they were engulfed in jungle. Stephens, a lawyer, and Catherwood, an architect, were the first English-speaking travellers to explore the regions originally settled by the Maya. They are credited with recording the existence of many of the ruins in the Maya area. Some of the finest examples of sculpture from Copán are now in London and Boston.

In the 1930s, the Carnegie Institute cleared the ground and rebuilt the Hieroglyphic Stairway, and since then the ruins have been maintained by the government. Some of the most complex carvings are found on the 21 **stelae**, or 3-m columns of stones on which the passage of time was originally believed to have been recorded. Under many of the stelae was a vault; some have been excavated. The stelae are deeply incised and carved with faces, figures and animals. There are royal portraits with inscriptions recording deeds and the lineage of those portrayed as well as dates of birth, marriage and death. Ball courts were revealed during excavation, and one of them has been fully restored. The **Hieroglyphic Stairway** leads up a pyramid; its upper level supported a temple. Its other

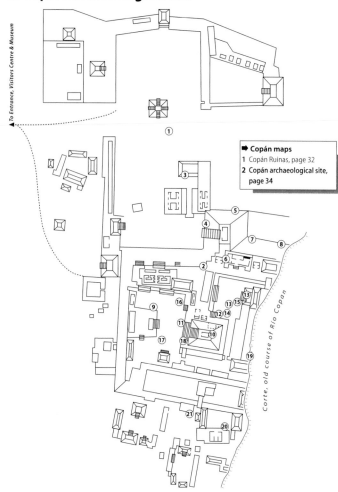

To Entrance, Visitors Centre & Museum

➡ **Copán maps**
1 Copán Ruinas, page 32
2 Copán archaeological site,
page 34

Corte, old course of Río Copán

N

50 metres
50 yards

	Ball Court **3**	Structure 16 **10**	East Court/Plaza
	Hieroglyphic Stairway **4**	Altar Q **11**	de los Jaguares **15**
	Structure 26 **5**	Rosalila Building	Plaza Occidental **16**
	Council House,	(within Structure 16) **12**	Altar I **17**
	Temple 22A **6**	Entrance to Rosalila &	Altar H **18**
	Temple of Meditation/	Jaguar tunnels **13**	Temple 18 **19**
	Temple 22 **7**	Hunal Building	Structure 32 **20**
Main Plaza with Stelae **1**	House of Knives **8**	(beneath Rosalila)	Zona Residencial **21**
Acropolis **2**	Structure 13 **9**	& Tomb of Founder **14**	

sides are still under excavation. The stairway is covered for protection, but a good view can be gained from the foot and there is access to the top via the adjacent plaza. After Hurricane Mitch, the **Rosalila Temple**, in Temple 16, was opened to the public, as were other previously restricted excavations, in an effort to attract more visitors. The Rosalila and Jaguar tunnels below the site are now open to visitors at an additional cost (see page 33). Much fascinating excavation work is now in progress, stacks of labelled carved stones have been placed under shelters, and the site looks like it is becoming even more interesting as new buildings are revealed. The most atmospheric buildings are those still half-buried under roots and soil. The last stela was set up in Copán between AD 800 and 820, after less than five centuries of civilized existence. The nearby river has been diverted to prevent it encroaching on the site when in flood.

Also near the ruins is a **sendero natural** (nature trail) through the jungle to the minor ball court; take mosquito repellent. The trail takes 30 minutes and has a few signposts explaining the plants, animals and spirituality of the forest to the Maya. After 1600 is the best time to see animals on the sendero natural, which is open until 1700. About 4 km from the main centre is the ceremonial site known as **Los Sapos** ① *entry US$2* (The Toads), a pre-Classic site with early stone carvings. The toad was a Maya symbol of fertility. East of the main ruins near Los Sapos is a stone, **Estela 12**, which lines up with another, **Estela 10**, on the other side of the valley at sunrise and sunset on 12 April every year.

One kilometre beyond the main ruins, along the road to San Pedro Sula, or connected by a stone path from the main site, is an area called **Las Sepulturas** ① *entrance is almost 2 km from the main site, entry to this site is included in the main Copán ticket,* a residential area where ceramics dating back to 1000 BC have been found. Exhibits from the site are on display in the Copán Museum. It is a delightful site, beautifully excavated and well maintained, peaceful and in lovely surroundings.

Around Copán Ruinas

There are many caves around Copán to visit – some of which have unearthed Maya artefacts; ask locally. Also here, and in the neighbouring part of Guatemala, are a few remaining Chorti indigenous villages, interesting to visit, particularly on 1 November, Día de Los Muertos, when there are family and communal ceremonies for the dead.

After all the trekking has exhausted you, a trip to the thermal springs **Agua Caliente**, ① *20 km north from Copán, T2651-4746, daily 0800-2000,* will be just what you need. Reached by a road through villages and beautiful scenery, it's a 45-minute journey by vehicle, pickups sometimes go for about US$25, shared between passengers. The cheapest option is local transport from beside the soccer field (three buses daily, US$1.50), though it's a very rough unpaved road, only advisable by 4WD in wet season. Best to use **Base Camp Adventures** for trips, US$15, plus entry to hot springs. Imaginatively designed as a Maya spiritual centre, complete with tunnel entry to a Xibalba 'underworld', Luna Jaguar offers a hedonistic treat, with 13 different hot pools, mud bath, hydrotherapy warm shower, DIY hot stone foot massage, nature trail and river bathing (US$10, plus extra for massage treatments), all set among the steamy lush forest with aloof Maya sculptures looking over the simmering bathers. Therapist on hand for advice; snacks and drinks served at the poolside. There are changing facilities, toilets, drinks and snacks in the park. Cold water pools before entrance to spa, US$3. Also on the road to Guatemala is the **Enchanted Wings Butterfly House** ① *0800-1700, US$5.50* (see page 32).

Nine kilometres east of Copán is **Santa Rita**, a small colonial town on the Copán River with cobblestones and red roofs (**Hospedaje Santa Rita** and unnamed outdoor restaurant recommended, off main road next to Esso; speciality *tajadas*, huge portions, cheap).

Also try the **Macaw Mountain** ⓘ *10 mins from town centre, T2651-4245, www.macawmountain.com, US$10 (valid for 3 days)*, an ecotourism project incorporating Honduras' largest bird park with 130+ parrots, toucans and macaws, all locally rescued or donated, including some injured and sick birds. There are also some birds of prey, including tiny pigmy owls, all lovingly cared for in clean, spacious enclosures; some tamer birds are in an open area. There are tours of the coffee *finca*, with expert bilingual naturalist guides; riverside restaurant serving good, hearty food,

Western Honduras

including excellent coffee and freshly baked cakes, a visitor centre and river swimming. Highly recommended.

Santa Rosa de Copán → *For listings, see pages 43-52. Altitude: 1160 m.*

Santa Rosa is an important regional town with a colonial atmosphere of cobbled streets and some of the best colonial architecture in Honduras. Originally known as Los Llanos, it was made a municipality in 1812 and became capital of the Department of Copán when it was split from Gracias (now Lempira). The town is set in some of the best scenery in Honduras and the fine weather makes it ideal for hiking, horses and mountain biking.

Santa Rosa owes its wealth to the fact that it's an agricultural and cattle-raising area. Maize and tobacco are grown here, and visitors can see traditional hand-rolling at the **Flor de Copán cigar factory** ① *3 blocks east of the bus terminal, T2662 0185, Mon-Fri until 1700, closed 1130-1300, tours in Spanish at 1000 and 1400, US$2 per person – ask the guard at the gate.* The central plaza and church are perched on a hilltop. There is a quieter plaza, the **Parque Infantil** ① *Calle Real Centenario y 6 Av SO*, a fenced playground and a nice place to relax. The main **market** ① *1 Calle and 3 Av NE*, has good leather items. **Farmers' markets** are held daily in Barrio Santa Teresa (take 4 Calle SE

Santa Rosa de Copán

Sleeping ▤
Blanca Nieves **1**
Continental **2**
Elvir **4**
Hospedaje Calle
 Real **5**
Maya Central **10**

Posada de Carlos
 y Blanca **7**
Rosario **11**
VIP Copán **3**

Eating ◑
El Rodeo **2**
Flamingos **3**
Las Haciendas **4**
Pizza Pizza **8**
Weekends Pizza **9**
Well **10**

Walking from San Manuel Colohuete to Belén Gualcho

There is a well-defined, well-used and easy-to-follow mule trail linking these two villages, which makes a good one- or two-day hike. Maps are not essential as there are communities at many points along the way where advice can be sought. If required, a map of the area is available from the Lenca Cultural Centre in Gracias.

The path leading away from the village leaves from opposite the *pulpería* and *comedor* where the bus drops you, heading west and downhill into a valley. The path is used by 4WD vehicles and continues to San Sebastián. Just after the community of San José, after passing the last house, the path to Belén branches off. A smaller path leaves the 4WD track and climbs steeply up to your right and more northwest.

One hour Just after Peña Blanca, the path direction becomes unclear after it crosses an area of white chalky rocks. There are several other paths here. The main path heads north and steeply downhill at this point.

Two hours There is water all the year round in the Quebrada de Rogán.

Three hours All year round water in Río Gualmite, a short descent. After this there is a longish, steep ascent.

Four hours Just after this point the path branches on a large flat grassy area. Both paths lead to Belén Gualcho. The one to the left drops and crosses the river and then you are faced with a long, arduous and very steep ascent. We would recommend taking the path to the right, which exits to the far right of a grassy area by three small houses.

Five hours The path climbs as it skirts around the Cerro Capitán. Just after passing the steepest part, a small landslide forces the path into a descent almost to the river. From here, only 2 m above the river, you can walk steeply down off the path to the river bank where there is the most perfect camp site. Flat sandy soil in some shade on the edge of a coffee plantation and 2 m from the river.

Six hours From the camping site there is a long, continuous climb before dropping down sharply to cross the river. It is possible, but difficult, to cross the river at the point the path meets it. Take a small path off to the right just before the river, which leads to a suspension bridge. From the river it is a long continuous climb, not especially steep, to Belén Gualcho. It is between two small peaks that can be seen clearly after crossing the river. There are more houses after crossing the river and the odd *pulpería* where you can buy refrescos or food.

past 5 Avenida SE), and at 4 Calle SE and 5 Avenida SE on Sunday 0500 to 1000.
▶▶ *For further information, visit www.visitesantarosadecopan.org.*

Around Santa Rosa de Copán

Taking time to explore some of the forested hills around Santa Rosa will lead you through spectacular scenery and give an insight into the life of agricultural Honduras.

There are buses from Santa Rosa west to the small town of **Dulce Nombre de Copán** (US$0.55). There are rooms available next to the Hondutel office. Hikers heading for Copán and the border can continue west through the mountains to stay at **San Agustín** (buses and pickups from Santa Rosa), take a hammock or sleeping bag, continuing next day through Mirasol to reach the Ruinas road at El Jaral, 11 km east of Copán ruins (see above).

South of Santa Rosa, buses pass through **Cucuyagua**, with a scenic river, good swimming and camping on its banks, and **San Pedro de Copán**, an attractive village and an entry point into the Parque Nacional Celaque, see below.

A mule trail (see box, page 38) connects **Belén Gualcho**, a Lenca village in the mountains and a good base for exploring the surrounding area, with **San Manuel de Colohuete** (1500 m), which has a magnificent colonial church whose façade is sculpted with figures of saints. Buses go to San Manuel from Gracias at 1300, four hours, and there's usually a pickup returning in the evening. There are no hotels so you must ask villagers about places to stay. There is an equally fine colonial church 30 minutes by 4WD vehicle to the southwest at **San Sebastián Colosuca** (1550 m). The village has a mild climate (two *hospedajes*; or try Don Rubilio; food at Doña Clementina García or Doña Alicia Molina). The Feria de San Sebastián is on 20 January. An hour's walk away is the Cueva del Diablo and 6 km away is Cerro El Alta with a lagoon at the top. From San Sebastián, a mule trail goes via the heights of **Agua Fría** to reach the route near the border at **Tomalá**.

Gracias → *For listings, see pages 43-52.*
Altitude: 765 m.

One of the oldest settlements in Honduras, dominated by Montañas de Celaque, Puca and Opulaca – the country's highest peaks – Gracias is a charming, friendly town. Just 50 km from Santa Rosa, both the town and the surrounding countryside are worth a visit. Gracias was the centre from which Francisco de Montejo, thrice Governor of Honduras, put down the great indigenous revolt of 1537-1538. Alonso de Cáceres, his lieutenant, besieged Lempira the indigenous leader in his impregnable

Gracias

To Santa Rosa de Copán

Río Arcagual

Cohdefor

C Principal

Las Mercedes

Palacio Municipal

Parque Central

San Marcos

To Castillo San Cristóbal

To Santa Lucía & Celaque

San Sebastián

To La Esperanza & Aguas Termales

To La Campa

N

200 metres
200 yards

Guancascos **3**
Hospedaje Corazón de Jesús **4**
Posada de Don Juan **5**
Rosario **6**
San Antonio **7**

Sleeping
Colonial **1**
Erick **2**

Eating
El Señorial **1**
La Fonda **2**

mountain-top fortress at Cerquín, finally luring him out under a flag of truce, ambushed him and treacherously killed him. When the Audiencia de los Confines was formed in 1544, Gracias became for a time the administrative centre of Central America.

A helpful **tourist office** in the Parque Central can store luggage and arrange transport to Parque Nacional Celaque.

There are three colonial churches, **San Sebastián**, **Las Mercedes** and **San Marcos** (a fourth, Santa Lucía, is southwest of Gracias), and a restored fort, with two fine Spanish cannon, on a hill five minutes' walk west of the centre. The fort, **El Castillo San Cristóbal**, has been well restored, and at the foot of the northern ramparts is the tomb of Juan Lindo, President of Honduras 1847-1852, who introduced free education through a system of state schools.

Around Gracias → *For listings, see pages 43-52.*

Balneario Aguas Termales
① *Daily 0600-2000, US$2.50, rental of towels, hammock, inner tube, restaurant/bar.*
Some 6 km from Gracias along the road to Esperanza (side road signposted), are hot, communal thermal pools in the forest for swimming (one hour by a path, 1½ hours by road). To find the path, walk 2 km beyond the bridge over Río Arcagual to a second bridge before which turn right by a white house. Climb the hill and take the first path on the left (no sign), cross the river and continue for about 15 minutes to the pools. Good place to barbecue.

Parque Nacional Celaque
It takes at least a day to climb from Gracias to the summit of **Monte Celaque** (2849 m, the highest point in Honduras). Most people allow two days to enjoy the trip. The trail begins from behind the visitor centre of the Parque Nacional Celaque (1400 m), which is 8 km from Gracias, two hours' walk. There are several intersections, best to ask at each. You can also enjoy a day walk to **Mirador La Cascada** ① *entry fee US$3 plus US$3 per night camping in the mountain*, about three hours from the visitor centre, 1½ hours downhill going back. Transport can be arranged with the tourist office in the Plaza Central (US$10 per vehicle for up to four people). **Comedor Doña Alejandrina** just before the visitor centre, provides excellent breakfasts. Not much of the 8-km road from Gracias to the park is passable when wet, without a high-clearance or 4WD vehicle. Transport can be arranged through the Lenca Centre. **Armando Mondragón** (Texaco station, T2898-4002) does trips, including lunch. At the centre there are seven beds, shower and cooking facilities, drinks available, well maintained. There is another cabin nearby with 10 beds. Take a torch and sleeping bag. Behind the centre is a trail going down to the river where a crystal-clear pool and waterfall make for wonderful bathing. For guides to the park, contact **Dona Mercedes' Comedor** in Villa Verde (T2994-96681), **Don Luis Melgar**, or **Don Cándido** (T2997-15114), or one of their brothers; all recommended. Ask the guide the exact way or pay US$6 for the guide. There is a warden, Miguel, living nearby who can supply food and beer but it is safer to take supplies from Gracias. Contact **Cohdefor** or **CIPANAC** in Gracias before leaving for full information. There is a trail all the way to the summit (trees are marked with ribbons) which takes at least six hours: the first three are easy to a campsite at 2000 m (**Campamento Don Tomás**) where there is small hut, the rest of the way is steep. A better

campsite if you can make it is **Campamento Naranjo**, with water, at about 2500 m – but you'll need a tent. Between these two sites, the climb is particularly steep and in cloud forest. Look out for spider monkeys. Above 2600 m quetzals have been seen. Many hikers don't bother with the summit as it is forested and enclosed; it's four hours down to the visitor centre. Don't forget good hiking boots, warm clothing, insect repellent and, given the dense forest and possibility of heavy cloud, a compass is also recommended for safety. Also, beware of snakes. There is a trail westward from the summit to Belén Gualcho which is steep towards Belén. It takes a couple of days, a guide might be a good idea.

Visiting the other peaks around Gracias is more complicated but interesting. Information, maps that you can photocopy, camping gear and guided tours can be found at the Lenca Cultural Centre.

Gracias to Erandique

After Gracias, the road runs 52 km to **San Juan del Caite** (a few *hospedajes*, Lempira, Sánchez, and the comfortable Hacienda, two restaurants nearby, helpful people and Peace Corps workers). From here a dirt road runs 26 km south to the small town of Erandique. Founded in 1560 and set high in pine-clad mountains not far from the border with El Salvador, it is a friendly town, and very beautiful. Lempira was born nearby, and was killed a few kilometres away. The third weekend in January is the local **Fiesta de San Sebastián**. Best time to visit is at the weekend. Market days are Friday and Sunday. Each of the three barrios has a nice colonial church. Ask around as there are lakes, rivers, waterfalls, springs and bathing ponds in the vicinity. Nearby is **San Antonio** where fine opals (not cut gems, but stones encased in rock) are mined and may be purchased. The many hamlets in the surrounding mountains are reached by roads that have been either resurfaced or rebuilt and the landscapes are magnificent.

There are several roads radiating from Erandique, including one to **Mapulaca** and the border with El Salvador (no immigration or customs or bridge here, at the Río Lempa), a road to San Andrés and another to Piraera (all passable in a car).

La Esperanza → *Altitude: 1485 m.*

Beyond San Juan del Caite the main, but still rough and stony, road winds through beautiful mountain pine forests to La Esperanza. It is 43 km from San Juan del Caite and another 98 km on a good road to Siguatepeque. Capital of Intibucá Department, La Esperanza is an old colonial town in a pleasant valley. It has an attractive church in front of the park. There is a grotto carved out of the mountainside west of the town centre, a site of religious festivals. There is a market on Thursdays and Sundays when the Lenca from nearby villages sell wares and food but no handicrafts. Nearby is the indigenous village of **Yaramanguila**. It's an excellent area for walking in forested hills, with lakes and waterfalls, although very cold December/January. You can hike to **Cerro de Ojos**, a hill to the northwest and visible from La Esperanza. It is forested with a clearing on top littered with many cylindrical holes; no one knows how they were formed, and they are a strange phenomenon. The turning to this hill is on the La Esperanza to San Juan road. Ask for directions.

Marcala and around → *For listings, see pages 43-52. Altitude: 1300 m.*

From La Esperanza, an unpaved road runs southeast to Marcala in the Department of La Paz (a paved road goes to La Paz). During the hotter months from March to May, a cooler climate can be found in the highlands of La Paz, with pleasant temperatures during the day and cold (depending on altitude) at night. Ideal for hiking and with beautiful scenery and dramatic waterfalls in the surrounding area, Marcala is a good base from which to visit Yarula, Santa Elena, Opatoro, San José and Guajiquiro. The Marcala region is one of the finest coffee-producing areas of Honduras and a visit to **Comarca**, at the entrance to town, gives an idea of how coffee is processed. Semana Santa is celebrated with a large procession through the main street and there is a **fiesta** in honour of San Miguel Arcángel in the last week of September.

Around Marcala

Near Marcala is **Balneario El Manzanal** ① *3 km on the road to La Esperanza, open weekends only*, which has a restaurant, two swimming pools and a boating lake. For panoramic views high above Marcala, follow this hike (one hour): head north past **Hotel Medina**, turn right (east) after the hotel and follow the road up into hills. After 2 km the road branches. Take the left branch and immediately on the left is a football field. A small path leaves from this field on the west side taking you through a small area of pine trees then out onto a ridge for excellent views. The track continues down from the ridge back to town, passing an unusual cemetery on a hill.

There are caves nearby on **Musula** mountain, the Cueva de las Animas in Guamizales and Cueva de El Gigante and El León near La Estanzuela with a high waterfall close by. Other waterfalls are El Chiflador, 67 m high, Las Golondrinas, La Chorrera and Santa Rosita. Transport goes to La Florida where there is good walking to the village of **Opatoro** and climbing **Cerro Guajiquiro**. Between Opatoro and Guajiquiro is the **Reserva las Trancas**, a heavily forested mountain where quetzales have been seen.

Yarula and **Santa Elena** are two tiny municipalities, the latter about 40 km from Marcala, with beautiful views (bus Marcala–Santa Elena 1230 returns 0500 next day, 2¾ hours, enquire at Gámez bus office opposite market; truck daily 0830 returns from Santa Elena at 1300). Sometimes meals are available at *comedores* in Yarula and Santa Elena. The dirt road from Marcala gradually deteriorates, the last 20 km being terrible, high clearance essential, 4WD recommended. In **La Cueva Pintada**, south of Santa Elena, there are pre-Columbian cave paintings (*pinturas rupestres*) of snakes, men and dogs; ask for a guide in Santa Elena. Ask also in this village about the **Danza de los Negritos**, performed at the annual **Fiesta de Santiago**, 24-25 March, in front of the church. A special performance may be organized, the dancers wearing their old wooden masks, if suitable payment is offered.

The village of **San José** (altitude: 1700 m) is a Lenca community where the climate can be cool and windy even in the hottest months. The scenery is superb, there's good hill walking (see box, page 38 for two examples; there are many others) and also rivers for swimming. Frequent pickups from Marcala, and two daily minibuses at about 0815 and 0900; from San José to Marcala minibuses depart at 0615 and 0645, one hour, US$1.

Nueva Ocotepeque → *For listings, see pages 43-52.*

Heading south from Santa Rosa, Nueva Ocotepeque gives access to good hiking and leads to the borders with Guatemala and El Salvador. The old colonial church of La Vieja (or La Antigua) between Nueva Ocotepeque and the border, is in the village of Antigua Ocotepeque, founded in the 1540s, but destroyed by a flood from Cerro El Pital in 1934.

The **Guisayote Biological Reserve** protects 35 sq km of cloud forest, about 50% virgin and is reached from the Western Highway, where there are trails and good hiking. Access is from El Portillo, the name of the pass on the main road north. El Portillo to El Sillón, the park's southern entrance, three to five hours. Twice daily bus from El Sillón to Ocotepeque. **El Pital**, 3 km east of Nueva Ocotepeque, at 2730 m is the third highest point in Honduras with several square kilometres of cloud forest. The park has not been developed for tourism.

The **Parque Nacional Montecristo** forms part of the Trifinio/La Fraternidad project, administered jointly by Honduras, Guatemala and El Salvador. The park is quite remote from the Honduran side, two to three days to the summit, but there are easy-to-follow trails. Access is best from Metapán in El Salvador. From the lookout point at the peak you can see about 90% of El Salvador and 20% of Honduras on a clear day. The natural resources office, for information, is opposite Texaco, two blocks from **Hotel y Comedor Congolón** at the south end of town. Raymond J Sabella of the US Peace Corps has written a very thorough description of the natural and historical attractions of the Department, including hikes, waterfalls and caves.

Western Honduras listings

For Sleeping and Eating price codes and other relevant information, see pages 10-11.

🛏 Sleeping

San Pedro Sula to Copán *p31*
$$-$ San Carlos, La Entrada, at junction to Copán Ruinas, T2898-5228. A/c, modern, cable TV, bar, swimming pool, restaurant (T2661-2187), excellent value.
$ Central, by Shell, La Entrada. With 2 beds (cheaper with 1), bath, cold water, fans.
$ Hospedaje Golosino Yessi, La Entrada. Parking, small rooms, OK.
$ Hospedaje María, La Entrada. Good, limited food.

Copán Ruinas *p31, map p32*
$$$$ Hacienda San Lucas, south out of town, T2651-4495, www.haciendasan lucas.com. Great spot for calm and tranquillity. 8 rooms with hot water bath,

restaurant, renovated hacienda home, lovely views of Copán river valley and hiking trails.
$$$ Camino Maya, corner of main plaza, T2651-4646, www.caminomayahotel.com. With bath, good restaurant, rooms bright and airy, cable TV, a/c, fans, rooms on courtyard quieter than street, English spoken, free internet, balconies on some upstairs rooms.
$$$ La Casa de Café, 4½ blocks west of plaza, T2651-4620, www.casadecafecopan.com. Renovated colonial home, with breakfast, coffee all day, library, expert local information, beautifully designed garden, lovely views over valley, friendly and interesting hosts, English spoken. Popular so best to reserve in advance, protected parking. **Bamboo Patio** massage pavilion offers 1-hr relaxation massage. Wi-Fi. Recommended.
$$$ Terramaya, 2 blocks uphill from main plaza, T2651 4623, www.terramayacopan.com. The town's 1st boutique-style hotel, with

6 small but tasteful rooms, glorious countryside views from those upstairs, leafy little garden with massage area and outdoor shower; lounge areas and library. Breakfast included. Owners of **Casa del Café** (see above) very helpful and knowledgeable for local tours and activities.

$$$-$$ Marina Copán, on the plaza occupying almost an entire block, T2651-4070, www.hotelmarinacopan.com. Swimming pool, sauna, restaurant, bar, live marimba music at weekends, also caters for tour groups, large rooms with TV, a/c, suites, very tasteful and spacious, friendly atmosphere. Recommended.

$$ Brisas de Copán, T2651-4118. Terrace, modern rooms with bath, hot water, quiet, limited parking. Recommended.

$$ Plaza Copán, on southeast corner of main plaza, T2651-4508. Clean, bright rooms with kitschy decor, cable TV and a/c, restaurant facing plaza, pool, laundry, safe parking.

$$ Posada Honduras, central location, T2651-4059, www.laposadacopan.com. Private bath, ceiling fan and hot water.

$ Café Via Via Copán, T2651-4652, www.viaviacafe.com. Great rooms, part of a worldwide Belgian network of cafés, breakfast US$2.75, special price for students with card and discounts for more than 1 night, hot water, good beds, bar and great vegetarian food.

$ En la Manzana Verde, T2651-4652, www.enlamanzanaverde.com. Great shared bunk rooms, shared bath, kitchen, same owners as **Via Via**. Good budget choice.

$ Hospedaje Los Gemelos, 1 block down from **Banco de Occidente**, T2651-4077. With shared bath, clean, fans, good value, friendly, pleasant patio. Recommended.

$ Hostel Iguana Azul, next to **La Casa de Café** and under same ownership, T2651-4620, www.iguanaazulcopan.com. Dormitory-style bunk beds in 2 rooms, shared bath, also 3 more private double rooms, hot water, free purified water, lockers, laundry facilities, garden patio, colonial decor, clean, comfortable, common area, books, magazines, travel guides (including Footprint), maps, garden, fans, safe box, English spoken. Good for backpackers.

Apartments

Casa Jaguar Rental Home, just 5 blocks from Parque Central, T2651-4620, www.casa jaguarcopan.com. Comfortable village residence with 2 double bedrooms with a/c, fully equipped for self-catering. Available for the night, week or month. Contact **La Casa de Café**, see above.

La Casa de Don Santiago, T2651-4620, www.casadedonsantiagocopan.com. Same owners as **Casa Jaguar**, with 2 bedrooms, hot water bath, balconies with valley views, garden, fully equipped for self catering and available per night, week and month. Sparkling clean, comfortable and centrally located. Wi-Fi.

Santa Rosa de Copán *p37, map p37*

$$$ Continental, 2 Calle NO y 2-3 Av, T6262-0801, on 2nd floor. Good value with bath, hot water, fan, cable TV, friendly management.

$$$ Elvir, Calle Real Centenario SO, 3 Av SO, T2662-0805, hotelelvir@globalnet.hn. Safe, clean, quiet, all rooms have own bath, TV, hot water, drinking water; free internet in lobby good but pricey meals in *cafetería* or restaurant; gym and rooftop pool and bar.

$$ Posada de Carlos y Blanca, Calle Centenario between 3 and 4 Av NO, T2662-4020, posadacarlosyb@yahoo.com. Cosy family-run B&B with 6 comfy rooms with firm beds and bath; homely lounge with internet use, pretty enclosed back garden, quiet and secure.

$$ VIP Copán, 1 Calle, 3 Av, T2662-0265. With bath, TV, cheaper without, cell-like rooms but clean, safe, hot water in morning.

$$-$ Rosario, 3 Av NE No 139, T2662-0211. Cold water, with bath, cheaper without, friendly.

$ Blanca Nieves, 3 Av NE, Barrio Mercedes, T2662-1312. Safe, shared bath with cold water, laundry facilities. Going down hill but worth a look.

$ Hospedaje Calle Real, Real Centenario y 6 Av NE. Clean, quiet, friendly, best of the cheaper places but sometimes water failures.

$ Maya Central (not to be confused with **Hospedaje Maya**), 1 Calle NO y 3 Av NO, T2662-0073. With bath, cold shower, pleasant.

Around Santa Rosa de Copán *p38*
In Belén Gualcho hotels fill up quickly on Sat as traders arrive for the Sun market.

$ Hospedaje, east of Santa Rosa de Copán Lepaera, opposite market. Very basic.

$ Hotelito El Carmen, Belén Gualcho, 2 blocks east down from the church in the plaza. Friendly, clean, good views. Recommended.

$ Pensión, Corquín. Good *pensión* with a charming garden. Recommended.

Gracias *p39, map p39*
$$$ Posada de Don Juan, Calle Principal opposite **Banco de Occidente**, T2656-1020, www.posadadedonjuanhotel.com. Good beds, great hot showers, nice big towels, laundry, some rooms have TV, a pool and parking. Recommended.

$$ Guancascos, at the west end of Hondutel road, T2656-1219, www.guancascos.com. Bath, hot water, TV, also rents 2-room cabin at **Villa Verde** adjacent to Monte Celaque visitor centre.

$$ Hotel Rosario, T2656-0694. Hot water, private bath, pool, clean and friendly.

$ Colonial, 1 block south of Erick, T2656-1258. With bath, fan, bar, restaurant, very good.

$ Erick, same street as bus office, T2656-1066. With bath, cheaper without (cold shower), TV, comfortable beds, fresh, bright, clean, good value with helpful, friendly owners. Laundry facilities, stores luggage, shop selling basic supplies and can arrange

transport to Mt Celaque. Very convenient and recommended.

$ Finca Bavaria, quiet place at the edge of town, T2656-1372. Good breakfasts. German/Honduran owned. Parking.

$ Hospedaje Corazón de Jesús, on main street by market. Clean, OK.

$ San Antonio, main street, 2 blocks from Texaco station, T2656-1071. Clean, pleasant, friendly, good.

La Esperanza *p41*
Simple but pleasant *pensiones*.

$$ Hotel Mina, 1 block south of east side of market, T2783-1071. Good beds, clean, very friendly, food available.

$$ La Esperanza, T2783-0068. With bath, cheaper without, warm water, clean, TV, friendly, good meals.

$ El Rey, in Barrio La Morera, T2783-2083. Clean, friendly.

$ Mejía Batres, ½ block from Parque Central, T2783-0051. With bath, clean, friendly, excellent value.

Marcala and around *p42*
$ Hospedaje Edgar, main street, beginning of town. Clean, basic, no sheets.

$ Hospedaje Jairo, 2 blocks east of main square. With bath.

$ Medina, on main road through town, T2898-1866. The most comfortable, clean, modern with bath, *cafetería*, free purified water. Highly recommended.

$ Unnamed hotel, San José. Run by Brit Nigel Potter ('Nayo'). Basic but comfortable and clean, with meals. He also takes groups to stay in Lenca villages, US$5 per person plus US$10 per person for accommodation in a village; ask for the house of Doña Gloria, Profe Vinda, Nayo or Ruth. At least one of these will be present to meet visitors.

Nueva Ocotepeque *p43*
$$ Maya Chortis, Barrio San José, 4 Calle, 3 Av NE, T2653-3377. Nice rooms with bath,

double beds, hot water, fan, TV, minibar, phone, room service, quieter rooms at back, including breakfast, good restaurant, good value.

$$ Sandoval, opposite **Hondutel**, T2653-3098. Rooms and suites, breakfast included, private bath, hot water, cable TV, minibar, phone, room service, restaurant attached, good value.

$ Gran, about 250 m from town at the junction of the roads for El Salvador and Guatemala, just north of town, at Sinuapa. With bath, cold water, pleasant, clean, single beds only.

$ Ocotepeque, by **Transportes Toritos**. Clean but noisy.

$ San Antonio, 1 Calle, 3 Av, T2653-3072. Small rooms but OK.

Eating

Copán Ruinas *p31, map p32*
$$$ Café Welchez, next to Hotel Marina Copán. Good cakes but expensive and coffee 'unpredictable'.

$$$ Hacienda San Lucas, south out of town, T2651-4106. Set menu by reservation, with 5-course meal, local ingredients, candlelight – great place for a special meal.

$$$ Twisted Tanya's, T2651-4182, www.twistedtanya.com. Mon-Sat 1500-2200. Happy hour 1600-1800. Lovely open-air setting, 2nd floor. Fine dining and quirky retro decor (ie mirrorballs) big portions, but overpriced and scatty service.

$$ Café Vamos a Ver, 1 block from plaza. Open daily 0700-2200. Lots of vegetables, good sandwiches and snacks, complete dinner US$5, pleasant, good value.

$$ Café Via Via Copán (see Sleeping, above). Food, fresh bread, bar, lodging.

$$ Elisa's at Camino Maya (see Sleeping, above). Excellent food at reasonable prices, pleasant, good service.

$$ La Casa de Todo, 1 block from Parque Central in a pleasant garden setting, www.casadetodo.com. Open 0700-2100.

Restaurant, internet, craft shop, internet, book exchange. What more could you want?

$$ Llama del Bosque, 2 blocks west of plaza. Open for breakfast, lunch and dinner, pleasant, large portions of reasonable food, try their *carnitas típicas*. Recommended.

$$ Pizza Copán, locally known as Jim's, US expat Jim cooks up good old US of A fare: grilled chicken, BBQ steaks, burgers and good pizza.

$ Carnitas Nía Lola, 2 blocks south of Parque Central, at end of road. Open daily 0700-2200. *Comida típica*, busy bar, relaxed atmosphere and book exchange.

$ Espresso Americano, Parque Central location for a café serving great coffee, ideal for people-watching.

$ Picame (see map). Good hearty food, good value, huge portions, popular with travellers. Recommended.

$ Pupusería y Comedor Mari, ½ block from market. The best cheap, typical food in town. Clean, decent service, very popular with locals at lunchtime. Daily specials like seafood soup. Food is fresh, cheap and plentiful, popular with locals.

Santa Rosa de Copán *p37, map p37*
$$ El Rodeo, 1 Av SE. Good menu, specializes in steaks, nice atmosphere, plenty of dead animals on the walls, pricey.

$$ Flamingos, 1 Av SE, off main plaza, T2662-0654. Reasonably priced and good pasta and chop suey, popular with locals; upstairs lounge bar, painted flamingos on walls.

$$ La Gran Villa, on the *carretera*. Some of the tastiest meats and meals in Santa Rosa, run by Garífuna family. Recommended.

$$ Las Haciendas, 1 Av Calle SE. Steak and seafood, varied menu, filling *comida corriente*, and an attractive patio bar. Recommended.

$$ Well, 3 Calle 2 Av SE, Chinese, a/c, huge portions, good value and service.

$ Merendero El Campesino, at the bus terminal. Good *comedor*.

$ Pizza Pizza, Real Centenario 5 Av NE, 4½ blocks from main plaza. Good pizza and pasta, great coffee, but rather stark and soulless, US owned, book exchange.

$ Weekends Pizza, 3 Av SO and 3C, T2662-4221. Downhill on edge of town but worth the walk for good-value pizzas, pastas and unusual extras like cheese straws; bright and colourful with lime green and marigold yellow walls. Home-made bread, local honey and coffee for sale. Wed-Sun 0900-2100. Recommended.

Around Santa Rosa de Copán *p38*
In Belén Gualcho there are 2 *comedores* on south side of plaza and east side on corner with store.

$ Comedor Mery, Belén Gualcho. 1 block northwest of plaza. Good food in a welcoming family atmosphere.

$ Las Haciendas, Belén Gualcho. Good.

Gracias *p39, map p39*
For breakfast, try the *comedores* near the market or, better, the restaurant at **Hotel Iris** (good *comida corriente* too) or **Guancascos**.

$$ Comedor Graciano and **Pollo Gracianito**, main street. Good value.

$$ La Fonda (see map). Good food, good value, attractively decorated, but no written menu – good practice for your Spanish. Recommended.

$ El Señorial, main street. Simple meals and snacks, once house of former president Dr Juan Lindo.

$ Rancho de Lily, 3 blocks west of Hondutel. Value for money, rustic cabin, bar service, good snacks.

La Esperanza *p41*
$$ Pizza Venezia, on edge of town towards Marcala. Good Italian dishes.

$ Café El Ecológico, corner of Parque Central. Home-made cakes and pastries, fruit drinks, delicious home-made jams.

$ Restaurant Magus, 1 block east of plaza, Good food in a video bar atmosphere.

$ Unnamed restaurant in front of church. Very good *comida corriente*.

Marcala and around *p42*
$$ Riviera Linda, opposite **Hotel Medina**. Pleasant atmosphere, spacious, a little pricey but good food.

$ Café Express, beside Esso. Good breakfast and *comida corrida*. Recommended.

$ Darwin, main street in centre. Cheap breakfasts from 0700. Recommended.

$ El Mirador, on entering town by petrol station. Nice views from veranda, good food. Recommended.

$ Jarito, opposite market entrance. Good.

Around Marcala *p42*
$ Comedor, 500 m before plaza on main road. Good, clean and cheap.

Nueva Ocotepeque *p43*
$$ Sandoval and **Don Chepe**, at **Maya Chortis**. The best options. Excellent food, small wine lists, good value. Recommended. Comedor Nora (**$**), Parque Central, and **Merendera Ruth** (**$**), 2 Calle NE, just off Parque Central, both offer economical *comida corriente*, preferable to *comedores* around bus terminal.

☻ Entertainment

Copán Ruinas *p31, map p32*
Barcito, 1 block down from southwest corner of main square, small, cosy, laid-back bar on upstairs open terrace; 1700-1900 Happy Hour; also serves great and inexpensive gourmet snacks and tapas.

Papa Changos, located a few blocks from downtown. After hours spot, popular with young locals and traveller crowd. Gets going at midnight on Fri and Sat. The place to let loose and party till dawn.

Via Via, see Sleeping, every night till 2400. European chill-out lounge vibe, comfortable and popular, food until 2100.

Santa Rosa de Copán *p37, map p37*
Bars and clubs
Extasis, shows videos Mon-Thu night.
Luna Jaguar, at 3 Av, between 1 Calle SE and Calle Real Centenario, is the hottest disco in town, but proper dress required.
Manzanitas, is on the corner of 3 Av SE and Calle Real Centenario, if you fancy singing your heart out to a little karaoke.

Cinema
Plaza Saavedra, opposite Blanca Nieves, nightly at 1900.

Santa Rosa de Copán *p37, map p37*
21-31 Aug Festival de Santa Rosa de Lima; the 'Tobacco Queen' is crowned at the end of the week.

La Esperanza *p41*
3rd week in Jul Festival de la Papa.
8 Dec Fiesta de la Virgen de la Concepción.

Copán Ruinas *p31, map p32*
Selling all sorts of local crafts are **La Casa de Todo**, down the street from **Banco de Occidente**, is one of Copán's best crafts shop, with a popular café for light meals and snacks; **Yax Kuk Mo** on southwest corner of plaza has biggest selection; **Mayan Connection**, opposite Barcito (see Entertainment, above) is a bit more expensive but better than average quality. **La Casa del Jade**, 1 block uphill from **Hotel Marina Copán** (with another branch in lobby) specializes in high-class designer jewellery.

Santa Rosa de Copán *p37, map p37*
Supermercado Manzanitaz, C Centenario.

Copán Ruinas *p31, map p32*
Animal and birdwatching
Birding guide and naturalist **Bob Gallardo** (T2651-4133, rgallardo32@hotmail.com) is the owner of the Butterfly Garden and an expert on Honduran flora and fauna. He leads birding trips, **natural history tours**, orchid and serpent tours around Copán and other parts of Honduras, including La Mosquitia.
Alexander Alvarado, T9751-1680, alexander2084@hotmail.com, based in Copán Ruinas, also leads birdwatching and hiking tours around the country; knows his stuff and speaks good English.

Coffee tours
Copán Coffee Tour, Finca Santa Isabel, 40 mins' drive from Copán Ruinas, www.cafe honduras.com, T2651-4202. Run by family producers of high-quality Welchez coffee for 3 generations. 3- to 4-hr tour of grounds shows whole production process in lovely hillside setting, with terrace restaurant overlooking river; expert multilingual guides; US$25-30. Horse riding also available, through countryside rich with flora and fauna, including some 80 bird species and medicinal plants. The best tour of its kind in the area, highly recommended.

Horse riding
You will probably be approached with offers of horse hire, which is a good way of getting to nearby attractions. Riding trips are available to **Los Sapos** and **Las Sepulturas**, US$15 for 3 hrs. Watch out for taxi and on the street recommendations as the quality and price can be poor.
Finca El Cisne, T2651-4695, www.fincael cisne.com. Full-day tours to the coffee plantation high in the mountains including horse riding, lunch and transport. Also trips to hot springs on this working hacienda. Accommodation (**$$$**). Good trip.

Tour operators
Base Camp Adventures, T2651-4695. Nature hikes US$8, treks, motocross tours US$40, horse riding US$15, expedition hikes US$20 and transport including shuttles to Guatemala City, Antigua US$12.

Copán Connections, T2651-4182, www.copanconnections.com. Tours, hotels, transport, specializing in Copán and Bay Islands. Run by Tanya of Twisted Tanya fame.

MC Tours, across the street from **Hotel Marina**, T2651-4453, www.mctours-honduras.com. Local and countrywide tours.

Santa Rosa de Copán *p37, map p37*
Tour operators
Lenca Land Trails, at Hotel Elvir, T2662-1375, www.lenca-honduras.com. Run by Max Elvir, who organizes cultural tours of the Lenca mountain villages in western Honduras, hiking, mountain biking, the lot; including a fascinating visit to a *purería* (cigar workshop), pilgrimage shrine and archaeological site at Quezailica, a village 38 km north of Santa Rosa. Excellent source of information about the region. Highly recommended.

Gracias *p39, map p39*
Tour operators
Celaque Aventuras Tours, based in Guancascos, T2656-1219. Run by Christophe Condor who organizes walking tours, visits to **La Campa**, the national park, thermal baths, horse hire, US$8, includes horse riding, visit to thermal pools day or night, visiting natural caves. Hot springs only, US$4.

Guancascos Tourist Centre, at the **Guancascos Hotel**, arranges tours and expeditions to Monte Celaque Parque Nacional, local villages and other attractions.

Marcala and around *p42*
For trips to visit Lenca villages see unnamed hotel in San José, under Sleeping, page 45.

⊖ Transport

Copán Ruinas *p31, map p32*
Bus
Heading inland you normally have to go to San Pedro Sula before heading for the coast or south to the capital.

There is a 1st-class direct service to **San Pedro Sula** with connections to **Tegucigalpa** and **La Ceiba** with Hedman Alas (T2651-4037, www.hedmanalas.com), 3 a day, 3 hrs to San Pedro. US$16, at 1030 and 1430, with connections in San Pedro for Tegucigalpa and La Ceiba. Also 0515 daily connection to **Tela**, 8 hrs, US$22 and **San Pedro Sula Airport, US$21**. To **Guatemala City** (US$35) and **Antigua** (US$42) at 1420 and 1800. To **San Pedro Sula** Casasola Express for San Pedro Sula (T2651-4078) at 0400, 0500, 0600, 0700 and 1400. Both services are comfortable, efficient, good value and with reclining seats.

If heading for **Santa Rosa de Copán** or **Gracias** get a bus to the junction at La Entrada and change there. Buses for **La Entrada** leave Copán Ruinas every 30 mins, 1 hr, US$1.80.

Plus+ Agency daily shuttle bus service (www.plustravelguate.com, T2651-4088), main office in Copán Ruinas, Comercial Handal, Calle Independencia, to many destinations around Honduras and to Guatemala City and Antigua (US$8). If travelling in a group, private express minibuses can be hired to **San Pedro Sula**, **Tela**, **La Ceiba**, and airport from Hotel Patty and Yaragua Tours – US$120 regardless of number of people. Numerous boys greet you on arrival to carry bags or offer directions for a small fee, while most are good kids, some will tell you hotels are closed when they aren't.

Tuk-tuk
As in much of Honduras, tuk-tuks have arrived, providing cheap, easy transport.

Short trips around town cost US$0.50, **Macaw Mountain Bird Park** US$1.10, **ruins** US$0.80, **Hedman Alas** terminal US$1.10.

Santa Rosa de Copán and around
p37, map p37
Bus
Buses depart from the city bus station on Carretera Internacional.
Local 'El Urbano' bus to centre from bus station (on Carretera Internacional, 2 km below town, opposite Hotel Mayaland), US$0.15, 15 mins; taxi US$1.40.

Long distance If coming from the Guatemalan border at Nueva Ocotepeque, the bus will stop at the end of town near Av Centenario, 2 km below town, opposite **Hotel Mayaland**. To **Tegucigalpa**, Toritos leaves at 0400 from terminal Mon-Sat 0400 and 1000 Sun, US$6, 10 hrs; also **Empresa de Transportes la Sultana** (T2662-0940) has departures at 0500, 0700, and 0900. Alternatively, take an express bus to San Pedro Sula and an express bus on to Tegucigalpa (US$5, 6 hrs). To **Gracias**, Transportes Lempira, several 0630-1800, 1½ hrs, US$1.30. To **San Pedro Sula**, US$2.50, 4 hrs, every 45 mins 0400-1730, express service daily 2½ hrs, US$3.50 (**Empresa Torito**). Bus to **La Entrada**, 1 hr, US$1. To **Copán Ruinas**, 4 hrs on good road, US$2.90, several direct daily 1100, 1230 and 1400. Alternatively, take any bus to La Entrada, 1 hr, US$1, and transfer to a Copán Ruinas bus. South on paved road to **Nueva Ocotepeque**, 6 daily, US$1.80, 2 hrs. There you change buses for El Salvador and Guatemala (1 hr to border, US$1, bus leaves hourly until 1700).

Around Santa Rosa de Copán *p38*
Bus Numerous buses head south daily from Santa Rosa to **Corquín** (US$0.75, 2 hrs). **Belén Gualcho** to **Santa Rosa** daily at 0430 (Sun at 0930). To **Gracias** from main plaza at 0400, 0500 and 1330.

Gracias *p39, map p39*
Bus
A bus goes to **La Esperanza** at 0530 and 0730, or take bus to Erandique (they leave when full from La Planta) get off at San Juan from where frequent buses goes to La Esperanza (1 hr, US$2)There is a bus service to **Santa Rosa de Copán**, US$1.30, from 0530 to 1630, 5 times a day, 1½ hrs; beautiful journey through majestic scenery. Also to **San Pedro Sula** at 0500, 0800 and 0900, US$3, 4 hrs. Daily bus service to **Lepaera** 1400, 1½ hrs, US$1.50; daily bus to **San Manuel de Colohuete** at 1300. **Cotral** bus ticket office is 1 block north of Parque Central. **Torito** bus, a few metres from the main terminal, has buses to the Guatemalan border at **Agua Caliente**, one at 1000, change buses at Nueva Ocotepeque.

Gracias to Erandique *p41*
Bus
There are minibuses to Erandique from the bridge on the road to La Esperanza, 1100 daily, although most people go by truck from Gracias (there is sometimes a van service as far as San Juan) or La Esperanza (change trucks at San Juan intersection, very dusty). Return minibus to Gracias at 0500 daily, which connects with the bus to La Esperanza in San Juan. Trucks leave Erandique 0700 daily, but sometimes earlier, and occasionally a 2nd one leaves around 0800 for Gracias, otherwise be prepared for a long wait for a pickup.

La Esperanza *p41*
Bus
To **Tegucigalpa** several daily, 3½ hrs, US$5 (Cobramil, also to **San Pedro Sula**, and **Joelito**, 4 hrs, US$2.60). To **Siguatepeque** 0700, 0900, last at 1000, US$1.50, 1 hr; also to **Siguatepeque**, **Comayagua** at 0600; and to the **Salvadorean border**; bus stops by market. Hourly minibuses to **Yaramanguila**, 30 mins. Daily bus to **Marcala**, 2 hrs at 1230

(but check), US$0.80 (truck, US$1.20, 2¼ hrs). Minibus service at 1130, US$1.50. Daily minibus service to **San Juan**, departs between 1030-1200 from a parking space midway between the 2 bus stops, 2½ hrs, pickups also do this journey, very crowded; for **Erandique**, alight at Erandique turn-off, 1 km before San Juan and wait for truck to pass (*comedor* plus basic *hospedaje* at intersection). If going to Gracias, stay on the La Esperanza–San Juan bus until the end of the line where a pickup collects passengers 15 mins or so later, 1 hr San Juan–Gracias. Buses to **Lake Yojoa** (see page 55), 2 hrs, US$2.50.

Marcala and around *p42*
Bus

To **Tegucigalpa** 0500, 0915 and 1000 daily via La Paz, 4 hrs, US$2.40 (bus from Tegucigalpa at 0800 and 1400, **Empresa Lila**, 4-5 Av, 7 Calle, No 418 Comayagüela, opposite Hispano cinema); bus to **La Paz** only, 0700, 2 hrs, US$1; several minibuses a day, 1½ hrs, US$1.50. Bus also from Comayagua. Pickup truck to **San José** at around 1000 from market, ask for drivers, Don Santos, Torencio, or Gustavo. Bus to **La Esperanza** at about 0830, unreliable, check with driver, Don Pincho, at the supermarket next to where the bus is parked (same street as Hotel Medina), 1½-2 hrs, otherwise hitching possible, going rate US$1.20. Bus to **San Miguel**, El Salvador, **Transportes Wendy Patricia**, 0500, 1200, 7 hrs, US$3.50.

Nueva Ocotepeque *p43*
Bus

Transportes Escobar daily service **Tegucigalpa** to Nueva Ocotepeque/Agua Caliente, via La Entrada and Santa Rosa de Copán (12 Av entre 8 y 9 Calle, Barrio Concepción, Comayagüela, T2237-4897; **Hotel Sandoval**, T2653-3098, Nueva Ocotepeque). Buses to **San Pedro Sula** stop at La Entrada (US$1.70), 1st at 0030, for connections to Copán. There are

splendid mountain views. From **San Pedro Sula** there are regular buses via Santa Rosa south (6 hrs, US$4.50); road is well paved.

❶ Directory

Copán Ruinas *p31, map p32*
Banks Banco Atlántida with an ATM and Banco de Occidente are both on the plaza and take Visa. **BAC**, has similar services and an ATM for MasterCard and Amex. It is possible to change Guatemalan currency in Copán but not at the banks; try where buses leave for the border or with money changers behind Hotel Marina. **Internet** Yaragua Tours, off southeast corner of Parque Central, daily 0700-2200 per hr. **Maya Connections**, inside handicraft shop one block downhill from southwest corner of Parque Central US$1.50 per hr, daily 0730-1800. **Casa de Todo**, internet and much more. Open daily 0700-2100. **Language schools** Academia de Español Guacamaya, T2651-4360, www.guacamaya.com, classes US$140 a week, with homestay US$225, recommended. Ixbalanque, T2651-4432, www.ixbalanque.com, 1-1 teaching plus board and lodging with local family, US$210 for classes and 7 days homestay. **Post** Next to the market, Mon-Fri 0800-1200, 1300-1700, Sat 0800-1200, beautiful stamps available. Max 4 kg by airmail. **Telephone** Phone calls can be made from the office of **Hondutel** 0800-2100.

Santa Rosa de Copán *p37, map p37*
Banks Atlántida (has Visa ATM, maximum withdrawal US$30) and **Banco de Occidente** (has ATM), both are on main plaza. **Cultural centre** ½ block south of Parque Central with live music and singing, sculpture and picture galley. **Immigration** Av Alvaro Contreras y 2 Calle NO, helpful, extensions available. **Internet** Pizza Pizza, has email at US$4 per hr, good machines. **Prodigy**, C Centenario, US$1 per hr, also across the

road from the Hotel Copán, US$2 per hr. **Laundry** Lavandaría Florencia, Calle Centenario. **Medical services** Dentist: Dr Wilfredo Urquía, at Calle Real Centenario 3-4 Av NE, speaks English. Recommended. Doctors: Clínica Médica Las Gemas, 2 Av NO, near Hotel Elvir, T2666-1428, run by Dr Soheil Rajabian (speaks English among other languages), 1st-class attention. Hospital: Médico Quirúrgico, Barrio Miraflores, Carretera Internacional, T2662-1283, fast and efficient, but not cheap. **Post and telephone** The post office and **Hondutel** are on the park, opposite side to the cathedral. **Voluntary work** **Hogar San Antonio**, run by nuns across the street from the Parque Infantil (city playground), welcomes volunteers, as does the Cultural Centre.

Gracias *p39, map p39*
Banks Bancafé, Bancrecer and Banco de Occidente, but none take Visa yet. **Cultural centres** Music lessons including marimba, available from Ramón Alvarenga, 2 blocks west of Parque Central on the same side as Iglesia San Marcos. **Internet** plenty to choose from. **Post and telephone** Hondutel and post office 1 block south of Parque Central, closes 1100 on Sat.

La Esperanza *p41*
Banks Banco de Occidente, Banco Atlántida and Banadesa. **Internet** Couple of places, one near the cathedral, US$4 per hr.

Marcala and around *p42*
Banks Banco de Occidente and Bancafé.

Nueva Ocotepeque *p43*
Banks Banco de Occidente will change TCs. Banco Atlántida has Visa facilities.

Tegucigalpa to San Pedro Sula

The main road connecting Tegucigalpa and the country's second largest city, San Pedro Sula, heads north through beautiful scenery along the shore of Lago Yojoa, skirting villages of the Lenca communities. Alhough the tendency is to head north for the warmth and beauty of the beaches, a slow journey along the road is very rewarding.

Támara and Zambrano → *See Around Tegucigalpa map, page 21.*

The Northern Highway between Tegucigalpa and San Pedro Sula leaves the capital and enters the vast valley of Támara, with the village of the same name. A turning leads to the **San Matías waterfal**, in a delightful area for walking in cool forested mountains.

The road climbs to the forested heights of **Parque Aventuras** ① *open at weekends*, at Km 33, good food, swimming pools, horses, bikes, then to **Zambrano** (altitude: 1450 m) at Km 34 and, at Km 36, midway between Tegucigalpa and Comayagua, **Parque Aurora** ① *camping US$0.50 per person, admission US$0.70, food supplies nearby*. It has a small zoo, good swimming pools and a picnic area among pine-covered hills, a lake with rowing boats (hire US$1 per hour), a snack bar and lovely scenery. The birdwatching is good too.

Before descending to the Comayagua Valley, the Northern Highway reaches another forested mountainous escarpment. Stalls selling home-made honey and garish chunky pottery line the roadside. A track leads off to the right (ask for directions), with about 30 minutes' climb on foot to a tableland and the natural fortress of **Tenampua**, where the indigenous inhabitants put up their last resistance to the *conquistadores*, even after the death of Lempira. It has an interesting wall and entrance portal.

Comayagua and around → *For listings, see pages 59-65. Altitude: 550 m.*

Founded on 7 December 1537 as Villa Santa María de Comayagua on the site of an indigenous village by Alonzo de Cáceres, Comayagua is a colonial town in the rich Comayagua plain, 1½ hours' drive (93 km) north from the capital. On 3 September 1543, it was designated the Seat of the Audiencia de los Confines by King Felipe II of Spain. President Marco Aurelio Soto transferred the capital to Tegucigalpa in 1880.

There are many old colonial buildings in Comayagua, reflecting the importance of Honduras' first capital after Independence in 1821. The centre has had an impressive makeover recently, and is worth a visit for the impressive colonial architecture in and around the main square, Plaza León Alvarado. Comayagua was declared a city in 1557, 20 years after its founding. Within a couple of centuries a rash of civic and religious buildings were constructed. The former university, the first in Central America, was founded in 1632 and closed in 1842 (it was located in the Casa Cural, Bishop's Palace, where the bishops have lived since 1558). Others include the churches of **La Merced** (1550-1588) and **La Caridad** (1730), **San Francisco** (1574) and **San Sebastián** (1575). **San Juan de Dios** (1590 but destroyed by earthquake in 1750), the church where the

Inquisition sat, is now the site of the Hospital Santa Teresa. **El Carmen** was built in 1785. The wealth of colonial heritage has attracted funds for renovation, which have produced a slow transformation in the town. The most interesting building is the **cathedral** in the Parque Central, inaugurated in 1711, with its plain square tower and façade decorated with sculpted figures of the saints, which contains some of the finest examples of colonial art in Honduras (daily 0700-1900). Of the 16 original hand-carved and gilded altars, just four survive today. The clock in the tower was originally made over 800 years ago in Spain and is the oldest working clock in the Americas. It was given to Comayagua by Felipe II in 1582. At first it was in La Merced when that was the cathedral, but it was moved to the new cathedral in 1715. You can climb the tower to see the clock and the old bells, with tour guides on hand in the cathedral (Ever Villanueva, T2994-77551, is knowledgeable and friendly). A huge floor mosaic of the cathedral façade has been built on the square, best seen from the tower. Half a block north of the cathedral is the **Ecclesiastical Museum** ① *daily 0930-1200, 1400-1700, US\$0.60.* One block south of the cathedral, the **Museo de Arqueología** ① *at the corner of 6 Calle and 1 Av NO, Wed-Fri 0800-1600, Sat and Sun 0900-1200, 1300-1600, US\$1.70,* housed in the former Palacio de Gobernación, is small scale but fascinating, with six rooms each devoted to a different period. Much of the collection came from digs in the El Cajón region, 47 km north of Comayagua, before the area was flooded for the hydroelectricity project. The **Casa Cultural** on a corner of the plaza, left of the cathedral, has permanent and temporary exhibitions of the city history and art, also **tourist information** ① *Tue-Thu 0900-1700, Fri and Sat 0900-2100, Sun 0900-1200, T2772-2028,* with a city map for sale, US\$1.20. City tours are available in an open-topped tram from outside the Casa Cultural, daily every 30 minutes, US\$1.50.

There are two colonial plazas shaded by trees and shrubs. A stone portal and a portion of the façade of **Casa Real** (the viceroy's residence) still survives. Built in 1739-1741, it was damaged by an earthquake in 1750 and destroyed by tremors in 1856. The army still uses a quaint old fortress built when Comayagua was the capital. There is a lively market area.

Parque Nacional Montaña de Comayagua is only 13 km from Comayagua, reached from the villages of San José de la Mora (4WD necessary) or San Jerónimo and Río Negro (usually passable). Contact **Fundación Ecosimco** ① *0 Calle y 1 Av NO in Comayagua, T772-4681,* for further information about the trails which lead through the cloud forest to waterfalls. The mountain (2407 m) has 6000 ha of cloud forest and is a major watershed for the area.

Siguatepeque → *Altitude: 1150 m.*

The Northern Highway crosses the Comayagua plain, part of the gap in the mountains which stretches from the Gulf of Fonseca to the Ulúa lowlands. Set in forested highlands 32 km northwest of Comayagua is the town of Siguatepeque, which has a cool climate. It is the site of the Escuela Nacional de Ciencias Forestales (which is worth a visit) and, being exactly halfway between Tegucigalpa and San Pedro Sula (128 km), is a collection point for the produce of the Intibucá, Comayagua and Lempira departments. The Cerro and Bosque de Calanterique, behind the Evangelical Hospital, is a 45-minute walk from the town centre. The Parque Central is pleasant, shaded by tall trees with the church of San Pablo on the north side and the cinema, **Hotel Versalles** and Boarding House Central on the east; **Hondutel** and the post office are on the south side.

Southwest from Siguatepeque, the route to La Esperanza is a beautiful paved road through lovely forested mountainous country, via **Jesús de Otoro**, where there are two basic *hospedajes* and **Balneario San Juan de Quelala** ① *US$0.30*, which has a *cafetería* and picnic sites. North from Siguatepeque, the highway goes over the forested escarpment of the continental divide, before descending towards Lago Yojoa. Just south of Taulabé on the highway are the illuminated **Caves of Taulabé** ① *daily, US$0.40, guides available*, with both stalactites and bats. North of Taulabé, and 16 km south of the lake is the turn-off northwest of a paved road to Santa Bárbara.

Lago Yojoa → *Altitude: 635 m.*

① *For local information contact Enrique Campos or his son at Hotel Agua Azul (see page 59). For more information, contact Proyecto Humuya, behind Iglesia Betel, 21 de Agosto, Siguatepeque (T2773-2426), or Proyecto de Desarrollo Río Yure, San Isidro, Cortés, Apdo 1149, Tegucigalpa.*

Sitting pretty among the mountains is the impressive Lake Yojoa, 22.5 km long and 10 km wide. To the west rise the Montañas de Santa Bárbara which include the country's second highest peak and the **Parque Nacional de Santa Bárbara** (see page 56). To the east is the **Parque Nacional Montaña Cerro Azul-Meámbar**. Pumas, jaguars and other animals live in the forests, pine-clad slopes and the cloud forest forming part of the reservoir of the Lago Yojoa basin. The national parks also have many waterfalls. The 50-sq-km Azul-Meámbar park is 30 km north of Siguatepeque and its highest point is 2047 m. To get to any of the entry points (Meámbar, the main one, Jardines, Bacadia, Monte Verde or San Isidro) a 4WD is necessary. A local ecological group, **Ecolago** ① *Edificio Midence Soto, Parque Central (Tegucigalpa), T2237 9659*, has marked out the area and is to offer guided tours. Ecolago has guides who are expert in spotting regional birds; at least 373 species have been identified around the lake. At one time the lake was full of bass, but overfishing and pollution have decimated the stocks. Tilapia farming is now very important.

The Northern Highway follows the eastern margin to the lake's southern tip at **Pito Solo**, where sailing and motor boats can be hired. Frustratingly, there is no public access to the lakeshore, which is fenced off by farms and private properties. Lake excursions are also available at several of the waterfront hotels and restaurants (see pages 59 and 61), which also offer the best views.

On the northern shore of Lago Yojoa is a complex of pre-Columbian settlements called **Los Naranjos** ① *US$5*, which are believed to have had a population of several thousand. It is considered to be the country's third most important archaeological site spanning the period from 1000 BC to AD 1000, and includes two ball courts. The site is slowly being developed for tourism by the Institute of Anthropology and History and has a visitor centre, small museum and coffee shop and a number of forest walking trails. Excavation work is currently in progress. The local office of the institute (T2557-8197) is at the **Hotel Brisas de Lago**. From the lake it is 37 km down to the hot Ulúa lowlands.

A paved road skirts the lake's northern shore for 12 km via Peña Blanca. A road heads southwest to **El Mochito**, Honduras' most important mining centre. A bus from 2 Avenida in San Pedro Sula goes to Las Vegas-El Mochito mine for walks along the west side of Lago Yojoa. Buses will generally stop anywhere along the east side of the lake. Another road heads north from the northern shore, through Río Lindo, to **Caracol** on the Northern Highway. This road gives access to the Pulhapanzak waterfall, with some unexcavated ceremonial mounds adjacent, and to Ojo de Agua, a pretty bathing spot near Caracol. **Peña Blanca** is, according to one reader, a "very ugly town" on the north side of the lake. Almost makes you want to stay.

Pulhapanzak waterfall

ⓘ *www.letsgopulha.com, T9995-1010, daily 0600-1800, US$2.80. The caretaker allows camping for US$0.85.*

The impressive 42-m waterfall at Pulhapanzak is on the Río Lindo. The waterfall is beautiful during, or just after the rainy season, and in sunshine there is a rainbow over the gorge. A path leads down to the foot of the falls, thick with spray, and very slippery; you can swim in river just before the edge – if you dare! There is a picnic area, a small *cafetería* and a good *comedor* 15 minutes' walk away down in the village, but the site does get crowded at weekends and holidays. There is also a large zip-wire course inside the grounds, with 13 sections, including one breathtaking stretch over the falls (US$32).

Santa Bárbara and around → *Altitude: 290 m.*

Santa Bárbara, surrounded by high mountains, forested hills and rivers, lies in a hot lowland valley 32 km west of Lago Yojoa. One of the nicest main towns in Honduras, it has little of architectural or historical interest compared with Gracias, Ojojona or Yuscarán, but it is here that you will find Panama hats and other goods made from junco palm. The majority of the population is fair-skinned (some redheads). In addition to being a pleasant place to stay, Santa Bárbara is also a good base for visiting villages throughout the Santa Bárbara Department. Nearby, the ruined colonial city of **Tencoa** has been rediscovered. A short local trek behind the town climbs the hills to the ruined site of **Castillo Bogran**, with fine views across the valley and the town. Heading south out of Santa Bárbara, the paved road joins the Northern Highway south of Lago Yojoa.

The Department of Santa Bárbara is called the Cuna de los Artesanos (cradle of artisans), with over 10,000 craftspeople involved in the manufacture of handicrafts. The main products come from the small junco palm, for example fine hats and baskets. The main towns for junco items are **La Arada**, 25 minutes from Santa Bárbara on the road to San Nicolás, and then branching off south, and **Ceguaca**, on a side road off the road to Tegucigalpa. Flowers and dolls from corn husks are made in Nueva Celilac. Mezcal is used to make carpets, rugs and hammocks, which are easy to find in towns such as **Ilama**, on the road to San Pedro Sula, which has one of the best small colonial churches in Honduras (no accommodation). People here also make *petates* (rugs) and purses.

Between Santa Bárbara and Lago Yojoa is the **Parque Nacional de Santa Bárbara** which contains the country's second highest peak, Montaña de Santa Bárbara at 2744 m. The rock is principally limestone with many subterranean caves. There is little tourist development as yet, with just one trail, and you can track down a guide in Los Andes, a village above Peña Blanca and Las Vegas. The best time to visit is the dry season, January-June. For information contact **Asociación Ecológica Corazón Verde** ⓘ *Palacio Municipal, Santa Bárbara*. There is a **Cohdefor** office just below the market (look for the sign) but they are not helpful.

San Pedro Sula and around

→ *For listings, see page 59-65. Altitude: 60-150 m. Population: 900,000.*

San Pedro Sula is the second largest and most industrialized city in the country and a centre for the banana, coffee, sugar and timber trades. It is a distribution hub for northern and western Honduras with good road links. Its business community is mainly of Arab origin, and it is considered the fastest-growing city between Mexico and Panama. By Central American standards, San Pedro Sula is a well-planned, modern city, but it's not a city you'll be inclined to stay in for long.

Ins and outs

Getting there San Pedro Sula is a more important international gateway than Tegucigalpa. Its airport, **Ramón Villeda Morales** (SAP) is 15 km from the city centre along a good

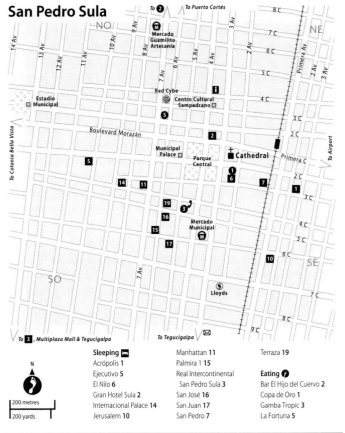

San Pedro Sula

Sleeping		
Acrópolis **1**	Manhattan **11**	Terraza **19**
Ejecutivo **5**	Palmira **1 15**	
El Nilo **6**	Real Intercontinental	**Eating**
Gran Hotel Sula **2**	San Pedro Sula **3**	Bar El Hijo del Cuervo **2**
Internacional Palace **14**	San José **16**	Copa de Oro **1**
Jerusalem **10**	San Juan **17**	Gamba Tropic **3**
	San Pedro **7**	La Fortuna **5**

four-lane highway. The **Gran Central Metropolitana** central bus terminal opened in March 2008. It's a short US$3 taxi from the centre of San Pedro Sula. ▸▸ *See Transport, page 64.*

Getting around The city is divided into four quadrants: Noreste (Northeast, NE), Noroeste (Northwest, NO), Sudeste (Southeast, SE) and Sudoeste (Southwest, SO), where most of the hotels are located, although newer hotels, shopping malls and restaurant chains are in the Noroeste. There are buses, minibuses and taxis for getting around town.

Best time to visit Although pleasant in the cooler season from November to February, temperatures are very high for the rest of the year. It is, nevertheless, a relatively clean city and the traffic is not too bad. The higher and cooler suburb of Bella Vista, with its fine views over the city, affords relief from the intense heat of the town centre.

Background
The city was founded in 1536 by Pedro de Alvarado in the lush and fertile valley of the Ulúa (Sula) River, beneath the forested slopes of the Merendón mountains. There are many banana plantations.

Sights
The large neocolonial-style **cathedral** was completed in the 1950s. **Museo de Antropología e Historia** ① *3 Av, 4 Calle NO, Mon, Wed-Sat 0900-1600, Sun 0900-1500, US$0.75, first Sun of the month is free,* has displays of the cultures that once inhabited the Ulúa Valley up to Spanish colonization and, on the first floor, local history since colonization. There is a museum café in the adjacent garden with fine stelae and a good set lunch. **Museo Jorge Milla Oviedo** ① *3 Av 9 Calle NE, Barrio Las Acacias, T552-5060*, is run by the foundation that cares for the Cuero y Salado wildlife reserve.

Parque Nacional Cusuco
① *Entrance is US$15, which includes a guided trip; you cannot go on your own. Contact the HRPF at 5 Av, 1 Calle NO, San Pedro Sula, T552-1014. Also contact Cohdefor, 10 Av, 5 Calle NO, Barrio Guamilito, San Pedro Sula, T553-4959, or Cambio CA, who run tours. Permission from HRPF is required to walk through the park to Tegucigalpita on the coast. There is a visitor centre but bring your own food. You cannot stay or camp in the park, but camping is possible outside. Access by dirt road from Cofradía (Cafetería Negro, one block northwest of plaza, good food), on the road to Santa Rosa de Copán, then to Buenos Aires: 2 hrs by car from San Pedro Sula, 4WD recommended. See Transport, page 65.*

Parque Nacional Cusuco, 20 km west of San Pedro Sula, offers some excellent hikes, trails and birdwatching in cloud forest. Now managed by the Fundación Ecológica Héctor Rodrigo Pastor Fasquelle (HRPF), the park was exploited for lumber until the 1950s. It was declared a protected area in 1959 when the Venezuelan ecologist, Geraldo Budowski, reported the pine trees there were the highest in Central America. Cutting was stopped and the lumber company abandoned the site. It is a splendid location and well worth the effort. The area includes tropical rainforest and cloud forest with all the associated flora and fauna. It includes both **Cerro Jilinco**, 2242 m, and **Cerro San Ildefonso**, 2228 m. There are four trails, ranging from 30 minutes to two days. They use old logging roads traversing forested ridges with good views. HRPF produces a bird checklist that includes the quetzal.

Tegucigalpa to San Pedro Sula listings

For Sleeping and Eating price codes and other relevant information, see pages 10-11.

Sleeping

Támara *p53*
$ Posada Don Willy, 500 m southwest of the toll station near Balneario San Francisco. With bath (electric shower), clean, quiet, fan, excellent value.

Zambrano *p53*
$$$-$$ Caserío Valuz, 1.5 km from the highway, 20 mins' walk on the road to Catarata Escondida, T9996-4294 (mob). 15 rooms with bath, most with balconies, 1- to 3-night packages including meals, also rooms for backpackers, with use of kitchen, volunteer work in exchange for room and board possible, a great place to relax, hike, read, paint.
$$$-$$ Casitas Primavera, Barrio La Primavera, 1.5 km west of main road, T2898-26625/ T2239-2328. Cosy houses, lovely setting, sleeps 6 (arrangements can be made for 1-2 people, **$**).

Comayagua and around *p53*
$$$ Santa María, Km 82 on the Tegucigalpa highway, T2772-7872. Private bath, a/c, cable TV. Best in town, although not in the centre.
$$ América Inc, 2 Av y 1 Calle NO, T2772-0360. A/c, private bath, hot water, cheaper with fan.
$$ Quan, 8 Calle NO, 3 y 4 Av, T2772-0070, hquan@hondutel.hn. Excellent, with private bath, popular.
$ Libertad, south side of Parque Central, T2772-0091. Nice courtyard, much choice of room size, clean apart from the toilets, cold water shower outside, helpful, good restaurant 2 doors away.
$ Norimax, Calle Central y 3 Av SO, Barrio Torondón, T2772-1210. Bath, a/c and TV, hot water, cheaper rooms available and car park.

$ Galaxia, Miramar, Primavera, Terminal and **Tío Luis**, are *pensiones*, all within a couple of blocks of the bus stop on the *Panamericana*.

Siguatepeque *p54*
$ Boarding House Central, Parque Central, T2773-2108. Very basic but good value; beware of the dog, which bites.
$ Internacional Gómez, 21 de Junio, T2773-2868. With bath (cheaper without), hot water, clean, parking.
$ Mi Hotel, 1 km from highway on road into town. With bath, parking, restaurant.
$ Versalles, on Parque Central. Excellent, with restaurant, use of kitchen on request.
$ Zari, T2773-2015. Hot water, cable TV, own generator, parking.

Lago Yojoa *p55*
$$$$ Gualiqueme, cottage at edge of lake, for information contact Richard Joint at **Honduyate**, T2882-3129. Has 4 bedrooms in main house, 2 in annexe. Daily, weekly, monthly rental, weekend packages include ferry and fishing boat.
$$ Brisas del Lago, close to Peña Blanca at the northern end of the lake, T2608-7229. Large, 1960s-era concrete hotel now looking a bit dated and mildewed, but with spacious rooms with a/c, cable TV and balcony, good value family suites; great lake views from gardens and pool. Good restaurant but overpriced, launches for hire and horse riding.
$$-$ Boarding House Moderno, Barrio Arriba, T643-2203. Rooms with fan better value than with a/c, with hot shower, quiet, parking. Recommended.
$$-$ Gran Hotel Colonial, 1½ blocks from Parque Central, T2643-2665. Fans in all rooms, some with a/c, cold water, sparsely furnished, friendly. Good view from roof. Recommended.
$$-$ Hotel Agua Azul, at north end of lake, about 3 km west from junction at Km 166,

T2991-7244. Basic clean cabins for 2 or more persons, meals for non-residents, but food and service in restaurant is poor, beautiful gardens, manager speaks English, swimming pool, fishing, horse riding and boating, launches, kayaks and pedalos for hire, around US$6 for 30 mins; mosquito coils. Good reduction in low season. Recommended (except when loud karaoke is in full swing).

$$-$ Los Remos, Pito Solo, at the south end of the lake, T2557-8054. Has cabins and camping facilities (**$**). Clean, beautiful setting, good food, nice for breakfasts, no beach but swimming pool, boat trips, parking US$3.

$ D&D Brewery and Guesthouse, T2994-9719, dndbrew@yahoo.com. Good rooms, with a garden with a small pool, book exchange and home brewed beer.

Santa Bárbara and around *p56*
$ Pensión, near the church, Colinas. Basic.
$ Ruth, Calle La Libertad, T2643-2632. Rooms without windows, fan.

San Pedro Sula and around *p57, map p57*
$$$$ Real Intercontinental San Pedro Sula, Blv del Sur at Centro Comercial Multiplaza, T2545-2500, www.ichotels group.com. Full service and the best in town.
$$$ Ejecutivo, 2 Calle 10 Av SO, T2552-4289, www.hotel-ejecutivo.com. A/c, cable TV, café/bar, phone, own generator.
$$$ Gran Hotel Sula, Parque Central, T2545-2600, www.hotelsula.hn. Rooms small and old-fashioned, but cosy, with all mod-cons. Good 24-hr restaurant, as well as bar, pool, gym and small shop. Charming and efficient service. Highly recommended.
$$ Acrópolis, 3 Calle 2 y 3 Av SE, T2557-2121. A/c, cable TV, parking, café, comfortable, friendly, good value.
$$ Hotel San Pedro, 3 Calle 2 Av SO, T2550-1513, www.hotelsanpedrosa.com. Private bath, a/c, cheaper with fan, popular,

clean, good value, rooms overlooking street are noisy, stores luggage, secure parking.
$$ Internacional Palace, 3 Calle 8 Av SO, Barrio El Benque, T2550-3838. A/c, helpful, internet service, parking, pool, bar, restaurant OK.
$ El Nilo, 3 Calle 2 Av SO, T2553-4689. Nice rooms, friendly.
$ Jerusalem, 6 Calle 1 Av SE, T2946-8352. Safe, good value.
$ Manhattan, 7 Av 3-4 Calle SO, T2550-2316. A/c, a bit run-down.
$ Palmira 1, 6 Calle 6 y 7 Av SO, T2557-6522. Clean, very convenient for buses, parking.
$ San José, 6 Av 5 y 6 Calle SO, just round corner from **Norteños** bus station, T2557-1208. Friendly, clean, safe, cheap and cheerful.
$ San Juan, 6 Calle 6 Av SO, T2553-1488. Modern, very noisy, clean, helpful, good value.
$ Terraza, 6 Av 4-5 Calle SO, T2550-3108. Friendly, cheaper without a/c. Dining room dark.

🍴 Eating

Comayagua and around *p53*
Parque Central is surrounded by restaurants and fast-food establishments.
$$$ Villa Real, behind the cathedral, T2772-0101. Mixes colonial atmosphere with good international and Honduran cuisine.
$$ Hein Wong, Parque Central. Chinese and international food, good, a/c, reasonably priced.
$$ Las Palmeras, south side of Parque Central, T2772-0352. Good breakfasts, open for dinner and lunch, good portions, reasonable prices.
$ Fruty Tacos, 4 Calle NO, just off southwest corner of Parque Central. Snacks and *licuados*.
$ Juanis Burger Shop, 1 Av NO 5 Calle, near southwest corner of Parque Central. Friendly, good food, OK.
$ Venecia, Calle del Comercio, in front of **Supermercado Carol**, T2772-1734. Popular café-style restaurant.

Siguatepeque *p54*

$$ Granja d'Elia, one of several restaurants on the Northern Hwy. Open all day, lots of vegetables, also meat, all-you-can-eat buffet, French chef, veg from own market garden and bread on sale outside.

$$ Juanci's, main street. Open until 2300. US-style hamburgers, good steaks and snacks.

$ Bicos, southwest corner of Parque Central. Nice snack bar/patisserie.

$ Cafetería Colonial, 4 Av SE (behind church). Good pastries and coffee, outside seating.

$ Pollos Kike, next door. Pleasant setting, fried chicken.

$ Supermercado Food, south side of plaza. Has a good snack bar inside.

Lago Yojoa *p55*

Roadside stalls near Peña Blanca sell fruit.

$$ Brisas del Canal, Peña Blanca, local food. Recommended, but small portions.

$$-$ Comedores, on the roadside. Serve bass fish caught in the lake, with **Atenciones Evita** being a popular choice.

$ Comedor Vista Hermosa, Peña Blanca. Has good, cheap food.

Cafés and bakeries

Panadería Yoja, 1 block from **Hotel Maranata**, Peña Blanca, good juices and pastries.

Santa Bárbara and around *p56*

$$ Doña Ana, 1 block above Parque Central. No sign but restaurant in Ana's dining room, crammed with bric-a-brac, only meat, rice, beans and bananas, plentiful and good food if a little boring.

$$ El Brasero, ½ block below Parque Central. Extensive menu of meat, chicken, fish, Chinese, good food, well prepared. Recommended.

$$ Pizzería Don Juan, Av Independencia. Very good pizzas.

$ Comedor Everest, by bus stop on Parque Central. Friendly, good *comida corriente*.

$ Las Tejas, near **Rodríguez**. Friendly, good pizzeria.

$ McPollo, main street. Clean, smart, good.

$ Repostería Charle's, Parque Central. Excellent cakes, pastries, about the only place open for breakfast.

San Pedro Sula and around *p57*, *map p57*

International restaurants in all the top hotels.

$$$ Bar El Hijo del Cuervo, 13 Calle 7-8 Av NO, Barrio Los Andes. Mexican cuisine, informal setting of *champas* in tropical garden with fountain, à la carte menu, tacos, *quesadillas*.

$$$ La Huerta de España, 21 Av 2 Calle SO, Barrio Río de Piedras, 4 blocks west of Av Circunvalación. Daily until 2300. Supposedly the best Spanish cuisine in town.

$$$ Las Tejas, 9 Calle 16 y 17 Av, Av Circunvalación. Good steaks and fine seafood, as also at nearby sister restaurant **La Tejana**, 16 Av 19 Calle SO, Barrio Suyapa, T2557-5276.

$$$ Pamplona, on plaza, opposite **Gran Hotel Sula**. Pleasant decor, good food, strong coffee, excellent service.

$$ Applebees, Circunvalación. Good food, service and prices. Highly recommended.

$$ Chef Mariano, 16 Av 9-10 Calle SO, Barrio Suyapa, T2552-5492. Garífuna management and specialities, especially seafood, Honduran and international cuisine, attentive service, a/c, not cheap but good value, open daily for lunch and dinner.

$$ Gamba Tropic, 5 Av 4-5 Calle SO. Delicious seafood, good wine, medium prices, a/c.

$$ La Espuela, Av Circunvalación, 16 Av 7 Calle. Good grilled meats. Recommended.

$$ La Fortuna, 2 Calle 7 Av NO. Chinese and international, very good, not expensive, smart, good service, a/c.

$$ Sim Kon, 17 Av 6 Calle NO, Av Circunvalación. Arguably the best Chinese in town. Enormous portions. Try *arroz con camarones* (prawns with rice).

$ Copa de Oro, 2 Av 2 y 3 Calle SO. Extensive Chinese and Western menu, a/c, pleasant. Recommended.

Cafés
Café Nani, 6 Av 1-2 Calle SO. Good *pastelería*.
Café Skandia, ground floor, **poolside at the Gran Hotel Sula**. Open 24 hrs, best place for late night dinners and early breakfasts, good club sandwiches, good service.
Café Venecia, 6 Av 4-5 Calle. Good juices, **Espresso Americano**, 2 branches, in Calle Peatonal, 4 Av, off southwest corner of Parque Central, and in Megaplaza shopping mall. Closed Sun, great coffee, cookies.

☻ Entertainment

San Pedro Sula and around *p57*, *map p57*
Bars and clubs
A thriving nightlife exists beyond the casinos.
Mango's, 16 Av 8-9 Calle SO, Barrio Suyapa. Open 1900 onwards. Open terrace, pool tables, dance floor, rock music, snacks. An exclusive option is **El Quijote**, 11 Calle 3-4 Av SO, Barrio Lempira, cover charge.

Cinemas
There are 8 cinemas, all showing Hollywood movies, look in local press for details.

Theatre
The Círculo Teatral Sampedrano stages productions (see Cultural centres, page 65).

Proyecto Teatral Futuro, is a semi-professional company presenting contemporary theatre of Latin American countries and translations of European playwrights, as well as ballet, children's theatre, and workshops. Offices and studio-theatre at 4 Calle 3-4 Av NO, Edif INMOSA, 3rd floor, T2552-3074.

☻ Festivals and events

San Pedro Sula and around *p57*, *map p57*
End Jun Feria Juniana, the city's main festival.

☻ Shopping

Siguatepeque *p54*
Leather goods A good leatherworker is **Celestino Alberto** Díaz, Barrio San Antonio, Casa 53, 2 Calle NE, 6 Av NE. 1 block north of Celestino's is a good shoemaker, leather shoes made for US$25.

San Pedro Sula and around *p57*, *map p57*
Bookshops La Casa del Libro, 1 Calle 5-6 Av SO. Comprehensive selection of Spanish and English-language books, good for children's books and game, just off Parque Central. **Librería Atenea**, Edif Trejo Merlo, 1 Calle 7 Av SO. Wide choice of Latin American, US and British fiction, philosophy, economics and so on. **Librería Cultura**, 1 Calle 6-7 Av SO. Cheap paperbacks, Latin American classics. **Librería Editorial Guaymuras**, 10 Av 7 Calle NO. Wide range of Hispanic authors.

Food Supermercado Los Andes, good supermarket at the intersection of Calle Oeste and Av Circunvalación.

Handicrafts Large artisan market, Mercado Guamilito Artesanía, 6 Calle 7-8 Av NO. Daily 0800-1700. Typical Honduran handicrafts, cigars and 'gifiti' – local moonshine, at good prices (bargain), with a few imported goods from Guatemala and Ecuador; also good for fruit and vegetables, and baleada comedores. **Danilo's Pura Piel**, factory and shop 18 Av B/9 Calle SO. **Honduras Souvenirs**, Calle Peatonal No 7, mahogany woodcraft. The **IMAPRO Handicraft School** in El Progreso has a retail outlet at 1 Calle 4-5 Av SE, well worth visiting, fixed prices, good value, good mahogany carvings. The **Museum Gift Shop**, at the Museo de Antropología e Historia has lots of cheap *artesanía* gifts open during museum visiting hours.

▲▲ Activities and tours

Comayagua and around *p53*
Comalhagua Tours, Plaza León Alvarado (entrance upstairs through Eskimo ice cream parlour), T9988-7101, city tours, and to El Rosario mine and Comayagua National Park; very informative and helpful.
Cramer Tours in Pasaje Arias.
Inversiones Karice's, 4 Av NO, very friendly and helpful.
Rolando Barahona, Av Central.

San Pedro Sula and around *p57*, *map p57*
Maya Temple, www.mayatempletours.com, also offers travel services.

⊖ Transport

Zambrano *p53*
Bus From the capital take any bus going north to Comayagua, Siguatepeque or La Paz and tell the driver where you want to get off.

Comayagua and around *p53*
Bus To **Tegucigalpa**, US$1.10, every 45 mins, 2 hrs (**Hmnos Cruz**, Comayagua, T772-0850), and with Comalhuacan (T2772-3889), from 0440 to 1720. To **Siguatepeque**, US$0.55 with **Transpinares**. To **San Pedro Sula**, US$1.50, 3 hrs, either catch a bus on the highway (very crowded) or go to Siguatepeque and change buses there. Incoming buses to Comayagua drop you on the main road outside town. From here you can walk or taxi into town. Buses depart from Torocagua: *colectivo* from Calle Salvador y Cervantes in town.

Siguatepeque *p54*
Bus To **San Pedro Sula**, from the west end of town every 35 mins, US$1.35.
Tegucigalpa with **Empresas Unidas** or **Maribel**, from west plaza, south of market, US$1.50, 3 hrs. Alternatively take a taxi, US$0.50, 2 km to the highway intersection and catch a Tegucigalpa–San Pedro Sula bus which passes every 30 mins. To **Comayagua**, **Transpinares**, US$0.50, 45 mins. To **La Esperanza** buses leave from near Boarding House Central, 1st departure 0530, several daily, taxi from town centre US$0.50.

Lago Yojoa *p55*
Bus To lake from **San Pedro Sula**, US$1, 1½ hrs; bus from lake to **Tegucigalpa** with Hedman-Alas, US$3, 3-5 hrs, 185 km.

Pulhapanzak waterfall *p56*
Bus By car it's a 1½-hr drive from San Pedro, longer by bus. There is a bus from **Peña Blanca** every 2 hrs to the falls, or take a **Mochito** or **Cañaveral** bus from **San Pedro Sula** from the bus station near the railway (hourly 0500-1700) and get off at the sign to the falls, at the village of Santa Buena Ventura, US$0.95. Alternatively stay on the bus to Cañaveral (take identification because there is a power plant here), and walk back along the Río Lindo, 2 hrs past interesting rock formations and small falls. Last bus returns at 1630 during the week.

Santa Bárbara and around *p56*
Bus To **Tegucigalpa**, 0700 and 1400 daily, weekends 0900, US$3, 4½ hrs with **Transportes Junqueños** (passing remote villages in beautiful mountain scenery). To **San Pedro Sula**, 2 hrs, US$1.90, 7 a day between 0500 and 1630. Bus to **San Rafael** at 1200, 4 hrs. Onward bus to **Gracias** leaves next day.

San Pedro Sula and around *p57, map p57*

Air

A taxi to the airport costs US$12 per taxi, but bargain hard. Yellow airport taxis cost US$18. Free airport shuttle from big hotels. Buses and *colectivos* do not go to the airport terminal itself; you have to walk the final 1 km from the La Lima road. Duty free, Global One phones, banks, restaurant on 2nd floor. Flights to **Tegucigalpa** (35 mins), **La Ceiba**, **Utila** and to **Roatán**. See page 8 for international flights.

Airline offices American, Ed Firenze, Barrio Los Andes, 16 Av 2-3 Calle, T2558-0524, airport T2668-3241. **Atlantic**, airport, T2668-7309. **Continental**, Plaza Versalles, Av Circunvalación, T2557-4141, airport T2668-3208. **Grupo Taca** 13 Av NO corner of Norte de la Circunvalación, Barrio Los Andes, T2557-0525, airport T2668-3333. **Isleña**, Edif Trejo Merlo, 1 Calle 7 Av SO, T2552-8322, airport T2668-3333. **Sosa**, 8 Av 1-2 Calle SO, Edif Román, T2550-6548, airport 668-3128.

Bus

Local Local buses cost US$0.10, smaller minibuses cost US$0.20.

Long distance Central bus terminal opened in 2008. The Gran Central Metropolitana is clean, safe and a short US$3 taxi from the centre of San Pedro Sula. **Heading south**, buses pass **Lago Yojoa** for **Tegucigalpa**, very regular service provided by several companies, 4½ hrs, 250 km by paved road. Main bus services with comfortable coaches in the town centre are **Hedman Alas**, T2516-2273, 0830, 1330 and 1730, US$18; **Transportes Sáenz**, T2553-4969, US$7; **El Rey**, T2553-4264, or **Express**, T2557-8355; **Transportes Norteños**, T2552-2145, last bus at 1900; **Viana**, T2556-9261.

Heading west from San Pedro the road leads to **Puerto Cortés**, a pleasant 45-min journey down the lush river valley. With **Empresa Impala**, T2553-3111, from 0430

until 2200, US$1, or **Citul**, and also on to **Omoa** from 0600.

Heading east buses go to **La Lima**, **El Progreso**, **Tela** and **La Ceiba** (Tupsa and Catisa, very regular to El Progreso, hourly to La Ceiba from 0600 and 1800, 3 hrs, US$3), some with a change in El Progreso, others direct. Also 1st class to La Ceiba with **Viana** at 1030 and 1730, and with **Hedman Alas** at 0600, 1030, 1520 and 1820. US$16 To **Trujillo**, 3 per day, 6 hrs, US$5, comfortable.

Heading southwest buses go to **Santa Rosa de Copán** through the Department of Ocotepeque, with superb mountain scenery, to the **Guatemalan border**. Congolón, and Empresa Toritos y Copanecos, serve **Nueva Ocotepeque** (US$8) and **Agua Caliente** on the Guatemalan border with 7 buses a day; Congolón, T2553-1174.

To **Santa Rosa de Copán**, with connections at La Entrada for **Copán Ruinas**, with **Empresa Toritos y Copanecos**, T2563-4930, leaving every 20 mins, 0345-1715, 3 hrs, US$3.70. Take a bus to the junction of La Entrada and change for connection to Copán Ruinas if you're not going direct. 1st-class bus to **Copán Ruinas** with Hedman Alas, T2516-2273, daily at 1030 and 1500, 3 hrs, US$16 with a/c, movie and bathrooms. Also direct service with **Casasola-Cheny Express** at 0800, 1300 and 1400.

International Services available from **Ticabus** covering the whole of Central America from Mexico to Panama.

Car

Car rentals Avis, 1 Calle, 6 Av NE, T2553-0888; **Blitz**, Hotel Sula and airport (T2552-2405 or 668-3171); **Budget**, 1 Calle 7Av NO, T2552-2295, airport T2668-3179; **Maya Eco Tours**, 3 Av NO, 7-8 Calle, and airport (T2552-2670 or 2668-3168); **Molinari**, Hotel Sula and airport (T2553-2639 or 2668-6178); **Toyota**, 3 Av 5 y 6 Calle NO, T2557-2666 or airport T2668-3174.

Car repairs Invanal, 13 Calle, 5 y 6 Av NE, T2552-7083. Excellent service from Víctor Mora.

Parque Nacional Cusuco *p58*
Bus San Pedro Sula–Cofradía, 1 hr, US$0.15, from 5 Av, 11 Calle SO (buses drop you at turn-off 1 km from town); pickup Cofradía-Buenos Aires 1½ hrs, US$1.75, best on Mon at 1400 (wait at small shop on outskirts of town on Buenos Aires road); the park is 12 km from Buenos Aires.

ⓘ Directory

Comayagua and around *p53*
Banks HSBC near Parque Central and others nearby include **Banco Pro Credit** **Banco Atlántida**, **Banco de Occidente**, **Bancafé**, **Ficensa**, **Banadesa**, **Bamer** and **Banffaa** All have ATMs, usually available 24/7 with security guard. **Immigration** Migración is at 6 Calle NO, 1 Av, good place to get visas renewed, friendly. **Medical services** Dentist: Dr José de Jesús Berlioz, next to Colegio León Alvarado, T772-0054.

Siguatepeque *p54*
Banks HSBC, Banco Atlántida and Banco de Occidente.

Santa Bárbara and around *p56*
Banks Banadesa, Bancafé, Banco Atlántida and Banco de Occidente.

San Pedro Sula and around *p57*, *map p57*
Banks HSBC, has a beautiful mural in its head office, 5 Av, 4 Calle SO and a branch at 5 Av, 6-7 Calle SO, changes TCs. **Banco Atlántida**, on Parque Central, changes TCs at good rates. **Banco de Honduras (Citibank)**. **Banco Continental**, 3 Av, 3-5 Calle SO No 7. **Banco de Occidente**, 6 Av, 2-3 Calle SO. **Bancafé**, 1 Calle, 1 Av SE and all other local banks. **BAC** for Visa, MasterCard and

Amex is at, 5 Av y 2 Calle NO. These are also at **Aval Card**, 14 Av NO y Circunvalación, and **Honducard**, 5 Av y 2 Calle NO. **Cultural centres** Alianza Francesa, on 23 Av 3-4 Calle SO, T2553-1178, www.afteguciga lpa.com, offers French and Spanish classes, has a library, films and cultural events. **Centro Cultural Sampedrano**, 3 Calle, 4 Av NO No 20, T2553-3911, USIS-funded library, cultural events, concerts, art exhibitions and theatrical productions. **Embassies and consulates** Belize, Km 5 Blv del Norte, Col los Castaños, T2551-0124, 2551-0707. **El Salvador**, Edif Rivera y Cía, 7th floor, local 704, 5 y 6 Av 3 Calle, T553-4604. **France**, Col Zerón, 9 Av 10 Calle 927, T2557-4187. **Germany**, 6 Av NO, Av Circunvalación, T2553-1244. **Guatemala**, 8 Calle 5-6 Av NO, No 38, T2553-3560. **Italy**, Edif La Constancia, 3rd floor, 5 Av 1-2 Calle NO, T2552-3672. **Mexico**, 2 Calle 20 Av SO 201, Barrio Río de Piedras, T2553-2604. **Netherlands**, 15 Av 7-8 Calle NE, Plaza Venecia, Local 10, T2557-1815. **Nicaragua**, Col Trejo, 23 Av A entre 11 Calle B y 11 Calle C No 145, T2550-3394. **Spain**, 2 Av 3-4 Calle NO 318, Edif Agencias Panamericanas, T2558-0708. **UK**, 13 Av 10-12 Calle SO, Suyapa No 62, T2557-2046. **Immigration** Calle Peatonal, just off Parque Central, or at the airport. **Internet** Internet cafés are found throughout town. **Internet Café**, Multiplaza centre, T2550-6077, US$1 per hr. **Red Cybe Café**, Calle 3, 1 block east of the Hedman Alas bus terminal, US$1per hr. **Laundry** Excelsior, 14-15 Av Blv Morazán. **Lava Fácil**, 7 Av, 5 Calle NO, US$1.50 per load. **Lavandería Almich**, 9-10 Av, 5 Calle SO No 29, Barrio El Benque. **Rodgers**, 4a Calle, 15-16 Av SO, No 114. **Medical services** Dentist: Clínicas Dentales Especializadas, Ed María Antonia, 3a Calle between 8 and 9 Av NO, apartamento L-1, Barrio Guamilito, T2558-0464. **Post** 3 Av SO between 9-10 Calle. **Telephone** Hondutel, 4 Calle 4 Av SO. Calls can be made from **Gran Hotel Sula**.

North coast

Honduras' Caribbean coast has a mixture of banana-exporting ports, historic towns and Garífuna villages. Working from west to east the main towns of interest are Omoa, Puerto Cortés, Tela, La Ceiba and Trujillo. In between the towns you will find isolated beaches and resorts, and national parks like Pico Bonito, which are perfect for hiking and whitewater rafting. The route west takes in the 'Jungle Trail' to Guatemala – which you can now do by bus.

Running parallel to the coast, a route from El Progreso runs south of the coastal mountain chain Cordillera Nombre de Dios leading to rarely visited national parks, pristine cloud forest and an alternative route to La Ceiba.

Puerto Cortés and around

Stuck out on the northwestern coast of the country and backed by the large bay of Laguna de Alvarado, Puerto Cortés is hot, tempered by sea breezes and close to many beautiful palm-fringed beaches. The success of the place is its location and most Honduran trade passes through the port, which is just 58 km from San Pedro Sula by road and rail, and

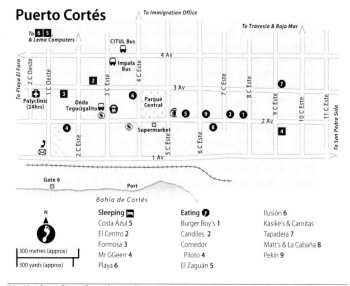

Puerto Cortés

To Immigration Office
To Travesía & Baja Mar
To **6** **5**, & Lema Computers
CITUL Bus
4 Av
Impala Bus
4 C Este
To Playa El Faro
2 C Oeste
3 C Oeste
3 Av
7 C Este
8 C Este
7
9 C Este
10 C Este
11 C Este
To San Pedro Sula
Polyclinic (24hrs)
Onda Tegucigalito
Parqué Central
6
3 C Este
2 Av
9 **1**
2
3
Supermarket
5 C Este
6 C Este
8
2 C Este
4
4
1 Av
Gate 6
Port
Bahía de Cortés

N
300 metres (approx)
300 yards (approx)

Sleeping 🛏
Costa Azul **5**
El Centro **2**
Formosa **3**
Mr GGeerr **4**
Playa **6**

Eating 🍴
Burger Boy's **1**
Candiles **2**
Comedor Piloto **4**
El Zaguán **5**

Ilusión **6**
Kasike's & Carnitas Tapadera **7**
Matt's & La Cabaña **8**
Pekín **9**

333 km from Tegucigalpa. It has a small oil refinery, a free zone and, being two days' voyage from New Orleans, is arguably now the most important port in Central America.

The Parque Central contains many fine trees but focuses on a huge Indian poplar, planted as a sapling in 1941, in the centre that provides an extensive canopy.

Getting there If entering Puerto Cortés by boat, go straight to immigration. Passports are often collected on the boat and returned as they are processed. The US$3 entry fee (make sure that you have the stamp) is the only official payment; if asked for more, demand a receipt.

Omoa

Omoa, 18 km from Puerto Cortés, is set in the beautiful Bahía de Omoa where the mountains, lusciously carpeted in jungle, tumble towards the sea. You can watch fine purple sunsets from the quiet laid-back bars on the beach, and if you're lucky see dolphins in the bay. It has an 18th-century castle, **Fortaleza de San Fernando**, now renovated and worth a visit. It was built by the Spaniards in 1759 to protect the coast and shipments of silver, gold and cacao from British pirates. There is a **visitor centre** and a small, interesting **museum** ⓘ *Mon-Sun 0900-1600, US$1.40, tickets on sale at gate, guides available.*

During the week Omoa is a quiet, friendly fishing village, but at weekends it gets a little busier with Hondurans from San Pedro and the place becomes littered, followed by a grand clean-up on the Monday morning. Near Omoa are two waterfalls (**Los Chorros**), with lovely walks to each, and good hiking in attractive scenery both along the coast and inland.

It's a fair walk from the main road. Get a tuk-tuk for US$0.50 to the beach.

East of San Pedro Sula → *For listings, see pages 75-85.*

Tela

Tela used to be an important banana port before the pier was partly destroyed by fire. Easily reached from San Pedro Sula with a bus service via El Progreso, it is pleasantly laid out with a sandy but dirty beach. Tela Viejo to the east is the original city joined by a bridge to Tela Nuevo, the residential area built for the executives of the American banana and farming company **Chiquita**. There is a pleasant walk along the beach east to Ensenada, or west to San Juan. More information is available at www.tela-honduras.com. **Note** Make sure you take a cab after midnight; Lps 30 per person at night.

Around Tela

Local buses and trucks from the corner just east of the market go east to the Garífuna village of **Triunfo de la Cruz**, which is set in a beautiful bay. Site of the first Spanish settlement on the mainland, a sea battle between Cristóbal de Olid and Francisco de Las Casas (two of Cortés' lieutenants) was fought here in 1524.

Beyond Triunfo de la Cruz is an interesting coastal area that includes the cape, **Parque Nacional Punta Izopo** (1½-hour walk along the beach, take water – 12 km from Tela) and the mouth of the Río León. This, and its immediate hinterland, is a good place to see parrots, toucans, turtles, alligators and monkeys as well as the first landing point of the Spanish conqueror Cristóbal de Olid. For information, contact **Prolansate**. To get right into the forest and enjoy the wildlife, it is best to take an organized tour (see Tour operators, page 81). A trip to Punta Izopo involves kayaking through mangrove swamps up the Río Plátano, Indiana Jones style.

Further northwest, along palm-fringed beaches is **Parque Nacional Punta Sal 'Jeannette Kawas'** ① *US$2*, 0800-1500 daily, contact **Prolansate** for information, a lovely place now protected within the park's 80,000-ha boundaries. It is one of the most important parks in Honduras and has two parts, the peninsula and the lagoon. During the dry season some 350 species of bird live within the lagoon, surrounded by forest, mangroves and wetlands. Once inhabited only by Garífuna, the area has suffered from the immigration of cattle farmers who have cleared the forest, causing erosion, and from a palm oil extraction plant on the Río San Alejo, which has dumped waste in the river and contaminated the lagoons. Conservation and environmental protection programmes are now underway. To get there you will need a motor boat, or take a bus (three a day) to Tornabé and hitch a ride 12 km, or take the crab truck at 1300 for US$0.40 (back at 1700), on to Miami, a small, all-thatched fishing village (two hours' walk along beach from Tornabé), beer on ice available, and walk the remaining 10 km along the beach. There are also pickups from Punta Sal to Miami, contact Prolansate for information.

Jardín Botánico at Lancetilla ① *T2448-1740, not well signposted – a guide is recommended, ask at the Cohdefor office; guide services daily 0800-1530, US$6; good maps available in English or Spanish US$0.30*, is 5 km inland, and was founded (in 1926) as a plant research station. Now, it is the second largest botanical garden in the world. It has more than 1000 varieties of plant and over 200 bird species have been identified. It has fruit trees from every continent, the most extensive collection of Asiatic fruit trees in the western hemisphere, an orchid garden, and plantations of mahogany and teak alongside a 1200-ha virgin tropical rainforest. But be warned, there are many mosquitoes.

To get to Lancetilla and the Jardín Botánico, take a taxi from Tela, US$4, but there are few in the park for the return journey in the afternoon, so organize collection in advance.

La Ceiba and around → *For listings, see pages 75-85.*

La Ceiba, the capital of Atlántida Department and the third largest city in Honduras, stands on the narrow coastal plain between the Caribbean and the rugged Nombre de Dios mountain range crowned by the spectacular Pico Bonito (2435 m) (see page 70). The climate is hot, but tempered by sea winds. Once the country's busiest port, trade has now passed to Puerto Cortés and Puerto Castilla, but there is still some activity. The close proximity to Pico Bonito National park, Cuero y Salado Wildlife Refuge and the Cayos Cochinos Marine Reserve gives the city the ambitious target of becoming an important ecotourism centre. While the opportunities aren't immediately obvious, there is definitely a buzz about town – watch out for developments. The main plaza is worth walking around to see statues of various famous Hondurans including Lempira and a couple of ponds.

A **butterfly and insect museum** ① *Col El Sauce, 2a Etapa Casa G-12, T2442-2874, http://butterflywebsite.com, Mon-Fri 0800-1600, closed Wed afternoon, Sat and Sun for groups only with advance reservation, US$1, student reductions*, has a collection of over 10,000 butterflies, roughly 2000 other insects and snakes. Good for all ages, you get a 25-minute video in both Spanish and English and Robert and Myriam Lehman guide visitors expertly through the life of the butterfly. There is also a **Butterfly Farm** ① *daily 0800-1530, entry US$6*, on the grounds of **The Lodge** at Pico Bonito.

Around La Ceiba

Fig Tree Medical Centre ⓘ *T2440-0041 (in La Ceiba), 25 km east of La Ceiba*, on the highway to Jutiapa, is a famous centre for alternative medicine. Operated by Dr Sebi, this facility is treating cancer and diabetes utilizing vegetarian diet, medications and the local hot springs. For more information or to visit call in advance. **Jutiapa** is a small dusty town with a pretty little colonial church. Contact Standard Fruit Company, Dole office in La Ceiba (off main plaza) to visit a local pineapple plantation. **Corozal** is an interesting

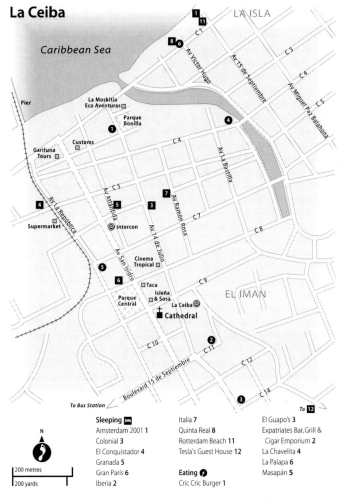

La Ceiba

Caribbean Sea

Sleeping 🛏	Italia **7**	El Guapo's **3**
Amsterdam 2001 **1**	Quinta Real **8**	Expatriates Bar, Grill &
Colonial **3**	Rotterdam Beach **11**	Cigar Emporium **2**
El Conquistador **4**	Tesla's Guest House **12**	La Chavelita **4**
Granada **5**		La Palapa **6**
Gran París **6**	Eating 🍴	Masapán **5**
Iberia **2**	Cric Cric Burger **1**	

Garífuna village near La Ceiba, at Km 209.5, with a beach, Playas de Sambrano and a hotel (see Sleeping, page 77). **Sambo Creek**, another Garífuna village, has nice beaches and a couple of hotels. Near the towns of **Esparta** and **El Porvenir**, thousands of crabs come out of the sea in July and August and travel long distances inland. The **Catarata El Bejuco** is a waterfall 7 km along the old dirt road to **Olanchito** (11 km from La Ceiba). Follow a path signposted to Balneario Los Lobos to the waterfall about 1 km upriver through the jungle. There is good swimming from a pebbly beach where the river broadens. Along this road is **El Naranjo** near Omega Tours Jungle Lodge and Adventure Company.

Yaruca, 20 km down the old road to Olanchito, is easily reached by bus and offers good views of Pico Bonito. **Eco-Zona Río María**, 5 km along the Trujillo highway (signposted path up to the foothills of the Cordillera Nombre de Dios), is a beautiful walk through the lush countryside of a protected area. Just beyond Río María is **Balneario Los Chorros** (signposted), a series of small waterfalls through giant boulders into a deep rock pool that is great for swimming (refreshments nearby). Upstream there is some beautiful scenery and you can continue walking through the forest and in the river, where there are more pools. Another bathing place, Agua Azul, with restaurant is a short distance away. The active can get on the **Río Cangrejal** for the exhilarating rush of Grade II, III and IV **whitewater rapids**, which can be combined with treks in to the wilderness of **Parque Nacional Pico Bonito** (see below).

Beaches around La Ceiba

Beaches in and near La Ceiba include **Playa Miramar** (dirty, not recommended), **La Barra** (better), **Perú** (across the Río Cangrejal at Km 205.5, better still, quiet except at weekends, deserted tourist complex, restaurant, access by road to Tocoa, 10 km, then signposted side road 1.5 km, or along the beach 6 km from La Ceiba) and **La Ensenada** (close to Corozal).

The beaches near the fishing villages of Río Esteban and Balfate are very special and are near Cayos Cochinos (Hog Islands) where the snorkelling and diving is spectacular. The Hog Islands (see page 91) can be reached by *cayuco* from Roatán, La Ceiba and **Nuevo Armenia**, a nondescript Garífuna village connected by road to Jutiapa. Take whatever you need with you as there is almost nothing on the smaller cayes. However, the Garífuna are going to and fro all the time.

Parque Nacional Pico Bonito

ⓘ *For further information on the park contact Leslie Arcantara at FUPNAPIB, at Calle 19, Av 14 de Julio, across from Suyapita Catholic church, Barrio Alvarado, T2442-0618. fupnapib@laceiba.com. Take care if you enter the forest: tracks are not yet developed, a compass is advisable. Tour companies in La Ceiba arrange trips to the park. A day trip, horse riding through the park, can be arranged through Omega Tours, see page 82. Trip includes food and guide, US$25. Recommended. Access to Public Trails in Pico Bonito is US$6. Go early in the morning for the best views, and to see birdlife and howler monkeys.*

Parque Nacional Pico Bonito (674 sq km) is the largest national park in Honduras and is home to Pico Bonito (2435 m). The Río Cangrejal, a mecca for whitewater rafting, marks the eastern border of the park. It has deep tropical hardwood forests that shelter, among other animals, jaguars and three species of monkey, deep canyons and tumbling streams and waterfalls (including Las Gemelas, which fall vertically for some 200 m).

Parque Nacional Pico Bonito has two areas open for tourism. The first is the Río Zacate area, located past the community of El Pino, 10 km west of La Ceiba; the second is on the Río Cangrejal, near the community of El Naranjo, about 7.5 km from the paved highway.

A hanging bridge over the Río Cangrejal provides access to the visitor centre and the **El Mapache Trail** up to the top of **El Bejuco** waterfall. Further up the road in **Las Mangas**, Guaruma (T2442-2693) there is a very nice trail with beautiful swimming holes in a pristine creek. The trail is well maintained and local guides are available.

For the Río Zacate area, access is just past the dry stream (*quebrada seca*) bridge on the main La Ceiba to Tela highway from where the road leads to the entrance through pineapple plantations to a steep trail leading up to the Río Zacate waterfall, about one hour 20 minutes' hiking. A good price range of accommodation is available in both areas.

Development of the park by **Curla** (Centro Universitario Regional del Litoral Atlántico) continues under the supervision of **Cohdefor**, the forestry office, and the **Fundación Parque Nacional Pico Bonito (FUPNAPIB)** ① *Calle 19, Av 14 de Julio, La Ceiba, T2442-0618.*

Cuero y Salado Wildlife Reserve

① *US$10 to enter the reserve, which you can pay at Fucsa, keep the receipt, plus US$5 per person for accommodation. The reserve is managed by the Fundación Cuero y Salado (Fucsa) Refugio de Vida Silvestre, 1 block north and 3 blocks west of Parque Central (see map) to the left of the Standard Fruit Company, La Ceiba, T2443-0329, Apartado Postal 674. The foundation is open to volunteers, preferably those who speak English and Spanish.*

Near the coast, between the Cuero and Salado rivers, 37 km west of La Ceiba, is the Cuero y Salado Wildlife Reserve, which has a great variety of flora and fauna, including manatee, jaguar, monkeys and a large population of local and migratory birds. It extends for 13,225 ha of swamp and forest.

Nilmo, a knowledgeable biologist who acts as a guide, takes morning and evening boat trips for those staying overnight, either through the canal dug by Standard Fruit, parallel to the beach between the palms and the mangroves, or down to the Salado lagoon. Five kayaks are available for visitors' use. In the reserve are spider and capuchin monkeys, iguanas, jaguar, tapirs, crocodiles, manatee, hummingbirds, toucans, ospreys, eagles and vultures. A five-hour trip will take you to Barra de Colorado to see the manatees. Fucsa's administration centre, on the banks of the Río Salado, has photos, charts, maps, radio and a two-room visitors' house. There is also a visitor centre, with a full-service cafeteria and bilingual guides.

Getting there Take a bus to La Unión (every hour, 0600 until 1500 from La Ceiba terminus, 1½ hours, ask to get off at the railway line, ferrocarril, or Km 17), an interesting journey through pineapple fields. There are several ways of getting into the park from La Unión. Walking takes 1½ hours. Groups usually take a *motocarro*, a dilapidated train that also transports the coconut crop. From near Doña Tina's house (meals available), take a *burra*, a flat-bed railcar propelled by two men with poles (a great way to see the countryside) to the community on the banks of the Río Salado. To return to La Unión, it is another *burra* ride or a two-hour walk along the railway, then, either wait for a La Ceiba bus (last one at 1500), or ask for the short cut through grapefruit groves, 20 minutes, which leads to the main La Ceiba–Tela road, where there are many more buses back to town.

Trujillo and around → *For listings, see pages 75-85.*

① www.trujillohonduras.com.

Once a major port and the former capital, Trujillo sits on the southern shore of the palm-fringed Bay of Trujillo. It is a quiet, pleasant town with clean beaches nearby and calm water that is ideal for swimming. Christopher Columbus landed close to the area on his fourth voyage to the Americas and the town was later founded in 1525 by Juan de Medina, making it the oldest town in Honduras. Hernán Cortés arrived here after his famous march overland from Yucatán in pursuit of his usurping lieutenant, Olid. Filibuster William Walker was shot near here in 1860; a commemorative stone marks the spot in the rear garden of the hospital, one block east of the Parque Central, and the old cemetery (near Hotel Trujillo) is his final resting place.

Fortaleza Santa Bárbara ① *US$1*, a ruined Spanish fortress overlooking the bay, is worth a visit. Most of the relics found there have been moved to the museum of Rufino Galán, but there are still a few rusty muskets and cannon balls. Twenty minutes' walk from Trujillo plaza is the **Museo y Piscina Rufino Galán Cáceres** ① *US$1, US$0.50 to swim*, which has a swimming pool filled from the Río Cristales with changing rooms and picnic facilities. Close by, the wreckage of a US C-80 aircraft that crashed in 1985 forms part of Sr Galán's museum. The rest of the collection is a mass of curios, some very interesting. The cemetery is rather overgrown, with collapsed and open tombs, but it does give a feel of the origins of early residents. The **Fiesta de San Juan Bautista** is in June, with participation from surrounding Garífuna settlements.

West of Trujillo, just past the football field on the Santa Fe road, is the **Río Grande**, which has lovely pools and waterfalls for river bathing, best during the rainy season. Take

Trujillo & the coast

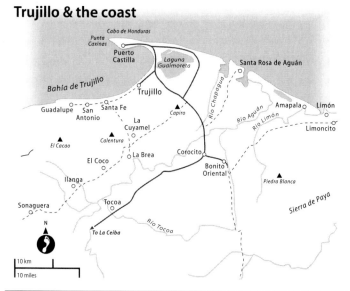

the path on the far side of river, after about 10 minutes cut down to the rocks and follow the river upstream along the boulders.

Beaches

Good beaches are found both on the peninsula and around Trujillo Bay. Before setting out ask which beaches are safe. Take a bus from near the Parque Central towards Puerto Castilla and ask the driver to let you off at the path about 1 km beyond the bridge over the lagoon. Other beaches around Puerto Castilla are separated by mangroves, are littered and have sandflies. The beaches in town tend to be less clean. If you're tempted to walk to find a cleaner stretch of sand don't walk alone; tourists here have been assaulted and robbed.

West of Trujillo

There are interesting Garífuna villages west of Trujillo. The road is rough, often impassable in wet weather, and jeeps are needed even in the dry season. **Santa Fe**, 10 km west of Trujillo, is a friendly place with several good Garífuna restaurants, for example **Comedor Caballero** and **Las Brisas de Santa Fe**, on the endless white sandy beach. The bus service continues to **San Antonio** (good restaurant behind the beach) and **Guadalupe**. Walk in the morning along the beach to Santa Fe and then get a bus back to Trujillo, taking plenty of water and sun block. This stretch of beach is outstanding, but watch out for *marea roja*, a sea organism that colours the water pink and can give irritating skin rashes to bathers. Also, be warned, local people consider this walk unsafe. It's best to go in a large group.

Santa Rosa de Aguán

One of the largest Garífuna communities, Santa Rosa de Aguán is an interesting coastal town, some 40 km east of Trujillo, with 7000 hospitable English- and Spanish-speaking inhabitants. The spreading settlement lies at the mouth of the Río Aguán, the greater part on the east of the bay. A white-sand beach stretches all the way to Limón, and the thundering surf is an impressive sight. Take drinking water, insect repellent, mosquito coils and high-factor sun screen.

If driving from Trujillo, turn left at Km 343, 20 km along the highway, where a good gravel road runs another 20 km to Santa Rosa. From where the road ends at the west bank, take a canoe ferry across to the east side.

Parque Nacional Capiro y Calentura

The Parque Nacional Capiro y Calentura encompasses these two mountains over-looking Trujillo. The four- to six-hour walk to the summit gives spectacular views and on a clear day Isla Roatán can be seen in the distance. The walk is best done early in the morning when the forest is alive with the sounds of birds, monkeys and other wildlife. The path can be reached by walking (or taking a taxi) up the hill past the **Villa Brinkley Hotel**. The road to the summit is in poor condition from the entrance of the park and can only be driven in a 4WD. Insect repellent is needed if you pause. As with all walks in this area, it's safest to go in a group. The park is run by the **Fundación Capiro Calentura Guaimoreto (FUCAGUA)** ① *Parque Central, Trujillo, Mon-Fri*. They have information on all the reserves in the area and also on hiking and tours. Until a new office is built in the park, entry tickets must be bought here before going to Capiro y Calentura. They are opening up trails, improving old ones and organizing guided tours through parts of the forest. The hike along the Sendero de la

Culebrina uses the remnants of a colonial stone road used to transport gold from the mines in the Valle de Aguán. Halfway up the **Cerro de las Cuevas**, 7 km beyond Cuyamel, are impressive caves showing traces of occupation by pre-Columbian Pech people.

Refugio de Vida Silvestre Laguna de Guaimoreto (RVSLG)

FUCAGUA, see above, also administers the Refugio de Vida Silvestre, Laguna de Guaimoreto (RVSLG), northeast of Trujillo, where there is a bird island (Isla de los Pájaros), monkeys and good fishing. To visit, either arrange a trip with Fucagua, a tour agency such as Turtle Tours, or take a bus from Trujillo towards Puerto Castilla, get off just after the bridge which crosses the lagoon, then walk away from the lagoon for about 200 m to a dirt track on the left. Follow this and cross a low bridge and on the left is the house of a man who rents dug-out canoes. The Isla de los Pájaros is about 3 km up the lagoon, a bit too far for a dug-out. Another alternative is to go down to the wharf and hire out a motorized canoe or launch(price depends on the number of passengers and length of trip). There are no roads, paths or facilities in the area.

El Progreso and east → *For listings, see pages 75-85.*

El Progreso, an important but unattractive agricultural and commercial centre on the Río Ulúa, is 30 minutes' drive on the paved highway southeast of San Pedro Sula, en route to Tela. While most people make straight for the coast at Tela, heading east from El Progreso leads through mountain scenery up to the small town of Yoro, beyond to Olanchito and a link to La Ceiba. With everyone else rushing to the Bay Islands, you could well have the place to yourself.

Parque Nacional Pico Pijol

This park protects the 2282-m summit of primary cloud forest that is home to many quetzales. It is 32 km from the town of **Morazán** in the Yoro Department, which is 41 km from Progreso (bus from Progreso or Santa Rita). In Morazán are **Hospedaje El Corazón Sagrado**, several restaurants and a disco. The lower slopes of Pico Pijol have been heavily farmed. Access by vehicle is possible as far as Subirana. A guide is needed from there to a large cave nearby; access is difficult. Another trail to the summit (2282 m) starts at **Nueva Esperanza** village (bus from Morazán, Parque Central); ask for the correct trail. The first day is tough, all uphill with no shade; the second is tougher and requires a lot of clearing. Take compass and topographical map. Also in the park is the waterfall at **Las Piratas** (bus Morazán–Los Murillos and then walk to El Ocotillo (ask for Las Piratas).

Yoro and around

The paved highway to the prosperous little town of Yoro passes through pleasant countryside surrounded by mountains and dotted with ranches and farms. The **Parque Nacional Montaña de Yoro** is 8 km to the southeast (access from Marale), comprising 257 sq km of cloud forest, home to the Tolupanes people, also known as Xicaques. The Asociación Ecológica Amigos de la Montaña de Yoro has an office in the Parque Central in Yoro. From Yoro a dirt road continues to **Olanchito** via **Jocón**, through attractive country as the road snakes along the pine-forested slopes of Montaña Piedra Blanca and Montaña de la Bellota, with fine views of the surrounding valleys and distant mountain ranges.

North coast listings

For Sleeping and Eating price codes and other relevant information, see pages 10-11.

😴 Sleeping

Puerto Cortés *p66, map p66*

Avoid 4 Calle between 1 and 2 Av and the area on 1 Av opposite the dockyards; it is unpleasant by day and dangerous at night.

$$$ Costa Azul, Playa El Faro, T2665-2260. Restaurant, disco-bar, billiards, table tennis, pool, horse riding, volley ball, good value.

$$$ Playa, 4 km west at Cienaguita, T2665-1105. Hotel complex, directly on beach, cable TV, good fish dishes in restaurant. Mountain bikes for rent, available to non-guests.

$$ Mr GGeerr, 9 Calle, 2 Av E, T2665-0444. No hot water, very clean, a/c, bar, video, satellite TV. Recommended.

$$-$ El Centro, 3 Av 2-3 Calle, T2665-1160. With bath, a/c, hot water, cable TV, parking, garden, café, pleasant, well furnished.

$ Formosa, 3 Av 2 Calle E. With bath (some without), no towel, but soap and toilet paper provided, clean, fan, good value, friendly Chinese owner.

$ Frontera del Caribe, Playas de Camaguey, road to Travesía, T2665-5001. Very friendly, quiet, safe, on beach, restaurant on 1st floor, open, airy, good food, 7 rooms on 2nd floor, private bath, cold water, linen changed daily, fan. Recommended.

Omoa *p67*

$$ Fisherman's Hotel, great small hotel by the beach, clean, handy location, restaurant out front. A/c, cheaper with fan.

$$ Sueño del Mar, T2658-9047, www.sueno sdemar.com. Newest hotel on the beach with a handful of rooms of differing sizes run by Canadian couple Karen and Mark. Great spot and the quiet end of the beach. Canadian breakfasts, laundry, Wi-Fi internet and a few steps from the beach. Recommended.

$$ Tatiana, on beach. With bath, clean and quiet.

$ Roli's Place, T2658-9082, http://yaxpactours.com. 80 m from beach, clean rooms with private bath and hot water, good information here of the region, bikes and kayaks for guests' use, games, shady garden and campground. Roli will change TCs, quetzals, euro and dollars. Quiet after 2200. Great, but not a party place.

Tela *p67*

During Easter week, the town is packed: room rates double; advance booking is essential.

$$$ Telamar, T2448-2196, www.hotel telamar.com. A large luxury resort of wooden bungalows, set on a palm-fringed, clean, white-sand beach. Rooms and villas available, also restaurants, bar, golf club, swimming pools, kids' activities and a conference centre.

$$$-$$ Maya Vista, top of hill, steep flight of steps starting opposite **Preluna**, T2448-1497, www.mayavista.com. Canadian-owned, French and English spoken, bath, a/c, hot water, bar, restaurant, delicious French-Canadian cuisine, fantastic views. Very highly recommended.

$$ Gran Central, just south of the centre of town, T448-1099, www.hotelgran central.com. French-owned, beautifully restored historic banana-port-era hotel. 1 suite, kitchen, hot water, cable TV, a/c, security, safe box in each room. Local excursions available. Highly recommended.

$$ Mango B&B, 8 Calle, 5 Av, T2448-0338, www.mangocafe.net. A/c, hot water, TV, comfortable, well-furnished rooms, friendly, efficient; Spanish tuition, and bike hire. Recommended.

$$ Tela, 9 Calle, 3-4 Av NE, T2448-2150. Clean, airy, fans, hot water, will do laundry, with restaurant, but meagre breakfast, otherwise very good.

$$-$ Bertha's, 8 Calle, 9 Av NE, T2448-1009. Near bus terminal, with bath, a/c, cheaper with fan, clean. Recommended.

$ Mar Azul, 11 Calle, 5 Av NE, T2448-2313. With fan and bath, charming helpful owner. Best backpacker place in town.

$ Sara, 11 Calle, 6 Av, behind the restaurant **Tiburón Playa**, T2448-1477. Basic in a rickety old building, with bath, or without, poor sanitation. Cheapest in town, popular with backpackers, friendly, noisy especially at weekends from all-night discos.

Around Tela p67

There are cheap houses and *cabañas* for rent in Triunfo de la Cruz. There is a small hotel in Río Tinto, near Parque Nacional Punta Sal; accommodation is available in private houses.

$$$-$$ Caribbean Coral Inn, Triunfo de la Cruz, T2669-0224, www.globalnet.hn/caribcoralinn. With bath, fan.

$$$-$$ The Last Resort, Tornabé, T2984-3964. Has 8 bungalows for rent, some a/c, some fan, hot water, with breakfast, several cabins for different size groups.

$ El Tucán, Triunfo de la Cruz. Backpacker place with *cabañas*.

La Ceiba p68, map p69

$$$ Quinta Real, Zona Viva, on the beach, T2440-3311, www.quintarealhotel.com. By far the best hotel in La Ceiba, with big, well-furnished rooms. Swimming pool, a/c, cable TV, beach, restaurant and bars, free Internet. (Taxi drivers sometimes confuse it with the **Hotel Quinta ($$$)** opposite the Golf Club on Tela–La Ceiba road, T2443-0223, which is modern and functional, also with pool, but not half as nice).

$$$-$$ Gran Hotel París, Parque Central, T2443-2391, hotelparis@psinet.hn. A/c, own generator, swimming pool, parking, good value.

$$ Iberia, Av San Isidoro, next door to **Ceiba**, T2443-0401. A/c, windows without screen. Recommended.

$$ Italia, Av Ramón Rosas, T2443-0150. Clean, a/c, good restaurant with reasonable prices, swimming pool, parking in interior courtyard.

$$ Tesla's Guest House, Calle Montecristo 212, Col El Naranjal, opposite Hospital La Fe, T2443-3893. 5 rooms, private bathrooms, hot water, a/c, pool, phone, minibar, BBQ, laundry, friendly family owners speak English, German, French and Spanish, airport collection.

$$-$ Posada Don Giuseppe, Av San Isidro at 13 Calle, T2442-2812. Bath, a/c (fan cheaper), hot water, TV, bar, restaurant. Comfortable.

$ Amsterdam 2001, 1 Calle, Barrio La Isla, T443-2311. Run by Dutch man Jan (Don Juan), good for backpackers, dormitory beds or rooms, with laundry, bit run-down, **Dutch Corner Café** for great breakfasts.

$ Colonial, Av 14 de Julio, between 6a and 7a Calle, T2443-1953. A/c, sauna, jacuzzi, cable TV, rooftop bar, restaurant with varied menu, nice atmosphere, tourist office, tours available. A bit run-down.

$ El Conquistador, Av La República, T2443-3670. Cheaper with fan, shared bath, safe, clean, TV.

$ Granada, Av Atlántida, 5-6 Calle, T2443-2451, hotelparis@psinet.hn. Bath, a/c, clean, safe, cheaper with fan.

$ Las 5 Rosas, Calle 8 near Av La Bastilla, opposite Esso. Clean, simple rooms, bath, fan, laundry, good value.

$ Rotterdam Beach, next door to **Amsterdam 2001** at 1 Calle, Barrio La Isla, T2440-0321. On the beach, with bath, fan, clean, friendly, pleasant garden, good value. Recommended.

Around La Ceiba p69

$$ Coco Pando, Km 188, T969-9663, www.cocopando.com. On seafront a few kilometres west of La Ceiba, this palm-roofed building has great sunset views from upper deck; simple rooms with showers, a/c and TV (mixed reports about cleanliness and availability of hot water); free shuttle to town and airport; good value **Iguana** bar/restaurant and discotheque next door.

$$ Hotel Canadien, Sambo Creek, T2440-2099, www.hotelcanadien.com. With double suite. Can arrange trips to Hog Islands for US$80 per boat.

$$ Villa Helen's, Sambo Creek about 35 mins east of La Ceiba, T2408-1137, www.villahelens.com. Good selection of rooms from simple to luxury. Pool and on the beach, with a variety of activities in the quiet seclusion.

$$ Villa Rhina, near the turn-off from the main road, Corozal, T2443-1222. With pool and restaurant.

$ Cabañas del Caribe, in Dantillo, 5 mins out of town on the road to Tela, T2441-1421, T2997-8746 (mob). 6 big cabins, some with jacuzzi, and 7 rooms on the beach, restaurant serving breakfast. Video screen in restaurant. Great place to relax. Call 1 day ahead to collect from town. Buses from La Ceiba for Dantillo every 30 mins.

$ Finca El Edén, in Santa Ana, 32 km west of La Ceiba, bertiharlos@yahoo.de. Rooms, dorms, hammocks and mattresses. Good views to the sea and good food.

$ Hermanos Avila, Sambo Creek. Simple hotel-restaurant, clean; food OK.

Beaches around La Ceiba *p70*
$ Chichi, Nuevo Armenia. 3 small rooms, fan, mosquito net, clean, good food available.

Parque Nacional Pico Bonito *p70*
Río Cangrejo area
$$-$ Jungle River Lodge, on Río Cangrejal overlooking Pico Bonito, T2440-1268, www.jungleriverlodge.com. Private rooms and dorms, natural swimming pools, restaurant and breathtaking views. Rafting, canopy tours, zip-wires, hiking and mountain biking tours available. Activities include a free night's accommodation. Take Yaruka bus from main bus terminal, get off at Km 7;

blue kayak marks entrance on river side of the road, call for arranged transport or join a tour.

$$-$ Omega Tours Jungle Lodge and Adventure Company, El Naranjo, T2440-0334, www.omegatours.info. With wide range of options from simple rooms to comfortable *cabañas* and good food. Rafting and kayaking are available on the Río Cangrejal and trips to La Mosquitia (see page 107).

$ Cabañas del Bosque, up the road from Jungle River at Las Mangas. Nice rustic cabins with spectacular views in rooms and dorms.

Río Zacate area
$$$$ The Lodge, Pico Bonito, 15 mins' drive west of La Ceiba, T2440-0388, T1-888-428-0221 (USA), www.picobonito.com. Honduras' 1st world-class ecolodge at the base of Parque Nacional Pico Bonito. Luxury wooden cabins – no TV, very peaceful – in 400 acres of grounds. Forest trails, with lookout towers, natural swimming holes and waterfalls; nature guides and tours, very popular with birders; butterfly farm and serpentarium; swimming pool and gourmet restaurant. Highly recommended.

$ Natural View Ecotourism Center, in El Pino, T2386-9678. Very rustic cabins with access to trails in the vicinity. Cabins are built of adobe walls and thatched room, with a private bath, mosquito screens, but no power. Set in the middle of a plant nursery with a nice restaurant on premises. Efraín can help arrange several good trips nearby including a boat trip down the lower Río Zacate through mangroves to a farm located next to the beach, adjacent to Cuero y Salado.

$ Posada del Buen Pastor, T2950-3404. Has 4 rustic rooms on the upper storey of a private home with private bath, cable TV and fan.

Cuero y Salado Wildlife Reserve *p71*
$ Refuge, T2443-0329, Fucsa's administration centre, on the banks of the Río Salado. Has photos, charts, maps, radio and a 2-room visitors' house, sleeping 4 in

basic bunks, electricity 1800-2100. No mosquito nets, so avoid Sep and Oct if you can. Don't wear open footwear as snakes and yellow scorpions can be found here. Book in advance. Food available. There's also tent space for camping at the refuge.

Trujillo and around *p72, map p72*
$$$-$$ Christopher Columbus Beach Resort, outside town along the beach, drive across airstrip, T2434-4966. Has 72 rooms and suites, a/c, cable TV, swimming pool, restaurant, watersports, tennis, painted bright turquoise.

$$ O'Glynn, 3 blocks south of the plaza, T2434-4592. Smart, clean, good rooms and bathrooms, a/c, TV, fridge in some rooms. Highly recommended.

$$ Resort y Spa Agua Caliente Silin, Silin, on main road southeast of Trujillo, T2434-4247. *Cabañas* with cable TV, pool, thermal waters, restaurant, massage given by Pech Lastenia Hernández, very relaxing.

$ Buenos Aires, opposite **Catracho**, T2434-4431. Monthly rates available, pleasant, clean, peaceful, but cabins damp and many mosquitos, organizes tours to national park.

$ Casa Kiwi, in Puerto Castilla, out of town, T2434-3050, www.casakiwi.com. A 5-km, 15-min bus journey from town in an isolated location. Private rooms and dormitories, with kitchen and restaurant facilities. On a secluded beach with the benefits of internet, book swap, boat rides, horse riding, local trips and perfect for true relaxation. Buses to Puerto Castilla from the bus station every couple of hours, US$0.40. Watch out when riding bikes in the area, especially at night.

$ Catracho, 3 blocks south of church, then a block east, T2434-4439. Basic, clean, noisy, no water at night, wooden cabins facing a garden, camping space US$1.50, parking.

$ Colonial, on plaza, T2434-4011. With bath, hacienda style, restaurant (**El Bucanero**, see Eating), a/c, safe and clean.

$ Mar de Plata, up street west, T2434-4174. Upstairs rooms best, with bath, fan, friendly and helpful, beautiful view from room.

Yoro and around *p74*
$ Aníbal, corner of Parque Central, Yoro. Excellent value, private or shared bath, clean, pleasant, wide balcony, restaurant.

$ Colonial, Calle del Presidio, Olanchito. Good value, bath, fan, cheaper with shared bath, restaurant, parking.

$ Hospedaje, Jocón. Clean and basic.

$ Hotel Olanchito, Barrio Arriba, Calle La Palma, Olanchito, T2446-6385. A/c.

$ Nelson, Yoro. Comfortable rooms with bath, fan, modern, good restaurant/bar and nice outdoor swimming pool on 3rd floor, bar/disco on roof with marvellous views. Warmly recommended.

$ Palacio, on main street, Yoro. All rooms with bath and fan and a good resaurant.

$ Valle Aguán y Chabelito, 1 block north of Parque Central, Olanchito, T2446-6718 (same management as **Hotel Olanchito**). Single rooms with a/c, doubles with fan, all rooms with cable TV, best in town, with best restaurant.

Eating

Puerto Cortés *p66, map p66*
$$ Candiles, 2 Av, 7-8 Calle. Good grills, reasonable prices, open-air seating.

$$ Pekín, 2 Av, 6-7 Calle. Chinese, a/c, excellent, good service, a bit pricey but recommended. **Supermercado Pekín** next door.

$ Burger Boy's, 2 Av 8 Calle. Lively, popular with local teenagers.

$ Comedor Piloto, 2 Av 1-2 Calle. Mon-Sat 0700-1800. Clean, satellite TV, fans, good value and service, popular.

$ El Zaguán, 2 Av 5-6 Calle, closed Sun. Popular with locals, good for refreshments.

$ Ilusión, 4 Calle E opposite Parque. Pastries, bread, coffee, nice for breakfast.

\$ Kasike's Restaurant-Bar-Peña, 3 Av y 9 Calle and **Carnitas Tapadera**, on same block. Recommended.

\$ Matt's, on same block as **La Cabaña**, a/c, nice bar, good food, not expensive.

\$ Wendy's, on the Parque. With inside play centre for children.

Cafés and ice cream parlours
\$ Repostería y Pastelería Plata, 3 Av and 2 Calle E, near Parque Central. Good bread and pastries, excellent cheap *almuerzo*, buffet-style, kids' playroom. Recommended.

Omoa *p67*
\$ Cayuquitos, on beachfront. Good-value meals all day, but service is very slow.

\$ Fisherman's Hut, 200 m to right of pier. Clean, good food, seafood, recommended. Don't expect early Sun breakfasts after the partying the night before.

\$ Sunset Playa, on beachfront at southern end of the beach. Good food, open all day.

Cafés and juice bars
\$ Stanley, on the beach next door to **Cayuquitos**. Good value, with good shakes and juices.

Tela *p67*
The best eating is in the hotel restaurants.

\$\$\$ Casa Azul, Barrio El Centro. Open till 2300. Run by Mark from Texas, subs, dinner specials, book exchange. Helpful.

\$\$ Arecifes. Calle Muelle de Cabotaje, on seafront road T441-4353. Open Tue-Sun. Best bar and grill in town.

\$\$ César Mariscos. Open from 0700. Nice location on the beach, serves good seafood, very good breakfast menu.

\$\$ Iguana Sports Bar, road between 2 town bridges leading out of town. Open-air, music.

\$\$ Luces del Norte, of Doña Mercedes, 11 Calle, 2 Av NE, towards beach from Parque Central, next to **Hotel Puerto Rico**. Delicious seafood and good typical

breakfasts, very popular, also good information and book exchange.

\$\$ Maya Vista, in hotel (see Sleeping, above). Run by Québécois Pierre, fine cuisine, 1 of the best in Tela. Highly recommended.

\$\$ Merendero Tía Carmen, at the the **Mango B&B** (see Sleeping). Good food, Honduran specialities including *baleadas*, good *almuerzo*.

\$ Bahía Azul, good fresh food, excellent sea food.

\$ Bella Italia, Italian-owned serving pizza, on walkway by the beach.

\$ El Pescador, San Juan. On the beach, great seafood in a fine setting.

\$ Sherwood. Good food, popular, enjoy the view from the terrace, also opens 0700 and serves excellent breakfast.

\$ Tuty's Café, 9 Calle NE near Parque Central. Excellent fruit drinks and good cheap lunch specials, but slow service.

Cafés and ice cream parlours
Espresso Americano, in front of Parque Central. Best place in town for coffee, latte, cappuccino, with internet and international calls. Very popular.

La Ceiba *p68, map p69*
\$\$ Cafetería Cobel, 7 Calle between Av Atlántida and 14 de Julio, 2 blocks from Parque Central. Could be the best *cafetería* in the entire country, very popular with locals, always crowded, good fresh food, daily specials, highly recommended. Unmissable.

\$\$ El Guapo's, corner of 14 de Julio and 14 Calle. Open daily for dinner. US-Honduran owned, good combination of international and typical Honduran cuisine.

\$\$ La Chavelita, end of 4 Calle E, overlooking Río Cangrejal. Open daily for lunch and dinner. Seafood, popular.

\$\$ La Palapa, Av Víctor Hugo, next to **Hotel Quinta Real**. Giant, palm-roofed, wood-beamed 'palapa', serving juicy steaks, grills, fish, seafood and burgers; also sports bar with half a dozen TV screens, ice-cold beer. Good value for money though indifferent service.

$$ La Plancha, Calle 9, east of the cathedral. Open daily for lunch and dinner. Best steak house in La Ceiba, with good seafood dishes.

$$ Toto's, Av San Isidro, 17 Calle. Good pizzas.

$ Cric Cric Burger, Av 14 de Julio, 3 Calle, facing attractive Parque Bonilla. Good fast food, several branches. Recommended.

$ Expatriates Bar, Grill and Cigar Emporium, Final de Calle 12, above **Refricón**, 3 blocks south, 3 blocks east of Parque Central. Thu-Tue 1600-2400. Honduran-American owners, very affordable, with good steak and shrimps. Free internet service for clients. Also have a branch at the Cangrejal River, Km 9.

$ Gallo Pinto, Calle 9, east of the cathedral. Affordable typical Honduran cuisine in a pleasant informal setting.

$ Mango Tango, on 1 Calle. The best Ceibeño cuisine in the Zona Viva. Open daily for dinner from 1730. Menu includes fish, pork, chicken and beef dishes, and the best salad bar in town! They also have a nice sports bar.

$ Masapán, 7 Calle, Av San Isidro and Av República. Daily 0630-2200. Self-service, varied, well-prepared choice of dishes, fruit juices, good coffee. Recommended.

$ Palace, 9 Calle, Av 14 de Julio. Large Chinese menu, surf 'n' turf. Recommended.

$ The Palm Restaurant, centrally located, half a block from Parque Central in the **Banco de Occidente** building. American-style food open daily for breakfast, lunch and dinner. TVs with international news and sports. Free internet service for clients.

$ Paty's, Av 14 de Julio between 6 and 7 Calle. Milkshakes, wheatgerm, cereals, donuts, etc, purified water, clean. Opposite is an excellent pastry shop. There are 2 more **Paty's**, at 8 Calle E and the bus terminal.

Around La Ceiba *p69*

$$ Kabasa, Sambo Creek. Seafood Garífuna-style, bar, delightful location.

Trujillo and around *p72, map p72*
Don't miss the coconut bread, a speciality of the Garífuna.

$$ Galaxia, 1 block west of plaza. Good seafood, popular with locals.

$$ Oasis, opposite HSBC. Outdoor seating, Canadian owned, good meeting place, information board, good food, bar, English books for sale, book exchange, local tours.

$ Bahía Bar, T2434-4770, on the beach by the landing strip next to **Christopher Columbus**. Popular with expats, also Hondurans at weekends, vegetarian food, showers, toilets.

$ Don Perignon, uphill from **Pantry**. Some Spanish dishes, good local food, cheap.

$ El Bucanero, on main plaza. A/c, video, good breakfast, *desayuno típico*.

$ Pantry, 1½ blocks from the park. Garífuna cooking and standard menu, cheap pizzas, a/c.

🎭 Entertainment

La Ceiba and around *p68, map p69*
Iguana Sports Bar Discoteque, in **Coco Pando** hotel (see Sleeping, above), is the place to go.

La Casona, 4a Calle. Thu-Sat 2000-0400. Most popular nightspot in town. Karaoke bar, good music.

Monaster, 1 Calle. Thu-Sat 2000-0400. Nice setting, good a/c. Several others along 1 Calle.

Trujillo and around *p72, map p72*
Head to **Rincón de los Amigos** or **Rogue's** if you're looking for drink at the end of the day. Also try the **Gringo Bar** and **Bahía Bar**. In **Barrio Cristales** at weekends there's *punta* music and lively atmosphere. Recommended.

The cinema shows current US releases (most in English with subtitles).

🎉 Festivals and events

Puerto Cortés *p66, map p66*
Aug Noche Veneciana on 3rd Sat.

Tela *p67*
Jun Fiesta de San Antonio.

La Ceiba and around *p68, map p69*
15-28 May San Isidro La Ceiba's patron
saint's celebrations continue for 2 weeks,
the highlight being the international carnival
on the 3rd Sat in May, when La Ceiba parties
long and hard to the Afro-Caribbean beat of
punta rock.

⚙ Shopping

Puerto Cortés *p66, map p66*
There is a souvenir shop, **Marthita's**, in the
customs administration building (opposite
Hondutel). The market in the town centre is
quite interesting, 3 Calle between 2 and 3 Av.
Supertienda Paico is on the Parque.

La Ceiba and around *p68, map p69*
Carrion Department Store, Av San Isidro
with 7A Calle. **Deli Mart** late-night corner
store on 14 de Julio, round corner from
internet café, shuts at 2300. **El Regalito**,
good-quality souvenirs at reasonable prices in
small passage by large Carrión store. **T Boot**,
store for hiking boots, Calle 1, east of Av San
Isidro, T2443-2499. **Supermarket Super
Ceibena**, 2 on Av 14 de Julio and 6A Calle.

Trujillo and around *p72, map p72*
Garí-Arte Souvenir, T2434-4207, in the
centre of Barrio Cristales, is recommended
for authentic Garífuna souvenirs. Owned
by Ricardo Lacayo and open daily.
Tienda Souvenir Artesanía next to
Hotel Emperador, handicrafts, hand-painted
toys. 3 supermarkets in the town centre.

⛰ Activities and tours

Puerto Cortés *p66, map p66*
Bahía Travel/Maya Rent-a-Car,
3 Av 3 Calle, T2665-2102.
Irema, 2 Av 3-4 Calle, T2665-1506.
Ocean Travel, Plaza Eng,
3 Av 2 Calle, T2665-0913.

Tela *p67*
Garífuna Tours, southwest corner of Parque
Central, T2448-2904, www.garifunatours.
com, knowledgeable and helpful with
mountain bike hire, US$5 per day. Day trips
to Punta Sal (US$31, meals extra), Los Micos
lagoon (US$31) and Punta Izopo (US$24).
La Ceiba– Cayos Cochinos (US$39),
La Ceiba–Cuero Salado (US$68), Pico Bonito
(US$33). Also trips further afield to La Ceiba,
Mosquitia (4 days, US$499) and a shuttle
service between San Pedro Sula and La Ceiba,
US$18 per person. Also La Ceiba–Copán,
US$45. Good value. Highly recommended.
Honduras Caribbean Tours, T2448-2623,
www.honduras-caribbean.com. Wide range
of tours and treks throughout Honduras
specializing in the north coast.

La Ceiba and around *p68, map p69*
Ask around to find a tour that suits your
needs and to verify credentials.
Caribbean Travel Agency, run by Ann
Crichton, Av San Isidro, Edif Hermanos Kawas,
Apdo Postal 66, T2443-1360, helpful, shares
office with **Ríos Honduras**, see below.
Garífuna Tours, Av San Isidro 1 Calle, T2440-
3252, www.garifunatours.com. Day trips into
Pico Bonito National Park (US$34 per person),
Cuero y Salado (US$49), rafting on the
Cangrejal (US$34), trips out to Cayos Cochinos
(US$49) and a shuttle service to Tela (US$1).
Junglas River Rafting, T2440-1268,
www.jungleriverlodge.com.
La Ceiba Ecotours, Av San Isidro, 1st block,
50 m from beach, T2443-4207, hiking and
riding in Parque Nacional Pico Bonito,
visits to other nearby reserves, whitewater
rafting, trips to La Mosquitia.
La Moskitia Eco Aventuras, Av 14 de Julio
at Parque Manuel Bonilla, T2442-0104,
www.lamoskitia.hn. Eco-adventure tours, run
by Jorge Salaverri, extremely knowledgeable
nature guide, enthusiastic and flexible.
Specializes in trips to Mosquitia, including
week-long expeditions to Las Marias and

hikes up Pico Baltimore and Pico Dama. Highly recommended.

Omega Tours, T2440-0334, www.omega tours.info, runs rafting and kayaking trips on the Río Cangrejal, jungle hikes, and own hotel 30 mins upstream. Also tours to La Mosquitia ranging from easy adventure tours of 4 days up to 13-day expeditions. Prices drop dramatically with more than 2 people.

Ríos Honduras, T2443-0780, office@ rioshonduras.com, offering whitewater rafting, trips on the Río Cangrejal, spectacular, reservations 1 day in advance.

Cuero y Salado Wildlife Reserve *p71*

Although it is possible to go to the Salado and hire a villager and his boat, a qualified guide will show you much more. It is essential to bring a hat and sun lotion with you. Travel agencies in La Ceiba run tours there, but **Fucsa** arranges visits and owns the only accommodation in the reserve. Before going, check with **Fucsa** in La Ceiba. Although the office only has basic information, the people are helpful and there are displays and books about the flora and fauna to be found in the park. A guide and kayak for a 1-hr trip costs about US$10. Boatmen charge about US$20 for a 2-hr trip or US$40 for 5 hrs (6-7 persons maximum), US$6-7 for the guide.

Trujillo and around *p72, map p72*
Hacienda Tumbador Crocodile Reserve is privately owned, accessible only by 4WD and with guide, US$5 entry.

☻ Transport

Puerto Cortés *p66, map p66*
Boat
To Guatemala Information from **Ocean Travel** at 3 Av, 2 blocks west of plaza.

To Belize Boats connecting to Belize leave from beside the bridge over the lagoon (Barra La Laguna), buy tickets at the blue wooden

shack next to *joyería* near **Los Coquitos** bar just before bridge. Daily 0800-1700. The **Gulf Cruza** launch leaves Puerto Cortés on Mon at 1100, for **Mango Creek** and on to **Placencia**, 4 hrs arriving around 1340, US$50.

Remember to get your exit stamp. To be sure of getting an exit stamp go to Immigration in town (see Directory, page 84). If arriving from Belize and heading on straight away you don't need to go into town to catch a bus. Get on to the bridge, cross over the other side and keep walking 200 m to the main road. Buses going past are going to San Pedro Sula and beyond.

Bus
Virtually all buses now arrive and leave from 4 Av 2-4 Calle. Bus service at least hourly to **San Pedro Sula**, US$2.30, 45 mins, **Citul** (4 Av between 3 and 4 Calle) and **Impala** (4 Av y 3 Calle, T2255-0606). **Expresos del Caribe**, **Expresos de Citul** and **Expresos del Atlantic** all have minibuses to **San Pedro Sula**. Bus to **Omoa** and **Tegucigalpita** from 4 Av, old school bus, loud music, very full, guard your belongings. **Citral Costeños** go to the Guatemalan border, 4-5 Av, 3C E. Regular buses leave for **Omoa** (US$0.70) at 0730 to get to **Corinto** at the Guatemalan border.

Omoa *p67*
Boat
Boats leave for **Lívingston**, Guatemala, on Tue and Fri around 1000. Ask around to confirm. Ask at **Fisherman's Hut** for Sr Juan Ramón Menjivar.

Bus
Frequent buses to the Guatemalan border at 1000, 1400 and 1700.

Tela *p67*
Bike
Hire from **Garífuna Tours**, 9 Calle y Parque Central (see page 81), and from Hotel Mango.

Bus

Catisa or **Tupsa** lines from San Pedro Sula to **El Progreso** (US$0.50) where you must change to go on to **Tela** (3 hrs in total) and **La Ceiba** (last bus at 2030 with Transportes Cristina). On **Catisa** bus ask to be let off at the petrol station on the main road, then take a taxi to the beach, US$0.50. Also 1st-class service with **Hedman Alas** at 1010, 1415 and 1810.

Bus from Tela to **El Progreso** every 25 mins; last bus at 1830, US$1.50. To **La Ceiba**, every 30 mins, from 0410 until 1800, 2 hrs, US$2. Direct to **Tegucigalpa**, Traliasa, 1 a day from Hotel Los Arcos, US$4.50, same bus to **La Ceiba** (this service avoids San Pedro Sula; 6 a day with **Transportes Cristinas** (US$9.20). To **Copán**, leave by 0700 via El Progreso and San Pedro Sula; to arrive same day. To **San Pedro Sula**, 1130 and 1715 with Diana Express (US$2.50), or 8 a day with **Transportes Tela Express**, last bus at 1700 (US$3). To **Trujillo** through Savá, Tocoa and Corocito.

Shuttle **Garífuna Tours**, see page 81, offers a shuttle service direct to **San Pedro**, US$18 and **Copán Ruinas**, US$45.

Around Tela *p67*
Bus

To **Triunfo de la Cruz**, US$0.40 (about 5 km, if no return bus, walk to main road where buses pass).

La Ceiba and around *p68, map p69*
Air

For La Mosquitia see page 107.

Golosón (LCE), 10 km out of town. See Getting there, page 8, for international services. For details of flights to Bay Islands, see page 86. **Isleña** (T2443-0179 airport), flies to **San Pedro Sula**, **Trujillo**, **Puerto Lempira**, **Roatán** and **Guanaja**; Taca fly to **Tegucigalpa** and **San Pedro Sula**. Sosa, the most reliable domestic airline flies to **Utila**, **Roatán**, **San Pedro Sula**, **Tegus**

and others. Office on Parque Central, T2443-1399. **Atlantic Air**, T2440-2347. **Sosa**, **Atlantic** and **Isleña** all have flights. At weekends there are some charter flights that may be better than scheduled flights. Taxi to town US$8 per person or walk 200 m to the main road and share for US$2 with other passengers, also buses from bus station near Cric Cric Burger at end 3 Av, US$0.15. Intercity buses pass by the entrance.

Boat

Ferry schedules from the Muelle de Cabotaje, T445-1795 or T445-5056, with daily services as follows: **La Ceiba–Utila** 0815, 0930 and 1630, **Utila–La Ceiba**, 0630, 0945 and 1430, US$15. **La Ceiba–Roatán**, 1000 and 1600, **Roatán–La Ceiba**, 0700 and 1300, US$18. Boats leave from Muelle de Cabotaje. Too far to walk, about 15-min taxi ride from town, US$2-3 per person if sharing with 4 people, buses available from centre of town.

Trips to the **Hog Islands** can be arranged, call T441-5987 or through **Garífuna Tours** (see Activities and tours, page 81), US$65 for a boat load.

Bus

Taxis from centre to bus terminal, which is a little way west of town (follow Blv 15 de Septiembre), cost US$1 per person, or there are buses from Parque Central. Most buses leave from here. **Traliasa**, **Etrusca** and **Cristina** bus service to **Tegucigalpa** via Tela several daily, US$6, avoiding San Pedro Sula (US$1 to Tela, 2 hrs); also hourly service to **San Pedro Sula**, US$2 (3-4 hrs). **Empresa Tupsa** direct to **San Pedro Sula** almost hourly from 0530 until 1800. Also 1st class with **Hedman Alas** – take taxi to separate terminal. To **Trujillo**, 3 hrs direct, 4½ hrs local (very slow), every 1½ hrs or so, US$3; daily bus La Ceiba–Trujillo–Santa Rosa de Aguán. To **Olanchito**, US$1, 3 hrs; also regular buses to **Sonaguera**, **Tocoa**, **Balfate**, **Isletas**, **San Esteban** and other regional locations.

Car

Car rental Maya Rent-a-Car, Hotel La Quinta, T2443-3071. **Dino's Rent-a-Car**, Hotel Partenon Beach, T2443-0404. **Molinari** in Hotel París on Parque Central, T2443-0055.

Beaches around La Ceiba *p70*
Bus

To **Nuevo Armenia** from La Ceiba at 1100 US$0.75, 2½ hrs. At the bus stop is the office where boat trips are arranged to **Cayos Cochinos**, US$10, trips start at 0700.

Trujillo and around *p72, map p72*
Boat

Cargo boats leave for **Mosquitia** (ask all captains at the dock, wait up to 3 days, see page 107), the **Bay Islands** (very difficult) and Honduran ports to the west. Ask at the jetty. The trip to **Puerta Lempira** costs about US$15.

Bus

Trujillo can be reached by bus from **San Pedro Sula**, **Tela** and **La Ceiba** by a paved road through Savá, Tocoa and Corocito. From La Ceiba it is 3 hrs by direct bus, 4 hrs by local. 3 direct **Cotraibal** buses in early morning from Trujillo. Bus from **Tegucigalpa** (Comayagüela) with **Cotraibal**, 7 Av between 10 and 11 Calle, US$6, 9 hrs; some buses to the capital go via La Unión, which is not as safe a route as via San Pedro Sula. To **San Pedro Sula**, 5 daily 0200-0800, US$5. Public transport also to **San Esteban** and **Juticalpa** (leave from in front of church at 0400, but check locally, arriving 1130, US$5.20). Bus to **Santa Fe** at 0930, US$0.40, leaves from outside **Glenny's Super Tienda**. To **Santa Rosa de Aguán** and **Limón** daily.

Yoro and around *p74*
Bus Hourly bus service to **El Progreso**, several daily to **Sulaco**.

Puerto Cortés *p66, map p66*
Banks Mon-Fri 0800-1700, Sat 0830-1130. HSBC, 2 Av, 2 Calle. Banco de Comercio cashes TCs. **Banco de Occidente**, 3 Av 4 Calle E, cashes Amex TCs, accepts Visa/ MasterCard. Banco Ficensa has ATM for MC and Amex only, 2 Av, 2C. Banks along 2 Av E, include **Atlántida** (2 Av, 3-4 Calle, has Visa ATM), Bamer, and HSBC. **Immigration** Migración 5 Av y 3-4 Calle next to Port Captain's office, 0800-1800. **Internet** Lema Computers, 5-6 Av, 2C, open Mon-Sat. **Medical services** Policlínica, 3 Av just past 1 Calle, open 24 hrs. **Post** Next door to Hondutel. **Telephone** Hondutel, dock entrance, Gate 6, fax and AT&T. Direct to USA.

Omoa *p67*
Banks Banco de Occidente does not take credit cards, but will cash TCs. Some shops will change dollars. Ask around. **Immigration** Migración office on the main road opposite Texaco. If you come from Guatemala by car you have to get a police escort from Corinto to Puerto Cortés. **Internet** Near the beach.

Tela *p67*
Banks Banco Atlántida (with ATM), HSBC, 9 C 3 Av, Visa and MasterCard cash advances and changes TCs. Also try **Bamer** and Atlantida. Casa de Cambio La Teleña, 4 Av, 9 Calle NE for US$, TCs and cash. Exchange dealers on street outside post office. **Immigration** Migración is at the corner of 3 Av and 8 Calle. **Internet** Service at the Mango Café. **Language classes** Mango Café Spanish School, US$115 for 4 hrs a day, Mon-Fri with a local tour on Sat, T2448-0338, www.mangocafe.net. **Laundry** El Centro, 4 Av 9 Calle, US$2 wash and dry. Lavandería Banegas, Pasaje Centenario, 3 Calle 1 Av. Lavandería San José, 1 block northeast of market. **Medical services** Centro Médico

CEMEC, 8 Av 7 Calle NE, T2448-2456. Open 24 hrs, X-rays, operating theatre, smart, well equipped. **Post and telephone** Both on 4 Av NE. Fax service and collect calls to Europe available and easy at **Hondutel**.

La Ceiba and around *p68, map p69*
Banks HSBC, 9 Calle, Av San Isidro, and **Banco Atlántida**, Av San Isidro and 6-7 Calle, have ATM that accepts Visa. Cash advances on Visa and MasterCard from **BAC** on Av San Isidro opposite Hotel Iberia between 5 and 6 Calle; also Amex. **Honducard**, Av San Isidro for Visa, next to Farmacia Aurora. Better rates for US$ cash from *cambistas* in the bigger hotels (and at travel agency next door to Hotel Príncipe). Money exchange, at back of Supermercado Los Almendros, 7 Calle, Av San Isidro with Av 14 de Julio, daily 0800-1200, 1400-1800, T2443-2720, good rates for US$ cash and TCs. **Internet** Hondusoft, in Centro Panayotti, 7A Calle between San Isidro and Av 14 de Julio, Mon-Fri 0800-2000, Sat 0800-1800, discount 1800-2000 when US$3 instead of US$6 per hr. La Ceiba **Internet Café**, Barrio El Iman, 9 Calle, T2440-1505, Mon-Sat 0900-2000, US$3 per hr. Iberia, next to Hotel Iberia, US$0.80 per hr. **Intercon Internet Café**, Av San Isidro, opposite Atlántida ATM. **Language schools** Best to do some research and look at the options. Worth considering are: **Centro Internacional de Idiomas**, T2440-1557, www.honduras spanish.com, provides a range of classes 5 days for US$150, with hotel option US$290, with branches in Utila and Roatán. **Central**

America Spanish School, Av San Isidro No 110, Calle 12 y 13, next to Foto Indio, T2440-1707, www.ca-spanish.com, US$150 for the week, homestay also an option adding US$70, also have branches on Utila and Roatán. **Medical services** Doctors: **Dr Gerardo Meradiaga**, Edif Rodríguez García, Ap No 4, Blv 15 de Septiembre, general practitioner, speaks English. **Dr Siegfried Seibt**, Centro Médico, 1 Calle and Av San Isidro, speaks German. Hospital: **Vincente D'Antoni**, Av Morazán, T2443-2264, private, well equipped. **Post** Av Morazán, 13 Calle O. **Telephone** Hondutel for international telephone calls is at 2 Av, 5 y 6 Calle E.

Trujillo and around *p72, map p72*
Banks Banco Atlántida on Parque Central and **HSBC**, both cash US$, TCs and handle Visa. **Banco de Occidente** also handles MasterCard and Western Union.
Immigration Opposite Mar de Plata.
Internet Available in town. **Laundry** Next to Disco Orfaz, wash and dry US$2.50.
Libraries Library in middle of square.
Medical services Hospital on main road east off square towards La Ceiba. **Post and telephone** Post office and Hondutel, F2434-4200, 1 block up from church.

Yoro and around *p74*
Banks Banco Atlántida on Parque Central.
Post and telephone Post office and Hondutel 1 block from Parque Central.

Bay Islands

A string of islands off the northern coast of Honduras, the Bay Islands are the country's most popular tourist attraction. Warm, clear Caribbean waters provide excellent reef diving – some of the cheapest in the Caribbean. Equally enjoyable are the white-sand beaches, tropical sunsets and the relaxed atmosphere which positively encourages you to take to your hammock, lie back and relax. The culture is far less Latino than on the mainland. English is spoken by many and there are still Black Carib – Garífuna – descendants of those deported from St Vincent in 1797.

Ins and outs

Getting there Transport to the Bay Islands is easy and there are regular flights with Isleña, Sosa and **Atlantic Airlines** from La Ceiba (T2440-2343) and San Pedro Sula (T2433-6016) to Utila and Roatán. **Taca** has an international service from Miami to Roatán. There is also a daily boat service from La Ceiba to Roatán and Utila. **Spirit Airlines** is going to provide direct flights from Fort Lauderdale (Miami) to La Ceiba from May 2009.

The islands → *www.caribbeancoast.com/bayislands/index.cfm.*

The beautiful Bay Islands (**Islas de la Bahía**), of white sandy beaches, coconut palms and gentle sea breezes, form an arc in the Caribbean, some 32 km north of La Ceiba. The three main islands are **Utila**, **Guanaja** and, the largest and most developed, **Roatán**. At the eastern end of Roatán are three smaller islands: **Morat**, **Santa Elena**, and **Barbareta**, with many islets and cayes to explore. Closest to the mainland are the small, palm-fringed **Hog Islands**, more attractively known as **Cayos Cochinos**.

The underwater environment is one of the main attractions and is rich and extensive; **reefs** surround the islands, often within swimming distance of the shore. **Caves** and caverns are a common feature, with a wide variety of **sponges** and the best collection of **pillar coral** in the Caribbean. There are many protected areas including the **Marine Parks** of Turtle Harbour on Utila, and Sandy Bay/West End on Roatán, which has permanent mooring buoys at the popular dive sites to avoid damage from anchors. Several other areas have been proposed as marine reserves by the Asociación Hondureña de Ecología: the Santuario Marino de Utila, Parque Nacional Marino Barbareta and Parque Nacional Marino Guanaja. The Bay Islands have their own conservation association (see under Roatán, page 88).

The traditional industry is fishing, mostly shellfish, with fleets based at French Harbour; but the supporting boat-building is a dying industry. Tourism is now a major source of income, particularly because of the scuba-diving attractions. English-speaking blacks constitute the majority of the population, particularly on Roatán. Utila has a population that is about half black and half white, the latter of British descent mainly from the settlers from Grand Cayman who arrived in 1830. Columbus anchored here in 1502, during his fourth voyage. In the 18th century the islands were the base for English, French and Dutch buccaneers. They were in British hands for over a century, but were finally ceded to Honduras in 1859. Latin Hondurans have been moving to the islands from the mainland in recent years.

The islands are very beautiful, but beware of the strong sun (the locals bathe in T-shirts), sandflies and other insects. Basic etiquette for snorkelling and diving applies. Snorkellers and divers should not stand on or even touch the coral reefs; any contact, even the turbulence from a fin, will kill the delicate organisms.

Utila → *For listings, see pages 92-103. Area: 41 sq km.*

Utila is the cheapest and least developed of the islands and has a very laid-back ambience. Only 32 km from La Ceiba, it is low lying, with just two hills, Pumpkin and the smaller Stewarts, either side of the town known as **East Harbour**. The first inhabitants were the Paya and there is scant archaeological evidence of their culture. Later the island was used by pirates; Henry Morgan is reputed to have hidden booty in the caves. The population now is descended from Black Caribs and white Cayman Islanders with a recent influx from mainland Honduras. Independence Day (15 September) festivities, including boxing and climbing greased poles, are worth staying for. ► *For more information, see www.aboututila.com.*

Around Utila

There are no big resorts on the island, although a couple of small, lodge-style, upmarket places have opened, otherwise the accommodation is rather basic. Sunbathing and swimming is not particularly good – people come for the diving. **Jack Neal Beach** has white sand with good snorkelling and swimming. **Chepee's White Hole** at the end of Blue Bayou peninsula has a beach for swimming. Snorkelling is also good offshore by the Blue Bayou restaurant, a 20-minute walk from town, but you will be charged US$1 for use of

Utila

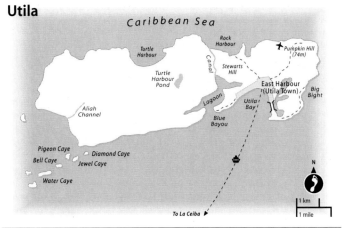

Utila's dive sites

There are currently around 50 dive sites around Utila, where permanent moorings have been established to minimize damage to the coral reef. Although the reef is colourful and varied, there are not a lot of fish, and lobster have almost disappeared. The dive sites are close to shore at about 20 m depth but they are all boat dives. Diving off the north coast is more spectacular, with drop-offs, canyons and caves. Fish are more numerous, helped by the establishment of the Turtle Harbour Marine Reserve and Wildlife Refuge.

the facilities. There are hammocks and a jetty, which is great for fishing at sunset, and the only place to get away from the terrible sandflies. **Bandu Beach** is another option on the northern end of the island. Sunchairs, drinks and clean toilets are provided. Buy a drink or pay a US$2 charge. There is also sandfly relief at **Big Bight**, **Redcliff** and **Rocky Point**.

You can hike to **Pumpkin Hill** (about 4 km down the lane by HSBC, bikes recommended) where there are some freshwater caves with a beach nearby (watch out for sharp coral). It is also possible to walk on a trail from the airfield to Big Bight and the iron shore on the east coast, about 2 km, exploring tidal pools; nice views and beach but it is rocky so wear sandals.

You can visit the **Iguana Station** ① *Mon, Wed and Fri 1400-1700, T2425-3946, www.utila-iguana.de, US$2.20*, a short walk up hill from the fire station – follow the signs. Paying volunteer options possible. They also offer great trips through the mangroves to explore the more hidden parts of the island for around US$10.

Utila's cayes

A 20-minute motorboat ride from East Harbour are the cayes, a chain of small islands populated by fisherfolk off the southwest coast of Utila, which are known as the Cayitos de Utila. **Jewel Caye** and **Pigeon Caye** are connected by a bridge and are inhabited by a fishing community, which reportedly settled there to get away from the sandflies on Utila. Basic accommodation and food is available. **Diamond Caye** is privately owned, the snorkelling offshore here is excellent. **Water Caye** is a coconut island with 'white hole' sandy areas and with wonderful bathing in the afternoons. It is the only place where you can camp, sling a hammock or, in an emergency, sleep in or under the house of the caretaker; take food and fresh water, or rent the caretaker's canoe and get supplies from Jewel Caye.

Roatán → *For listings, see pages 92-103. Area:127 sq km.*

Roatán is the largest of the islands and has been developed quite extensively. But its idyllic charm is still apparent and quiet beaches are often just a short walk away. There is a paved road running from West End through to French Harbour, almost to Oak Ridge, continuing unpaved to Punta Gorda and Wilkes Point, as well as other unmade roads.

Tourist offices Bay Islands Conservation Association (BICA) ① *Casa Brady, 1st floor, Sandy Bay, 200 m off road to Anthony's Key Resort, T2445-3117, www.bicaroatan.com, Irma Brady,* *director of BICA, which manages the Sandy Bay/West End Marine National Park and Port Royal National Park in eastern tip of island,* has lots of information about the reef and its conservation work; volunteers welcome. Local information maps are also available from **Librería Casi Todo**, West End. The **Voice Book** is a useful online directory of island services and businesses, as well as local news and reviews; monthly magazine edition available in most hotels: www.bayislandsvoice.com.

Coxen Hole

The capital and administrative centre of the department, Coxen Hole, or **Roatán City**, is on the southwest shore. Planes land and boats dock here and you can get transport to other parts of the island. It is a colourfully scruffy little town with not much of tourist interest but some souvenir shops are opening. Besides being the seat of the local government, it has immigration, customs and the law courts. There is a post office, supermarket, handicraft shops, restaurants, banks, travel agents, a bookshop and various other stores. Buses leave from outside the supermarket. All public transport starts or ends here. If taxis are shared, they are *colectivos* and charge the same as buses. A huge, swanky new cruise-liner dock has opened outside the western end of town, with the Town Center shopping mall, offering pricey cafés, gift shops, duty-free stores, and – probably unique on the island – free and spotless public toilets.

Sandy Bay

A short journey from Coxen Hole, en route to West End, is Sandy Bay, one of the quieter towns on the island. The **Carambola Botanical Gardens** ① *opposite Anthony's Key Resort, www.carambolagardens.com, daily 0800-1700, US$10, guided tours (US$5) or self-guided nature trails,* created in 1985, contain many flowering plants, ferns and varieties of trees which can be explored on a network of trails – it is well worth a visit. The **Roatán Museum** ① *T2445-3003, US$4,* has displays covering the history of the island, with plenty of information about the pirates who called Roatán home, and a collection of artefacts.

1 Roatán

West End

Five minutes by road beyond Sandy Bay, the popular community of West End, at the western tip of the island, is the most popular place to stay. It's a narrow beach on a palm-fringed bay with a distinctly laid-back atmosphere. The **Sandy Bay/West End Marine Park** protects marine life in the area and large numbers of fish have flourished along the coast creating spectacular snorkelling. There are numerous good foreign and local restaurants with lots of pizza/pasta places, as well as hotels, *cabañas* and rooms to rent for all budgets. It is a stiff walk from Coxen Hole over the hills (three hours)to West End, or take the bus on the paved road (US$1; 20 minutes). ▸▸ *See www.roatanmarine park.com for more details.*

West Bay

A beautiful clean beach with excellent snorkelling on the reef, particularly at the west end, where the reef is only 10-20 m offshore and the water is shallow right up to where the wall drops off 50-75 m out and scuba-diving begins. Biting sandflies – *jejenes* – can be a pest here at dusk, but since the hotel staff started raking the beach every day, which exposes their eggs to the sun and kills them, they are no longer such a nuisance. Developers have discovered the delights of West Bay and the atmosphere is changing fast. Apartments, hotels, bars and restaurants are springing up, though mostly low-rise, and hidden behind the palm trees, so it's still pretty quiet here during the week.

East of Coxen Hole

French Harbour, on the south coast, with its shrimping and lobster fleet, is the main fishing port of Roatán. There is no beach and there are two seafood-packing plants. The road passes Coleman's (Midway) Bakery, where you can buy freshly baked products. The bay is protected by the reef and small cayes, which provide safe anchorage. Roatan Dive and Yacht Club and Romeos Marina (at Brick Bay) offer services for visiting yachts. Several charter yachts are based here. There are a few cheap, clean places to stay, as well as expensive hotels and dive resorts. Eldon's Supermarket is open daily and has a range of imported US food. **Gios Restaurant** and **Casa Romeos** serve top-quality seafood.

Across the island

The main road goes across the mountain ridge along the island with side roads to Jonesville, Punta Gorda and Oak Ridge. You can take a bus on this route to see the island's hilly interior, with beautiful views from coast to coast. Alternatively, hire a small 4WD, which is almost as cheap if shared between four people and allows you to explore the dirt roads and empty bays along the island's northern tip. **Jonesville** is known for its mangrove canal, which is best reached by hiring a taxi boat in Oak Ridge. **Oak Ridge**, situated on a caye (US$1 crossing in a dory from the bus stop), is built around a deep inlet on the south coast. It is a sleepy little fishing port, with rows of dwellings on stilts built on the water's edge (a bus from Coxen Hole to Oak Ridge takes about one and a half hours, depending on passengers, US$1.70). Much of the town has been rebuilt after widespread destruction by Hurricane Mitch in 1998, but the new buildings have retained the same traditional stilt design and pastel colours. Boatmen offer tours around the bay and through mangroves to caves allegedly used by pirates; US$20 for 45 minutes, but it's worth bargaining.

Isla Guanaja → *For listings, see pages 92-103. Area: 56 sq km.*

Columbus called Guanaja the Island of Pines, but Hurricane Mitch swept most of them away. Since then, a great replanting effort has been completed and, until the pines have regrown, flowering and fruiting plants thrive on the island. The island was declared a forest reserve in 1961, and is now designated a national marine park. Good (but sweaty) clambering on the island gives splendid views of the jungle and the sea and there are several attractive waterfalls, which can be visited on the hills rising to the summit of 415 m. The first English settler was Robert Haylock, who arrived in 1856 with a land title to part of the island, the two cayes that now form the main settlement of Bonacca and some of the Mosquito coast. He was followed in 1866 by John Kirkconnell who purchased Hog Caye, where the Haylocks raised pigs away from the sandflies. These two families became sailors, boat builders and landowners, and formed the basis of the present population.

Much of Guanaja town, locally known as **Bonacca** and covering a small caye off the coast, is built on stilts above sea water, with boardwalks and concrete pathways, hence its nickname: the 'Venice of Honduras'. There are three small villages, **Mangrove Bight**, **Savannah Bight** and **North East Bight**, on the main island. Much of the accommodation is all-inclusive resorts, but you can visit independently as well. Sandflies and mosquitoes cannot be escaped on the island, and none of the beaches offer respite (coconut oil, baby oil or any oily suntan lotion will help to ward off sandflies).The cayes are better, including Guanaja town. South West Caye is especially recommended.

Cayos Cochinos (Hog Islands) → *For listings, see pages 92-103.*

The Hog Islands, 17 km northeast of La Ceiba, constitute two small islands and 13 palm-fringed cayes. **Cochino Grande** is the larger island, rising to an altitude of just 143 m, and **Cochino Pequeño** is the smaller. Both have lush tropical vegetation with primeval hardwood forests and there are fewer biting insects than in the Bay Islands. As part of a National Marine Reserve, Cayos Cochinos and the surrounding waters are protected. There is a fee to enter parts of the islands of US$10. There are Garífuna fishing villages of palm-thatched huts at Chachauate on Lower Monitor Cay, where you can organize basic accommodation, and East End Village on Cochino Grande. Transport to the Hog Islands can be sought on the supply *cayuco* from Nuevo Armenia (see page 70), or by boat from La Ceiba, Sambo Creek or Roatán. There is a small dirt airstrip. Dug-out canoes are the local form of transport. The islands are privately owned and access to most of the cayes is limited, being occupied only by caretakers.

Bay Islands listings

For Sleeping and Eating price codes and other relevant information, see pages 10-11.

🛏 Sleeping

Utila *p87, map p87*

$$$$-$$$ Laguna Beach Resort, on point opposite Blue Bayou, T2668-68452, www.utila.com. Comfortable lodge, with bungalows each with own jetty, 8-day package includes meals and diving US$970, non-diver US$840. Fishing offered, can accommodate maximum of 40.

$$$-$$ Mango Inn, La Punta, T2425-3326, www.mango-inn.com. With bath, cheaper without, fan, spotless, helpful, roof terrace, reduction for students with **Utila Dive Centre**. Pool, **Mango Café** and **La Dolce Vita Pizzeria** for brick-oven pizzas on premises. Recommended.

$$$-$$ Trudy's, 5 mins from airport, T2425-3103. Rooms with a/c and hot water. Also **Trudy's Suites**, with colour TV, fridge and microwave. Recommended. **Underwater Vision** dive shop on site.

$$ Bay View, 100 m from **Utila Lodge**, T2425-3114, bayviewinternet@yahoo.com. 2 apartments with kitchen, living and dining room. Located on the water. With or without bath, pier, family-run.

$$ Jade Seahorse, T2425-3270, www.jadeseahorse.com. 5 great cabins, artistic, unusual and very funky, restaurant, bar, fantastic artistic gardens. Recommended.

$$-$ Freddy's, off the boat and turn right, it's a long walk to just over the bridge, T2425-3142. Good rooms, kitchens, quiet end of town.

$ Bavaria, up towards **Mango Inn**, offers clean, simple rooms.

$ Celena, main street, T2425-3228. With bath, clean with fan. Recommended.

$ Countryside, 10 mins' walk out of town, T2425-3216. Shared bath, rooms and apartments, quiet, clean, friendly, fan, porch, ask in town for Woody and Annie.

$ Cross Creek (see also Dive operators, page 98), T2425-3334, www.crosscreekutila. com. Good, clean rooms, with shower and shared toilets, discount for divers on courses.

$ Harbour View, right on water, T2425-3159. **Parrot's Dive** on site, cheaper rooms with shared bathrooms upstairs, rooms with private bath downstairs, hot water, own generator, cleaning done only on arrival, TV, fans, run by Roger and Maimee.

$ Loma Vista, up road opposite the dock, T2425-3243. Clean, fan, shared bath, very friendly, washes clothes cheaply.

$ Margaritaville, in a pleasant location just outside town near the beach, T2425-3366. Very clean, big rooms with 2 double beds, private bathroom, friendly.

$ Seaside, opposite **Gunter's Dive School**, T2425-3150. Private and shared rooms, kitchen for use. Wi-Fi, nice place, clean, laundry service, hammocks, balcony. Popular with budget travellers. Recommended.

Utila's cayes *p88*

All hotels are small family-run affairs (**$**).

$ Hotel Kayla. Affiliated with **Captain Morgan's Dive Center** on Jewell Cay. Free accommodation at Jewell Cay with PADI courses. Jewell Cay and Pigeon Cay are linked by a bridge.

You can rent out **Little Cay** and **Sandy Cay** completely, details available from cayosutila@hotmail.com.

Roatán *p88, map p89*
Coxen Hole

$$ Cay View, Calle Principal, T2445-1202. A/c, bath, TV, phone, laundry, restaurant, bar, dingy rooms, one with seaview, no breakfast, overpriced, but just about adequate if desperate.

$$-$ Mom, on main road into Coxen Hole, above pharmacy, next to hospital. Private or shared bath, modern, clean, a/c, TV.

$ El Paso, next door to **Caye View**, T445-1367. Shared bath, restaurant.
$ Naomi Allen, near the bus depot. Fan, clean, good.

West End

$$$ Half Moon Bay Cabins, Half Moon Bay, T445-4242. Bungalows and cabins with bath, restaurant with excellent seafood.
$$$-$$ Coconut Tree, West End, T2445-4081, www.westbaycoconuttree.com. Private cabins (3 double beds) owned by Vincent Bush, a/c, kitchen, balcony, hot water, fan, fridge, clean, friendly, discounts in low season.
$$$-$$ Keifitos Plantation Resort, on hillside above beach, T2978-4472, www.keifitosplantation.com. Bungalows in a beautiful setting, short walk from village, mosquitoes, bar, good breakfasts to 1300, champagne breakfasts Sun, horses for rent with guide, friendly owners, very quiet, very clean. Recommended.
$$$-$$ Mermaid Beach, West End, T2445-4335, Clean, quiet, with bath, fan or a/c, dive shop next door.
$$ Casa Calico, north of Half Moon Bay, T2445-4231, www.casacalico.com. Comfortable, cable TV, videos, rooms and apartments, fan, 2 rooms with a/c, garden, huge balconies, apartments sleep 4 or more with kitchen, hot water, noisy in morning, friendly, helpful.
$$ Dolphin Resort, centre of Half Moon Bay, T2445-1280. Private bathroom, a/c and fan. Recommended.
$$ Posada Arco Iris, Half Moon Bay, T2445-4264, www.roatanposada.com. Apartments with kitchen, hot water, fan, large balcony, friendly owners. Restaurant specializing in grilled meats. Highly recommended.
$$ Sea Breeze, north of West End, T2445-4026, www.seabreezeroatan.com, Nice rooms, hot water, baths, a/c optional, suites and studios available with kitchens, windsurfers and kayaks for rent.
$$ Seagrape Plantation Resort, Half Moon Bay, T2445-4428, www.seagraperoatan.com.

Cabins, rooms with private bath, hot water, family atmosphere, friendly, Visa accepted, nice location on rocky promontory, no beach, but snorkelling possible, full-service restaurant and bar, inclusive packages available. Fun drives for US$30 with equipment.
$$-$ Anderson's, behind **Chris's Tienda**, West End, T2455-5365. Basic rooms, shared bath, clean, fan, lower rates for longer stays.
$$-$ Chillies, Half Moon Bay, T2445-4003, www.nativesonsroatan.com/chillies.htm. Double rooms and dormitory, clean, fully equipped kitchen, lounge, big balcony, camping and hammocks available. Excellent value for money.
$ Dora Miller (no sign), West End, 2 houses behind **Jimmy's Lodge**. Washing facilities, no fan, no mosquito nets, basic, noisy, friendly.

West Bay

$$$$ Las Sirenas, midway along the beach, T2445-5009, www.hmresorts.com. Rooms, suites and enormous apartments, with a/c, flat-screen cable TV, and kitchen; small swimming pool; full board and shared amenities with adjacent HM resorts: Henry Morgan, Mayan Princess and Paradise Beach. Quiet, clean and well run. Recommended.
$$$$-$$$ Island Pearl, on the beach, T2445-5005, www.roatanpearl.com. Double-storey apartments, a/c, hot water, tiled kitchen, handmade furniture, nicely decorated.
$$$ West Bay Lodge, south of West Bay beach, T2991-0694, www.westbaylodge.com. Cabins with hot water and fan, good breakfast.
$$$-$$ Bananarama, centre of West Bay beach, T2992-9679. With bath, hot water, fan, PADI dive courses available, breakfast included for guests, good value. Recommended.
$$$-$$ Las Rocas, next to **Bite on the Beach**, T2445-1841, www.lasrocasresort.com. Duplex *cabañas*, very close together, hot water, balcony, smaller cabins sleep 3, larger ones sleep 6, free boat transport to West End and back, dive shop and restaurant.

East of Coxen Hole

$$$$ Coco View Resort, French Harbour, T911-7371, www.cocoviewresort.com. Good shore diving, on lagoon.

$$$$ Reef House Resort, Oak Ridge, T2435-1482, www.reefhouseresort.com. Meals and various packages, including diving. Wooden cabins with sea-view balconies, seaside bar, private natural pool, dock facilities, good snorkelling from the shore.

$$$-$$ Executivo Inn, Mount Pleasant on the road to French Harbour opposite electricity plant, T2455-6708, www.executiveinn.org. Nice rooms, a/c, hot water, TV, pool, no beach.

$$ Palm Tree Resort, Brick Bay, T2445-1986. Cabins with bath, home cooking island style, quiet, diveshop, wall diving with boat.

$ Dixon's Plaza, French Harbour, past the **Buccaneer**. Good.

$ San José Hotel, Oak Ridge. With bath (2 rooms), cheaper without (3 rooms), clean, pleasant, good value, water shortages, good food, English-speaking owner, Luis Solórzano.

Elsewhere

$$ Ben's Restaurant, on coast road south out of Punta Gorda, T2445-1916. Nice cabins to rent, dive shop (US$35 per dive), limited equipment, disorganized, wooden deck over sea, local food, bar, friendly, safe parking.

Isla Guanaja *p91*

$$-$ Harry Carter, T2455-4303, ask for fan. Rooms are clean.

$ Miss Melba, just before **Hotel Alexander** sign on left, house with flowers. 3 rooms in boarding house, run by friendly old lady with lots of island information, shared bathroom, cold water, great porch and gardens.

Cayos Cochinos (Hog Islands) *p91*

$$$ Plantation Beach Resort, Cochino Grande, T2442-0974. VHF 12. Rustic cabins on hillside, hot water, fans, diving offshore, yacht moorings, good steep walk up to lighthouse for view over cayes to mainland, music festival end Jul, local bands and dancers, they charge US$30 for the trip from La Ceiba.

$ Cayo Timón (also known as **North Sand Cay**) can be visited from Utila, 1¼ hrs by boat; you can rent the caye (price per person), minimum 6, 8 is comfortable, A-frame, Polynesian style, do overnight diving trips, very basic, quiet, peaceful. Phone Roy and Brenda at **Thompson's Bakery**, Utila, T2425-3112, for information.

❷ Eating

Utila *p87, map p87*

Menus are often ruled by the supply boat: on Tue and Fri restaurants have everything, by the weekend some drinks run out.

$$$ Jade Seahorse. Fri-Wed 1100-2200, closed Thu. A variety of seafood home-made style and *licuados*, coolest decor in town, includes the very popular **Treetanic** bar, high up in the trees 1700-2400.

$$$-$$ Mariposa Restaurant. Lovely spot over the water, good views overlooking bay, nice atmosphere, bright, clean, airy. One of the nicest places in town. Offers fresh seafood. Expensive but good quality.

$$ Bundu Café. Fri-Wed, closed Thu. Regular typical menu. Mon is all-you-can-eat pizza and pasta. Broad selection of beach novels, romance and Western novels. Great spot to watch people on the street. Recommended.

$$ Driftwood Café. Texan BBQ-style place with good burgers. Airy setting above the water.

$$ El Picante, up towards **Mango Inn**. Upscale Mexican restaurant in a good location.

$$ Indian Wok, in front of **Tranquila Bar**. Open Mon, Wed and Fri. Variety of Asian dishes and home-made, good potato salad.

$$ La Piccola. Pastas, garlic bread, fish, pizza, great service. Upscale yet relaxed atmosphere offering lunch and dinner. One of the best places in town.

$ Big Mamas. Lovely place, the prettiest restaurant on Utila.

$ Dave Island Café. In front of **Coco Loco**. Tue-Sat, closed Sun and Mon. Very popular with locals and tourists. San Franciscan chef offers pork and chicken with a choice of sauces. Great curries and good vegetarian dishes. Great home-made chocolate cake. Big portions. Menu changes daily. Come early to get a seat.

$ Howells's Restaurant, near the UPCO building. Popular with locals, and often overlooked. Great lunch options with local dishes.

$ Mermaid Restaurant. Very nice building, airy, open, wood ceiling, buffet style, some of the quickest food on the island, economical prices, popular with divers and locals.

$ Munchie's. In a lovely restored historic building near the dock with a porch for people-watching. Nice snacks, good service. Daily specials. Also organize trips to the cayes.

$ RJ's BBQ and Grill House. Open Wed, Fri, Sun, 1730-2200. Great BBQ. Popular.

$ Skidrow Bar and Restaurant, in front of **Ecomarine Dive shop**. Great burritos, popular with expats. Mon night is pub quiz night.

$ Thompsons Bakery. Open 0600-1200. Very informal, friendly, good cakes, coconut bread, breakfasts, biscuits, cinnamon rolls, *baleadas*, cheap and with lots of information. Good lunch option.

$ Zanzibar Café. Funky ramshackle place typical of Utila. Breakfasts, shakes, burgers, sandwiches, pastas.

Utila's cayes *p88*

There are a few restaurants, a Sat night disco and little else.

Roatán *p88 map p89*

Evening meals cost US$4-10. There is a good seafood restaurant on **Osgood Caye** a few mins by free water taxi from wharf.

Coxen Hole

$$ El Paso, next to the **Caye View**. Good seafood soup.

$$ Le Bistro, 10 mins' walk along seafront between Coxen Hole and West Bay, T9527-3136. Perched on a rocky outcrop on the beach. Thai and Vietnamese cuisine, with spicy seafood and curries. Beautiful spot with deck overlooking the sea; French owner François also takes snorkelling trips.

$$ Qué Tal Café, on road to West End. Good coffee, herbal teas, sandwiches and pastries, shares space with bookstore.

$ Hibiscus Sweet Shop. Home-made fruit pies, cakes and biscuits.

$ Pizza Rey, opposite **Warren's**. Pizza slices.

West End

$$$ Half Moon Bay Restaurant, Half Moon Bay. Nice location to sit on terrace overlooking sea, more expensive than most, excellent food, service can be very slow.

$$$ Tong. Asian and Middle East specialities, good location, salad buffet, expensive but worth it.

$$ Belvedere's, on water, West End. Fri-Sun 1900-2100. Nice setting, tasty Italian food. Recommended.

$$ Brick Oven, about 15 mins out of West End (follow the signs). Good food and movies every night.

$$ Cannibal Café, in the **Sea Breeze**. Open 1030 until 2200, closed Sun. Excellent Mexican food, large helpings, good value.

$$ Cindy's Place, next to **Sunset Inn**. Local family breakfast, lunches and dinner in garden, fish caught same morning, also lobster and king crab. Recommended.

$$ The Cool Lizard, Mermaid Beach. Seafood, vegetarian and chicken, home-made bread, salads, nice atmosphere, good.

$$ Keifito's Hangout, West End. Good breakfast, champagne on Sun, well priced.

$$ Papagayos, Half Moon Bay, on a jetty, T445-1008. Good atmosphere for pre-prandial tipple, reggae music, basic meals, no sandflies, great sundeck, Thu is band/dance/party night, also rooms to rent (**$$**).

$$ Pinocchio's, West End, along same path as the **Lighthouse**, www.roatanpinocchios. com. Excellent pasta, great stir fry and delicious salads, run by Patricia and Howard.

$$ Rick's American Café, Sandy Bay. Open from 1700, except Wed. Tree-top bar, shows all sports events, best steaks on Roatán.

$$ Rudy's. Open all day. Good pancakes and cookies for breakfast, sandwich combos, good atmosphere but pricey.

$$ Salt and Pepper Club, entrance to West End. Supermarket, BBQ and live music.

$$ Tony's Pizzeria, in the **Sunset Inn**. Fresh fish, good food, big portions.

$$ Velva's Place, at the far end of Half Moon Bay. Island-style seafood and chicken dishes, try the conch soup, good prices.

$ Sunset Playa on the beach.

$ Tartines and Chocolate, Half Moon Bay. French bakery, good bread and pastries.

West Bay

$$$ Bite on the Beach, on the point over West Bay. Wed-Sun brunch, huge deck in gorgeous position, excellent, fresh food and great fruit punch. Nightly feeding of moray eels, which swim – or wriggle – up to the edge of the dock. A fun place, very friendly, recommended and very much what Roatán is about.

$$ Neptuno Seafood Grill, between **Fosters** and **Coconut Tree 2**. Seafood, paella, barbecued crab, extensive bar, open daily for lunch and dinner.

$$ West Bay Lodge, see Sleeping. Good breakfasts on a nice balcony with sea view.

East of Coxen Hole

There is a *taquería* close to HSBC on the main road in French Harbour serving good tacos, burritos and hamburgers.

$$$ Gios, French Harbour. Seafood, king crab speciality.

$$$ Roatan Dive and Yacht Club, French Harbour. Daily specials, pizza, salads, sandwiches, usually very good.

$$ BJ's Backyard Restaurant, Oak Ridge, at the harbour. Island cooking, fishburgers, smoked foods, reasonable prices. There is a pizzeria and, next door, a supermarket.

$$ Iguana Grill, French Harbour. International cuisine and suckling pig.

$$ Pirate's Hideaway, at Calabash Bay, east of Oak Ridge. Seafood, friendly owner.

$$ Romeo's, French Harbour. Romeo, who is Honduran-Italian, serves good seafood, and continental cuisine.

$$ Tres Flores, French Harbour, on the hill. Good views, Mexican specialities, they pick up groups from West End, T2245-0007.

Isla Guanaja *p91*

$$ Harbour Light, through **Mountain View** nightclub. Good food, reasonably priced for the island.

🎭 **Entertainment**

Utila *p87, map p87*
Bars and clubs

Bar in the Bush is the place to go, 100 m beyond the **Mango Inn**, very popular, lots of dancing and always packed, Wed 1800-2330, Fri (Ladies Night) and Sun 1800-0300.

Coco Loco, on jetty at harbour front near **Tranquila Bar**, very popular with young divers, together, these 2 places are the anchors and reigning kings of late night Utila night life.

La Pirata Bar, at the dock. High up, great views, breezy.

Treetanic Bar, Inside **Jade Seahorse**. Hot spot on the island.

Cinema

Reef Cinema, opposite Bay Islands Originals shop, shows films at 1930 every night, at US$3 per person. Popcorn, hotdogs, a/c, comfortable seats, big screen. Also inside the cinema is **Funkytown Books and Music**, an excellent bookshop to trade, sell and rent. Stock up here before you travel anywhere else. Also trades MP3s.

Utila Centre for Marine Ecology, opposite Trudy's, www.utilaecology.org. Offers free presentations on Tropical Marine Ecology, the 1st and 3rd Mon of each month, 1830-1930.

Roatán *p88, map p89*
Most clubs come alive about midnight, play reggae, salsa, *punta* and some rock.

Coxen Hole
Harbour View, Thu-Sun nights, late, US$0.50 entrance, very local, usually no problem with visitors, but avoid local disputes. Hot and atmospheric.
Sundowners Bar, popular happy hour from 1700-1900, Sun quiz followed by BBQ.

West End
Bahía Azul, Fri is party night, DJ, dancing.
C-bar, fantastic location on beachfront near Seagrape Plantation.
Foster's, the late night hotspot, dance music Thu night as well as band nights.
Lone's Bar, Mermaid Beach, nightly BBQ, reggae music.
Sundowners Bar, popular happy hour from 1700-1900, Sun quiz followed by BBQ.

East of Coxen Hole
Al's, Barrio Las Fuertes, before French Harbour. Closed Sat night, salsa and plenty of *punta*.

⚜ Festivals and events

Utila *p87, map p87*
Aug Sun Jam on Water Caye at a weekend at the beginning of Aug, www.sunjamutila.com. Look out for details locally. They charge a US$2.50 entrance fee to the island; bring your own tent/hammock, food and water.

○ Shopping

Utila *p87, map p87*
Arts and crafts
Bay Islands Original Shop sells T-shirts, sarongs, coffee, hats, etc. Mon-Fri 0900-1200 and 1300-1800, Sat and Sun 0900-1200.

Gunter Kordovsky is a painter and sculptor with a gallery at his house, good map of Utila, paintings, cards and wood carving.
Utila Lodge Gift Shop is also worth trying.

Roatán *p88, map p89*
Supermarkets
Best to buy supplies in Coxen Hole. **Coconut Tree** at West End is expensive. **Woods** is cheaper. **Eldon** in French Harbour is also expensive. **Ezekiel**, West End, opposite church, sells fruit and veg.
Mall Megaplaza, French Harbour. New shopping mall by roadside east of town, with fast-food outlets.

⛰ Activities and tours

Utila *p87, map p87*
The **Utila Snorkel Center**, for all those who do not want to dive, organizes trips. Inside Mango Tree Business building. See also **Bundu Café**, page 94.

Diving
Dive with care for yourself and the reef at all times; www.roatanet.com has plenty of information about Utila and its dive sites.

Utila is a very popular dive training centre. Learning to dive is cheaper here than anywhere else in the Caribbean, especially if you include the low living expenses. It is best to do a course of some sort; students come first in line for places on boats and recreational divers have to fit in. In recent years, Utila has developed a reputation for poor safety and there have been some accidents requiring emergency treatment in the recompression chamber on Roatán. Serious attempts have been made to change this by the diving community of Utila. The 3 or 4 accidents that happen annually are a result of cowboy divers and drug or alcohol abuse.

Instructors Choose an instructor who you get on with, and one who has small classes and cares about safety; follow the rules on alcohol/drug abuse and pay attention to the dive tables. There is a rapid turnover of instructors; many stay only a season to earn money to continue their travels, and some have a lax attitude towards diving regulations and diving tables. Check that equipment looks in good condition and well maintained. Boats vary, you may find it difficult to climb into a dory if there are waves. While a dive shop has a responsibility to set standards of safety, you also have a responsibility to know about diving times. If you don't, or are a beginner, ask.

Price There is broad price agreement across dive shops in Utila. Out of the revenues the **Utila Dive Supporters' Association** can budget for spending, facilities and eventually conservation. Whatever you may think of the idea, one benefit, is greater safety and better organized protection of the reef. Whether this works remains to be seen, but the price of saving a few dollars could end up costing lives. Dive insurance at US$3 per day for fun divers, US$9 for students (Advanced, or Open Water), US$30 for divemasters is compulsory and is available from the BICA office. It covers air ambulance to Roatán and the recompression chamber. Treat any cuts from the coral seriously, they do not heal easily.

PADI courses A PADI Open Water course costs US$320 (including certificate) with 4 dives, an Advanced course costs US$280 with 5 dives, US$256 if you do the Open Water course with the dive shop first. You can work your way up through the courses with rescue diver (US$350) and dive master (US$800). The Open Water usually comes with 2 free fun dives. Credit cards, if accepted, are 6% extra. Not permitted by credit cards but as all companies on the island do it you can't go elsewhere. Competition is fierce with over 15 dive shops looking for business, so you can pick and choose. Once qualified, fun dives are US$50 for 2 tanks. Dive shops offer free basic accommodation with packages. Most schools offer instruction in English or German; French and Spanish are usually available somewhere, while tuition handbooks are provided in numerous languages including Japanese. A variety of courses is available up to instructor level. If planning to do a diving course, it is helpful but not essential to take passport-sized photographs with you for the PADI card.

Dive operators
Altons Dive Center, T2425-3704, www.altonsdiveshop.com. Offers NAUI and PADI certification, weekly fish talk, recommended, popular, owned by the mayor of Utila.
Bay Islands College of Diving, on main street close to **Hondutel** tower, T425-3291, www.dive-utila.com. 5-star PADI facility, experienced and well qualified staff, good boats ranging from 50 ft, for large parties to skiff for smaller ones, environmentally sound. Only dive shop on the island with in-house pool and hot tub. The trauma centre and recompression chamber, shared by all dive shops, is located here. 5-star facility.
Captain Morgan's, T2425-3349, www.divingutila.com. Has been recommended for small classes, good equipment, friendly staff. The only dive shop that offers accomodation on nearby Pigeon Key. Popular with travelling couples.
Cross Creek, T2425-3397, www.crosscreek utila.com. 2 boats, maximum 8 people per instructor, 2-3 instructors, free use of kayaks, accommodation on site for students, 18 rooms, can also arrange transfers from the mainland.
Deep Blue Divers, T2425-3211, www.deep blueutila.com. One of the newer operators on the island. The friendly owners are getting good feedback through word of mouth.
Gunter's Ecomarine Dive Shop, T2425-3350, http://ecomarinegunters.blogspot.com. Dive school with 4 divers per group maximum,

7 languages spoken. Most laid-back dive shop and the only dive school that does not hassle divers arriving at the ferry dock.

Paradise Divers, on the seafront, T2425-3148. Relaxed and friendly.

Parrot Aqua Adventures, T2425-3772, tatianaluna22@yahoo.com, run by a dynamic local couple. Good reviews by divers with small classes.

Underwater Vision Dive Center at Trudy's, T2425-3103, www.underwatervision.net. With accommodation. Very nice location at the Bay.

Utila Dive Centre, Mango Inn, PADI CDC, T2425-3326, www.utiladivecentre.com. Well-maintained equipment, daily trips to north coast in fast dory, recommended. All boats covered and custom-built, surface interval on cayes.

Utila Watersports, T2425-3264, run by Troy Bodden. 4 students per class. Troy also hires out snorkelling gear, photographic and video equipment and takes boat trips. Good reports.

Whale Shark & Oceanic Research Centre (**WSORC**), T2425-3760, www.wsorc.com. A professional scientific organization committed to education and preserving Utila's oceans, offers speciality courses including whale shark research, naturalist courses, research diver, fish ID, Coral ID. Free presentation 1930 Sun nights about whale sharks.

Roatán *p88, map p89*
Boat trips
Kayak rentals and tours from **Seablades**, contact Alex at **Casi Todo**, 3- to 7-day kayak tours, US$150-250. Full and ½-day rental US$20 and US$12 (with instruction), kayaks available at **Tyll's**. From Rick's American Café, **Casablanca** charters on yacht *Defiance III*, sunset cruises, party trips, full-day snorkelling, also can be arranged through **Casi Todo**. At West Bay beach is a glass-bottomed boat, **Caribbean Reef Explorer**, US$20 per 1½ hrs, unfortunately

includes fish feeding, which upsets the reef's ecological balance. Glass-bottomed boat and 3-person submarine tours from the dock at Half Moon Bay, US$25 per person.

Diving
If you don't want to dive, the snorkelling is normally excellent. The creation of the Sandy Bay/West End Marine Park along 4 km of coast from Lawson Rock around the southwest tip to Key Hole has encouraged the return of large numbers of fish in that area and there are several interesting dive sites. Lobsters are still rare, but large grouper are now common and curious about divers. If the sea is rough off **West End** try diving around **French Harbour** (or vice versa) where the cayes provide some protection. There are more mangroves on this side, which attract the fish. **Flowers Bay** on the south side has some spectacular wall dives, but not many fish, and it is calm during the 'Northers' which blow in Dec-Feb. Few people dive the east end except the live-aboards (**Bay Islands Aggressor**, **The Aggressor Fleet**, **Romeo Tower**, French Harbour, T2445-1518) and people on camping trips to Pigeon Cay, so it is relatively unspoilt. Because fishing is allowed to the east, tropical fish are scarce and the reef is damaged in places. In addition to a few stormy days from Dec to Feb, you can also expect stinging hydroids in the top few feet of water around Mar and Apr which bother people who are sensitive to stings. Vinegar is the local remedy.

Courses As on Utila, the dive operators concentrate on instruction but prices vary (since Dec 1994 the municipal government has set minimum prices). You can normally find a course starting within 1 or 2 days. There is more on offer than in Utila; not everyone teaches only PADI courses. Prices for courses and diving vary with the season. In low season good deals abound. Open Water US$320, advanced US$280, fun dives US$40 (2-9 dives = US$35 each, 10+ = US$30 each). Despite the huge number of dive students, Roatán has a good safety record but it still pays to shop around and find an instructor you feel confident with at a dive shop which is well organized with well-maintained equipment. As in other 'adventure' sports, the cheapest is not always the best. Dive insurance is US$2 per day, and is sometimes included in the course price. If you do not have dive insurance and need their services, the hyperbaric chamber charges a minimum of US$800.

Dive operators

Anthony's Key Resort, Sandy Bay, T2445-3003. Mostly hotel package diving, also swim and dive with dolphins.

Aquarius Divers, West End. PADI courses, fun dives, excursions to the south walls in conjunction with Scuba Romance dive shop, Brick Bay.

Bananarama, West Bay, in centre of beach, next to Cabaña Roatana, T2445-5005. Small, friendly dive shop, run by young German family, boat and shore diving.

The Last Resort, Gibson Bight, T2445-1838 (in USA T305-893-2436). Mostly packages from the USA.

Native Son's Water Sports, next to Mermaid cabins, West End, T2445-4003. Run by Alvin, local instructor, PADI and PDSI courses and fun dives.

Ocean Connections at Sunset Inn, West End, T3327-0935, www.ocean-connections.com. Run by Carol and Phil Stevens with emphasis on safety and fun, good equipment, multilingual instructors, PADI courses, BSAC, the only shop with nitrox instruction, fast boats, also rooms and restaurant, dive/accommodation packages available. Recommended. Also at West Bay, entrance through Paradise Beach Resort – though not attached to the resort – one of the few independent operators, T2445-5017. Very friendly and highly recommended.

Scuba Romance, Dixon Cove. Shop and equipment, large diesel boat and compressor, diving the south wall and the reef at Mary's Place, overnight trips to Barbareta, 6 dives, US$80, sleeping on the boat, work with Palm Cove Resort, cabin-style accommodation, home cooking.

Sueño del Mar Divers, T2445-4343. Good, inexpensive, American-style operation, tends to dive the sites closest to home.

Tyll's Dive, West End, T9698-0416, www.tyllsdive.com. Multilingual instructors, PADI, SSI courses. Accommodation also available.

West End Divers, West End, T2445-4289, www.westendivers.com. Italian owned, competent bilingual instructors, PADI Dive Centre.

Fishing

Trips can be arranged through Eddie, contact at **Cindy's** next to Ocean Divers, West End, small dory, local expert, good results, US$30 per hr, but prices can vary. Alternatively, go fishing in style from French Harbour, **Hot Rods** sports fisher, US$500 per day charter, T445-1862. Contact **Casi Todo**, T2445-1347, for fishing tours, ½- and full day. Fishing trips also available on **Flame**, contact Darson or Bernadette, T445-1616, US$20 per hr.

Submarine trips

Karl Stanley offers a probably unique opportunity with deep-sea submarine trips down to 2000 ft. At US$600 per person, a little on the pricey side, but then it's not an everyday option. **Stanley Submarines**, www.stanleysubmarines.com.

Tour operators

At **Belvedere's Lodge** on the headland at Half Moon Bay, Dennis runs snorkelling trips to secluded bays beyond Antony's Key in a glass-bottomed yacht. He also takes charters and sunset cruises all along the coast. Horse riding available from **Keifitos** or **Jimmy's** in West End. Alex does day trips to Punta Gorda and 2- to 3-day trips in his sailboat *Adventure Girl*, which is moored at **Ocean Divers** dock, contact here or at **Tyll's**. **Far Tortugas** charters, trimaran *Genesis*, does sailing trips with snorkelling and reef drag (snorkellers towed behind slow-moving boat), US$45 per day, US$25 per ½ day, contact **Casi Todo**, West End, T2445-1347. **Coconut Tree** have a rainforest tour to Pico Bonito, US$112 (guide, transport, lunch and snorkelling).

Travel agents

Airport travel agency has information on hotels, will make bookings, no commission. **Bay Islands Tour and Travel Center**, in Coxen Hole (Suite 208, Cooper Building, T2445-1585) and French Harbour. **Casi Todo 1** in West End or **Casi Todo 2** in Coxen Hole can arrange tours, locally and on the mainland, including fishing, kayaking, island tours, trips to Barbareta and Copán. Local and international air tickets also sold here as well as new and second-hand books, Mon-Sat, 0900-1630. **Columbia Tours**, Barrio El Centro, T2445-1160, good prices for international travel, very helpful. **Tropical Travel**, in Hotel Caye View, T2445-1146. **Carlos Hinds**, T2445-1446, has a van for trips, reasonable and dependable.

Zip-wire

High-wire canopy tour circuits are the latest craze on Roatán, with half a dozen sites strung around the island, including **Pirates of the Caribbean**, T2455-7576, **Mayan Jungle Canopy**,www.boddentours.com, and**South Shore Canopy Tour**, on West Bay Rd, T9967-1381, www.southshorezipline.com.

Isla Guanaja *p91*
Diving and sailing

The most famous dive site off Guanaja is the wreck of the *Jado Trader*, sunk in 1987 in about 30 m on a flat bottom surrounded by some large coral pinnacles which rise to about 15 m. Big black groupers and moray eels live here, as does a large shy jewfish and many other fish and crustaceans.

End of The World, next to **Bayman Bay Club**, T2402-3016, www.guanaja.com. Diving instruction, beachfront bar, restaurant, cabins, kayaks, canoes, hobie cats, white-sand beach, fishing. Highly recommended resort.

Jado Divers, beside **Melba's**, T2453-4326. US$26 for 2 dives, run by Matthew from US. Preston Borden will take snorkellers out for US$25 per boat load (4-6 people), larger parties accommodated with larger boat, or for customized excursions, very flexible.

⊙ Transport

Utila *p87, map p87*
Air

Sosa, T2452-3161, www.aerolineasosa.com, flies on Mon, Wed and Fri to **La Ceiba**, US$50. Also to **Roatán** (US$40), **San Pedro** (US$51) and **Tegucigalpa** (US$64). **Atlantic Air**, have 3 flights a week to La Ceiba. There is local transport between airport and hotels.

Boat

Ferry services on the Princess Utila, **La Ceiba**– Utila at 0930 and 1600, and Utila–La Ceiba at 0620 and 1400. Automatic ticketing US$21. Daily sailings Utila–**Roatán**, on Captain Vern's catamaran *Nina Elisabeth II*, T3346-2600 (mob), or ask at **Gunter's Dive Shop** on Utila and **Coconut Divers**, Half Moon Bay, Roatán. US$55 one way, no fixed schedule. Dock fee required when leaving Utila (US$1)

Cycling

Bike hire about US$5 per day. Try **Delco Bike**.

Roatán *p88, map p89*
Air

The airport is 20 mins' walk from Coxen Hole, or you can catch a taxi from outside the airport for US$1.50. There is a hotel reservation desk in the airport, T2445-1930. Change in Coxen Hole for taxis to West End. US$1 per person for *colectivos* to West End, US$2 to Oak Ridge. If you take a taxi from the airport they charge US$10 per taxi; if you pick one up on the main road you may be able to bargain down to US$5. **Isleña**, **Sosa** and **Atlantic Air** fly from **La Ceiba**, US$20 1 way (fewer Sun); flights also to and from **Tegucigalpa**, US$60, via **San Pedro Sula** (Isleña), US$50, frequency varies according to season. No other direct flights to other islands, you have to go via **La Ceiba** (to **Utila** US$38.50, to **Guanaja** US$51). Always buy your ticket in advance (none on sale at airport), as reservations are not always honoured.

From the USA, Taca flies on Sat from **Houston**, on Sun from **Miami**. From Central America, daily flights from **Belize City** (Isleña), Sat from **San Salvador** (Taca).

Airlines Taca, at airport T2445-1387; Isleña, airport T2445-1088; **Sosa**, airport T2445-1154. **Casi Todo**, T2445-1347, sells all flights within Honduras at same price as airlines.

Boat

Galaxy Wave catamaran sails twice daily from **La Ceiba** to Coxen Hole. Roatán–**La Ceiba** 0700 and 1400, La Ceiba–Roatán 0930 and 1630, T2445-1795 (Roatán), T2440-7823 (La Ceiba), US$52 return. No sailings in bad weather. At times the crossing can be rough, seasickness pills available at ticket counter, and steward gives out sick bags; smart modern ship, with café, and 2 decks, comfortable seating. Irregular boats from **Puerto Cortés** and **Utila**. Cruise ships visit from time to time, mostly visiting **Tabayana Resort** on West Bay.

Bus

From Coxen Hole to Sandy Bay is a 2-hr walk, or a US$1.70 bus ride, every 30 mins 0600-1700 from market, a couple of blocks in from Calle Principal. **Ticabus** buses go to French Harbour, Oak Ridge and Punta Gorda, daily every 45 mins from 0600-1630, US$1.75; from parking lot opposite Centro Médico Euceda east end of Calle Principal.

Car

Car rental **Captain Van**, West End, vans, also mopeds and bicycles, good information about the islands; **Roatan Rentals**, West End, range of vehicles, pickups and vans for rent; **Sandy Bay Rent-A-Car**, US$42 per day all inclusive, jeep rental, T2445-1710, agency also in West End outside Sunset Inn; **Toyota**, opposite airport, have pickups, US$46, 4WD, US$65, Starlets US$35 per day, also 12-seater bus, US$56 per day, T2445-1166.

Cycling and mopeds

Captain Van's Rentals, West End; also from Ole Rentavan, T445-1819.

Taxi

If you take a private taxi, *privado*, negotiate the price in advance. The official rate from the airport to Sandy Bay/West End is US$15 per taxi regardless of the number of passengers; from ferry dock to West End is US$20. Luis (waiter at **Bite on the Beach** restaurant West End), runs taxi tours, very informative and knowledgeable, T9892-9846. Water taxis from West End to West Bay, every few minutes depending on passengers, US$3, from jetty next to **Foster's Bar**.

Isla Guanaja *p91*
Air

The airport is on Guanaja but you have to get a water taxi from there to wherever you are staying; there are no roads or cars; **Sosa** and Isleña (T2453-4208) fly daily from **La Ceiba**, 30 mins. Other non-scheduled flights available.

Boat

The *Suyapa* sails between Guanaja, **La Ceiba** and **Puerto Cortés**. The *Miss Sheila* also does this run and on to **George Town** (**Grand Cayman**). *Cable Doly Zapata*, Guanaja, for monthly sailing dates to Grand Cayman (US$75 1 way). Irregular sailings from Guanaja to **Trujillo**, 5 hrs.

Utila *p87, map p87*

Banks Dollars are accepted on the island and you can pay for diving courses with dollars, TCs and credit cards, although the latter carry an 8-10% charge. **Banco Atlántida** Mon-Fri 0830-1530, Sat 0830-1130. **HSBC** Mon-Fri 0830-1530, Sat 0830-1130, changes dollars and gives cash against a Visa, but not MasterCard. There are now 2 ATM machines on the island. **Thompson's Bakery** and **Henderson's Shack** (next to La Cueva) will change dollars and TCs. **Michel Bessette**, owner of **Paradise Divers**, does Amex, Visa and MasterCard advances plus 8%.

Internet Annie's Internet, near the dock, 0800-1730, closed Sat, extortionate at US$0.15 per min. **Seaside Internet**, next to Seaside Inn, Mon-Fri 0900-1400 and 1600-1800. Also **Internet Café** on road to Mango Inn, Mon-Sat 0900-1700. **Mermaids** offers good internet service for reasonable prices. **Language schools** Central American Spanish School, T2425-3788, www.ca-spanish.com. 20 hrs per week instruction, 4 hrs per day, US$200, Accommodation US$160 per week. Also have schools on Roatan and La Ceiba. **Medical services** Utila Community Clinic (Mon-Fri 0800-1200), has a resident doctor. **Post** At the pier opposite Captain Morgan's Dive Centre, Mon-Fri 0800-1200, 1400-1600, Sat 0800-1100. **Telephone** Hondutel office, Mon-Fri 0700-1100 and 1400-1700, Sat 0700-1100, is near Utila Lodge. The main service is reported as unreliable. **Hondutel** sends (and receives) faxes. The REMAX office in the Mango Tree business building offers phone calls and most internet places offer Skype services.

Roatán *p88, map p89*

Banks Banco Atlántida, Credomatic, and HSBC in Coxen Hole. There is also a **BAC** office where you can get a cash advance on your Visa/MasterCard, upstairs, before Caye View Hotel on the main street. 5 banks in French Harbour; **HSBC** in Oak Ridge, T2245-2210, MasterCard for cash advances. No banks in West End. No exchange facilities at the airport. Dollars and lempiras can be used interchangeably for most services. **Emergencies** Police, T9716-3837, Red Cross, T2445-0428. **Internet** Available at the **Sunset Inn**. The **Lucky Lemp**, opposite Qué Tal coffee shop, main street Coxen Hole, phone, fax and email services. **D & I Cyber Cafe**, Calle Principal, Coxen Hole, western edge of town, across river, Mon-Sat 0800-2100. **Cyber Planet**, Calle Principal, opposite Cay View Hotel, Coxen Hole, T2445-0194, US$3 per hr, daily 0800-2000. **Paradise Computer**, Coxen Hole, 10 mins' walk down road to West End. **Language School** West End Spanish School, T9927-44007. Weekly culture-based courses. **Medical services** Dentist: upstairs in the Cooper building for emergency treatment, but better to go to La Ceiba or San Pedro Sula. **Doctor**: Dr Jackie Bush has a clinic in Coxen Hole, no appointment necessary, for blood or stool tests, etc. **Ambulance and Hyperbaric Chamber**, Anthony's Key with full medical service. **Local hospital**, Ticket Mouth Rd, Coxen Hole, T2445-1499. **Post** In Coxen Hole, stamps not always available, bring them with you or try **Librería Casi Todo** in West End. **Telephone and fax** Very expensive, you will be charged as soon as a call connects with the satellite, whether or not the call goes through. **Hondutel** in Coxen Hole, fax is often broken. **Supertienda Chris**, West End, T2445-1171, 1 min to Europe US$10, USA, Canada US$5. Both **Librería Casi Todo** and **Rudy's Cabins** in West End have a fax, US$10 per page to Europe, US$5 to USA. Rudy's charges US$2 a min to receive phone calls.

Isla Guanaja *p91*

Banks HSBC and Banco Atlántida.

The Northeast

Through the agricultural and cattle lands of Olancho State, a road runs near to the Parque Nacional Sierra de Agalta and beyond to Trujillo on the Caribbean coast. To the west, accessible only by air or sea, is the Mosquitia coast – a vast expanse of rivers and swamps, coastal lagoons and tropical forests filled with wildlife but with few people.

Eastern Honduras

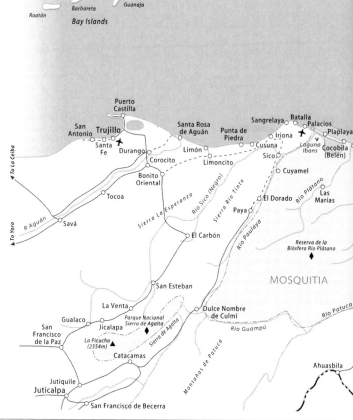

Tegucigalpa to the northeast coast → *For listings, see pages 110-113.*

The Carretera de Olancho runs from the capital northeast to the Caribbean coast. It passes through **Guaimaca** and **San Diego**, **Campamento**, 127 km, a small, friendly village surrounded by pine forests, and on to the Río Guayape, 143 km.

By the river crossing at **Los Limones** is an unpaved road north to **La Unión** (56 km), deep in the northern moutains passing through beautiful forests and lush green countryside. To the north is the **Refugio de Vida Silvestre La Muralla-Los Higuerales** ① *US$1*, where quetzales and emerald toucanettes can be seen between March and May in the cloud forest. For those that have made the effort to get to this spot, if you're

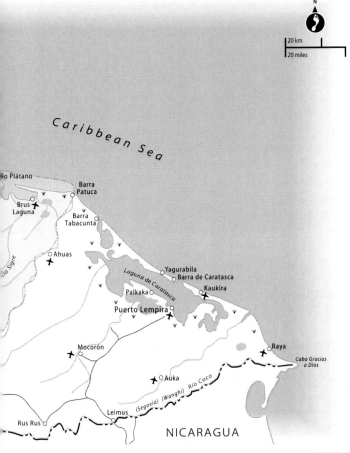

camping you may experience the frissonic pleasure of jaguars 'screaming' during the night. The park comprises the three peaks of **La Muralla**, 1981 m, **Las Parras**, 2064 m, and **Los Higuerales**, 1985 m. Cohdefor has an office on the main plaza for information, closed weekends. You are now required to take a guide with you on the trail. Cost is US$4, arrange in La Unión. Four trails range from 1-10 km and are recommended. There are two campsites in the forest (contact Cohdefor on T2222-1027 for prior arrangements), or there is accommodation for one or two at the visitor centre.

Juticalpa → *Altitude: 420 m.*
The main road continues another 50 km from Los Limones to Juticalpa, the capital of Olancho department, in a rich agricultural area for herding cattle and growing cereals and sugar cane. There is a paved road northeast through the cattle land of Catacamas, continuing to just beyond Dulce Nombre de Culmí.

Catacamas and around → *Altitude: 400 m.*
Catacamas lies at the foot of Agalta mountain in the Río Guayape valley in the Department of Olancho, 210 km from Tegucigalpa. The Río Guayape (named after an indigenous dress, *guayapis*) is famous for its gold nuggets.

The town was established by the Spaniards and the colonial church dates from the early 18th century. It is an agricultural and cattle-raising district. The National School of Agriculture (ENA) is based here, ask if you wish to visit their agricultural demonstration plots in the Guayape valley, 5 km south of the town.

Hiking in the mountains behind Catacamas is beautiful. From Murmullo there are trails to coffee farms. **Río Talgua**, 4 km east of Catacamas, is interesting with caves in which significant pre-Columbian remains have been found. The area and caves are worth a visit. Hiking to **El Boquerón**, stop off at the main road near Punuare, 17 km west of Catacamas, and walk up **Río Olancho**, which has nice limestone cliffs and a pretty river canyon. Through much of the canyon the stream flows underground.

Beyond Catacamas, a rough road continues northeast up the Río Tinto Valley to **Dulce Nombre de Culmí**. Further on is **Paya** where the road becomes a mule track but, in three to four days in the dry season, a route can be made over the divide (Cerro de Will) and down the Río Paulaya to Mosquitia (see below). Local police say that there is a path in the dry season from Dulce Nombre to San Esteban (about 30 km).

Juticalpa to Trujillo
There is a fine scenic road from Juticalpa to Trujillo. From Juticalpa head northeast and turn left where the paved road ends, to **San Francisco de la Paz**. Beyond San Francisco is **Gualaco**, which has an interesting colonial church (there are several places to stay, see Sleeping, page 110).

The town of **San Esteban** is 23 km from Gualaco. On the way you pass Agalta mountain, and some of the highest points in Honduras, and several waterfalls on the Río Babilonia.

After San Esteban the road continues to **Bonito Oriental** (via El Carbón, a mahogany collection point with the Paya communities in the vicinity). There are four hotels here. The final 38 km from Bonito Oriental to Trujillo are paved, through Corocito. There are many dirt roads between San Francisco and Trujillo. Fuel is available in the larger villages but there is none between San Esteban and Bonito Oriental.

Parque Nacional Sierra de Agalta

Between the roads Juticalpa–Gualaco–San Esteban and Juticalpa–Catacamas–Dulce Nombre de Culmí lies the cloud forest of the Parque Nacional Sierra de Agalta, extending over 1200 ha and reaching a height of 2590 m at **Monte de Babilonia**, a massif with a number of interesting mountains. Several different ecosystems have been found with a wide variety of fauna and flora: 200 species of bird have been identified so far. There are several points of entry. Contact **Cohdefor** in Juticalpa, Culmí, Gualaco, San Esteban or Catacamas for information on access, maps, guides, mules and lodging. There is no infrastructure in the park, but a base camp is being built. A good trail leads to **La Picucha** mountain (2354 m). Access is from El Pacayal, 750 m, a short distance towards San Esteban from Gualaco (bus at 0700 which goes on to Tocoa). There are two campsites on the trail, the first at 1060m is just short of **La Chorrera** waterfall, which has a colony of white-collared swifts that nest in the cave behind the falls. Four to six hours above is the second campsite at 1900 m. The final section is mainly dwarf forest with low undergrowth on the summit. There is much wildlife to be seen and a good viewpoint 1 km beyond at the site of two abandoned radio towers. Hiking time is two days.

La Mosquitia → *For listings, see pages 110-113.*

Forested, swampy and almost uninhabited, Mosquitia is well worth visiting if you have the time and energy. In the the Central American Little Amazon, you can hope to see rainforest wildlife including monkeys and incredible birdlife as you drift through the varied habitat that includes lowland tropical rainforest, coastal lagoons, undisturbed beaches, mangroves, grasslands and patches of pine savanna. Home to members of the Miskito and Pech tribes as well as the Garífuna ethnic group who live in small communities on the coast and along the major rivers. The Río Plátano Biosphere Reserve, a UNESCO World Heritage Site, covers an area over 5200 sq km – one of the largest protected areas in Central America.

Ins and outs

While certainly a challenging environment, many backpackers visit the reserve either alone or with professional guides. For those travelling alone, as long as you have basic Spanish and are a reasonably confident traveller this is the cheapest option. With access by air, sea and road, you can visit any time of the year but it is usually best to avoid the heavy rains from November to January. The driest months are March to May and August to October.

What to take It's a tough environment and you should go prepared. Take a mosquito net and repellent, clothing for rain and also for cooler temperatures at night, good walking shoes and a first-aid kit. Also enough cash in small denominations for your stay (there are no banks in the area) and plastic bags to keep things dry.

For study of the region MOPAWI (Mosquitia Pawisa, www.mopawi.org) is the best source of information about the indigenous communities in Mosquitia. It is a non-profit-making, non-sectarian organization dedicated to the development of the region and the conservation of the biodiversity of its flora and fauna; volunteer opportunities available. There is a **head office** ① *in Puerto Lempira, T898-7460*, another **office** ① *in Tegucigalpa, Residencias Tres Caminos 4b, lote 67, Apartado 2175, T235-8659*, plus offices in several other villages.

MOPAWI is concerned with the protection of natural and human resources throughout Mosquitia and the Department of Gracias a Dios. Among its programmes is the conservation of marine turtles and the green iguana. The Reserva Biósfera Río Plátano (525,100 ha) with the Reserva Antropólogica Tawahka, the Reserva Nacional Patuca and together with Mosquitia Nicaragüense, constitute one of the largest forest reserves north of the Amazon.

Coastal villages

A narrow strand of land divides the inland waterway and Ibans lagoon from the Caribbean. Along this pleasant setting lie a number of small native villages starting with the Garífuna village of Plaplaya and continuing through the Miskito villages of Ibans, Cocobila, Raistá, Belén, Nueva Jerusalem and Kuri. Trails connect all of these villages making exploration easy with vast expanses of unspoiled, white-sand beaches providing an easy route for getting from place to place, with the sea providing a wonderful way to cool off during the heat of the day.

Apart from generally relaxing in the slow-paced life along the coast there are several interesting things to do in the area. In **Raistá**, the butterfly farm was a pilot project, focusing on raising the colourful butterfly species of the area to sell to live butterfly exhibition houses throughout the world (closed at end of 2010 through lack of funds).

In **Plaplaya**, a community-run Sea Turtle Project aims to protect the leatherback and loggerhead turtles that nest along the coast. Each night during the breeding season (March-June) members of the village patrol the beaches to find nesting turtles, carefully gathering the eggs and re-burying them in a guarded area where they are watched over until they hatch. The newborn turtles are then released into the sea. Visitors can accompany the beach patrols for a small donation to the program. There are two traditional dance groups in Plaplaya that can provide an interesting evening's entertainment for visitors.

The Miskito village of **Kuri**, 1½ hours along the beach from Belén, is worth a visit. Here the traditional wooden and thatch houses sit behind the beach, sheltered from the sea breezes by the 'Beach Grape' and palm trees along the sand dunes.

Reserva de la Biósfera Río Plátano

The reserve was established by the Honduran government in 1980 to protect the outstanding natural and cultural resources of the Río Plátano valley and its environs. In 1982 UNESCO declared the reserve a World Heritage Site. The tropical jungles here shelter a number of endangered birds, mammals and fish, among them **scarlet macaws** and **harpy eagles**, **jaguars** and **tapirs**, and the **cuyamel**, a prized food fish fast becoming extinct throughout Honduras. In addition, there are a number of **archaeological sites** about which little is known, and the fabled lost White City of the Maya is said to be hidden somewhere in the thick jungles of the Plátano headwaters.

The Miskito and the Pech living along the lower Plátano cultivate yuca, bananas, rice, corn and beans, and also feed themselves by hunting and fishing. The upper (southern) portion of the Plátano watershed is being quickly populated by mestizo immigrants from the poverty-stricken south of Honduras. These new settlers are cutting down the forest to plant crops and raise cattle, hunting wildlife mercilessly and dynamite-fishing. The government's intention officially to allow settlers into the Sico and Paulaya valleys, on the western edge of the reserve, was roundly criticized. It was feared that the agrarian reform programme would lead to the desertification of the Río Plátano. Added to the damage being done by the settlers, there are now disturbing reports that drug smugglers are cutting landing strips deep in the jungle. Given the pressure the reserve is under, it is recommended to visit it sooner rather than later.

Along the Río Plátano

For those in search of a little more rugged adventure you should find a boat to take you up the Río Plátano to Las Marías, a small Miskito and Pech village that is the last outpost of civilization in this part of the reserve. Local boatman are trying to organize themselves with a view to regulating minimum standards, a fair price for the passage and a rotation system to ensure the work is shared more evenly between them.

Most people stay the night in Raistá before and after visiting Las Marías. Gasoline is very expensive in La Mosquitia and this is reflected in the high cost of transportation. The ride to Las Marías costs about US$130 so put together a group of four or five people to share the cost. That price should get you a boat and boatman for three days to take you on the round trip (four to six hours each way) from the coast with a day in Las Marías to look around. If you stay longer you should negotiate a fair price with the boatman to cover his extra time. Bring food and water for the trip as well as other jungle gear. The journey upstream to Las Marías, although beautiful, can become very tedious and uncomfortable. Birdwatching can provide a diversion; there are three species of toucan as well as several species of parrot, tanagers, herons, kingfishers, vultures, hawk eagles and oropendolas. If you are lucky you might see crocodiles, turtles or iguanas. On arrival in Las Marías, arrange return at once.

An alternative route to Las Marías is by boat across Ibans Lagoon, 45 minutes by tuk-tuk, then 6½ hours' walk through jungle (rough path, hot, mosquitoes, take lots of water and insect repellent, and wear good hiking boots). This is only recommended for fit walkers in drier weather. Expect to pay around US$30 for the guide, and if returning from Las Marías by boat you'll probably still have to pay the return fare even if you're only travelling one way.

Las Marías

This Miskito-Pech village is the furthest limit of upstream settlement. Once in Las Marías you're normally met by a member of the *saca guía*, a representative of the Las Marías Ecotourism Committee who will let you know what trips are available in the area and help make arrangements on a rotation system that shares the work among the community. This group was set up with the help of MOPAWI and Peace Corps with the aim of developing and coordinating a system of ecotourism that benefits the local people, protects the reserve and also offers extraordinary experiences to tourists. A number of guides have been trained in Las Marías to deal with international visitors. They are coordinated by the Committee, have a set price structure with prices and rules posted on the walls of all the *hospedajes*.

Typical guided trips include day hiking on trails around the village, a three-day hike to scenic **Pico Dama** (very strenuous), a day trip by *pipante* upriver to see the **petroglyphs** at **Walpulbansirpi** left by the ancestors of the Pech or multi-day trips upriver to visit other petroglyph sites and view wildlife in the heart of the reserve. Note that it's harder to advance upriver during the rainy season from June to December. ▶▶ *See Activities and tours, page 112.*

Brus Laguna

It is a 15-minute scenic flight from Puerto Lempira (see below) above Caratasca Lagoon and grassy, pine-covered savannahs to **Ahuas**, one-hour walk from the Patuca River (fabled for gold). There is a hospital here, four missions, some basic accommodation and a generally improving atmosphere. Irregular *cayucos* sail down to Brus Laguna for US$2.50, at the mouth of the Río Patuca, or US$12.50 (15 minutes) scenic flight in the mission plane. The airstrip is 4 km from village, take a lift for US$1. There is a disco at the riverside to the left of the bridge. Plagued by mosquitoes throughout summer and autumn.

Puerto Lempira

Puerto Lempira is on the large Caratasca Lagoon. The main office of MOPAWI (see page 107) is here. The airstrip is only five minutes' walk from town. Regular tuk-tuks (motorized canoes) cross the lagoon to **Kaukira**, US$1.20 (a nice place, but nothing there), **Yagurabila** and **Palkaka**. The tuk-tuks leave Kaukira daily except Sunday at 0500, returning during the morning. In the afternoon the lagoon is usually too rough to cross.

Inland by road from Puerto Lempira are **Mocorón** and **Rus Rus**, which may be visited with difficulty (there is no public transport but any vehicle will give a lift) and is a beautiful, quiet village (accommodation at Friends of America hospital's house; meals from Capi's next door, ask Friends about transport out). A branch off this road leads southeast to **Leimus** on the Río Coco and the border with Nicaragua. Ask for Evaristo López (at whose house you can get breakfast) who can arrange transport to Leimus, most days, three to four hours for about US$3.50. He is also knowledgeable about area safety.

The road continues south to the small town of **Ahuashbila** on the upper river of the Río Coco, which marks the border with Nicaragua.

The Northeast listings

For Sleeping and Eating price codes and other relevant information, see pages 10-11.

🛌 Sleeping

Tegucigalpa to the northeast coast *p105*
$ Hospedaje San Carlos, La Unión. Serves good vegetarian food.
$ Hospedaje Santos, Campamento. Basic.
$ Hotel, on plaza, Guaimaca, above restaurant **Las Cascadas**. Good value, clean and friendly.
$ Hotelito Granada, Campamento. Basic.

Juticalpa *p106*
$ Antúñez, 1 Calle NO y 1 Av NO, a block west of Parque Central, T2885-2250. With bath (cheaper without), friendly, clean, also annex in same street.
$ El Paso, 1 Av NE y 6 Calle NO, 6 blocks south of Parque (on way to highway), T2885-2311. Quiet, clean, bath, fan, laundry facilities. Highly recommended.
$ Familiar, 1 Calle NO between Parque and Antúñez. Bath, clean, basic. Recommended.

$ Fuente, 5 mins from bus station on left side of main road to town centre. Basic but large and clean rooms.
$ Las Vegas, 1 Av NE, T885-2700, central, ½ block north of Parque. Clean, friendly, with *cafetería*.
$ Regis, 1 Calle NO. Balcony, good value.

Catacamas and around *p106*
$ Central, Barrio El Centro, T899-4276. With bath, cheaper without, big mango tree in front.
$ Hospedaje Tania, on the main street, Dulce Nombre de Culmí. Very basic.
$ Juan Carlos, Barrio José Trinidad Reyes, T2899-4212. Good restaurant. Recommended.
$ La Colina, T2899-4488. With bath, hot water, fan, TV, parking.

Juticalpa to Trujillo *p106*
$ Calle Real, Gualaco, near Parque Central. Basic, friendly, will store luggage.
$ Centro, San Esteban. Very clean, nice family, best.

$ Hotel Hernández, San Esteban. Cheapest.

$ Hotel San Esteban, San Esteban.
Very friendly, clean.

$ Hotelito Central, Gualaco. Similar to
Calle Real.

Coastal villages *p108*
Plaplaya

$ Basilia, traditional and the cheapest,
15 mins west of centre.

$ Doña Sede, east of village centre with
good meals.

$ Doña Yohana, close to the village centre.

Raistá and Belén

Choose between **Eddie and Elma Bodden**
(**$**) on the lagoon and **Doña Cecilia Bodden**
(**$**), just up from the lagoon towards the sea.
Try the food at **Elma's Kitchen** (**$**) in Raistá,
thought by some to be the best on the coast.
Near the lagoon between Raistá and Belén is
Doña Exe (**$**), and in Belén there is **Doña
Mendilia** (**$**), near the grass airstrip.

Las Marías *p109*

Balancing the benefits of tourism are difficult in
such a sensitive area. Sharing the benefits is
one way of offsetting the negative impact of
tourism and, whenever possible, the Ecotourism
Committee tries to share tourists between the
4 basic but clean *hospedajes* (all **$**) of **Ovidio**,
Justa, **Tinglas** or **Diana**, with meals available
for US$3. Very friendly and with wonderful
community atmosphere, highly recommended
(no electricity after about 1900, bring torch).

Brus Laguna *p109*

$ Estancia, T2433-8043 and **Paradise**,
T2433-8039. Rooms with a fan and
optional private bath.

Puerto Lempira *p110*

$ Charly's restaurant, Mocorón.
Rooms available. Price per person.

$ Gran Hotel Flores. Some rooms with
bath. Recommended.

$ Pensión Moderno. Good, friendly,
with electricity from 1800-2230.

$ Villas Caratascas. Huts with bath,
restaurant, disco.

❷ Eating

Juticalpa *p106*

$ Casa Blanca, 1 Calle SE. Quite smart with
a good cheap menu, good paella.

$ Comedor Any, 1 Av NO. Good value
and friendly.

$ El Rancho, 2 Av NE. Specializes in meat
dishes, wide menu, pleasant.

$ El Tablado, 1 Av NE entre 3 y 4 Calle NO.
Good fish, bar.

Cafés

Helados Frosty, near Parque Central.
Ice creams.

La Galera, 2 Av NE. Specializes in *pinchos*.

Tropical Juices, Blv de los Poetas.
Good fruit juices.

Catacamas and around *p106*

In **Dulce Nombre de Culmí**, there are
several *comedores* on the main plaza.

$ As de Oro, Catacamas. Good beef dishes,
Wild West decor.

$ Asia, Catacamas. Chinese.

$ Comedor Ejecutivo, Catacamas. Buffet-
style meals US$2, local craft decorations.

$ Continental, Catacamas. Chicken dishes,
pizza, US beer.

Juticalpa to Trujillo *p106*

There are 3 nice *comedores* in **San
Esteban** near the Hotel San Esteban.

$ Comedor Sharon, Gualaco. One of
several places to eat.

Puerto Lempira *p110*

$ Delmy, 3 blocks north of main street.
Chicken and other dishes, noisy.

$ Doña Aida, north side of main road
to landing bridge. Fresh orange juice.

$ La Mosquitia, Centro Comercial Segovia in main street. Breakfasts and cheap fish.

☻ Entertainment

Catacamas and around *p106*
Fernandos and **Extasis Montefresco** are bars outside town towards Tegucigalpa, pool (US$1.20), live music 2 evenings a week.
   Cine Maya, Barrio El Centro, cinema.

Puerto Lempira *p110*
Hampu, is a bar by the landing bridge.

☻ Shopping

Juticalpa *p106*
From 0600 on Sat, the market in Parque Central has a good selection of food, fruit, vegetables and souvenirs, said to be the best outdoor market in Olancho.

▲ Activities and tours

La Mosquitia *p107*
Several commercial guides organize trips into the Río Plátano Biosphere Reserve and may be a good option for those with limited Spanish. All-inclusive packages range from 3-14 days and cost about US$100 per day. In order to support ecotourism in the reserve you are encouraged to check the tour operator you are considering works with local people. For other options, see under San Pedro Sula, La Ceiba and Trujillo.
Bob 'The Butterfly, Bird and Bug Guy'
Gallardo, based in Copán Ruinas, rgallardo32 @hotmail.com. Highly regarded birding and other specialized nature trips to La Mosquitia.
La Moskitia Eco Aventuras, with Jorge Salaverri, office in La Ceiba, T2442-0104, www.honduras.com/moskitia. Specializes in trips to La Mosquitia; excellent, possibly the best and most knowledgeable wildlife guide in all Central America.
Mesoamerica Travel (Col Juan Lindo, No 709, 8 Calle and 32 Av NO, San Pedro Sula, T2558-6447, www.mesoamerica-travel.com) and **Fundación Patuca** (Hauke Hoops)

(T236-9910), also specialize in travel in this region. **Mesoamerica** is the only company to run tours to the Zona Arriba of the Río Patuca (5 or 10 days).

Las Marías *p109*
The services of the *saca guía* are US$3.50. Guides are required even for day hikes due to the possibility of getting lost or injured on the faint jungle trails. The cost for a guide is US$6 per day for groups up to 5. Overnight hikes require 2 guides. River trips in a *pipante*, a shallow dug-out canoe manoeuvered with poles (*palancas*) and paddles (*canaletes*), require 3 guides plus US$4.20 for the canoe. 2 visitors and their gear will fit in each boat with the guides.

⊖ Transport

Tegucigalpa to the northeast coast *p105*
Bus From **Comayagüela** to La Unión, daily, take 4 hrs. To get to the park, hire a truck from La Unión for about US$18. There's little traffic so it's difficult to hitchhike. If driving from **San Pedro Sula**, take the road east through Yoro and Mangulile; from **La Ceiba**, take the Savá– Olanchito road and turn south 13 km before Olanchito.

Juticalpa *p106*
Bus Bus station is on 1 Av NE, 1 km southeast of Parque Central, taxis US$0.50. Hourly to **Tegucigalpa** from 0330 to 1800; to **San Esteban** from opposite Aurora bus terminal at 0800, 6 hrs, US$2.25. To **Trujillo** 0400, 9 hrs, US$5.20. To **Tocoa** at 0500.

Catcamas and around *p106*
Bus From **Tegucigalpa** to Juticalpa/ Catacamas, **Empresa Aurora**, 8 Calle 6-7 Av, Comayagüela, T237-3647, hourly 0400-1700, 3¼ hrs, US$2 to Juticalpa, 4 hrs US$2.75 to Catacamas. **Juticalpa**–Catacamas, 40 mins, US$0.60. To **Dulce Nombre de Culmí** (see below), 3 hrs, US$1.35, several daily.

Juticalpa to Trujillo *p106*

Bus To Juticalpa and to the north coast (Tocoa and Trujillo) buses are fairly frequent.

La Mosquitia *p107*

Air

Alas de Socorro fly to **Ahuas**, T2233-7025. This company charters planes for US$565, but per person it is US$60 1 way to Ahuas (see Medical services, below). **SAMi** flies to various villages from Puerto Lempira, eg **Ahuas**, **Brus Laguna**, **Belén**. There are expensive express flights to places like **Auka**, **Raya**, **Kaukira**.

    Airline offices Sosa, T898-7467.

Boat

Coastal supply vessels run between **La Ceiba** and the coastal villages of La Mosquitia. The *Corazón* and *Mr Jim* make the trip weekly and their captains can be found at the harbour east of La Ceiba. Prices vary (US$10-20); be prepared for basic conditions. There are no passenger facilities such as beds or toilets on board and the journey takes a good 24 hrs.

    Rivers, lagoons and inland waterways are the highways in the reserve and dug-out canoes provide the public transportation. Once in Palacios, you can catch *colectivo* boat transport at the landing near the **Río Tinto Hotel** to travel along the inland passage to coastal villages in the reserve such as Plaplaya, Raistá and Belén (about US$3.50 for a 1- or 2-hr trip). There is usually a boat to meet the planes that arrive in the morning and information on prices to different locations is posted in the airline offices. If you miss the *colectivo* you will usually have to pay extra for a special trip (about US$20).

Road

An upgraded road is the cheapest and most favoured route by locals. Take a bus from

La Ceiba to Tocoa (US$2). From the market in Tocoa take a series of pickups (US$16 per person) along the beach to Batalla, crossing the various creeks that block the way in launches that wait to meet the cars. The journey to **Batalla** takes about 5½ hrs. From Batalla cross the lagoon in a boat to **Palacios** (US$0.70) and continue from there. The trip is not possible in the wetter months of the year (Jul, Oct and Nov).

Note Some may suggest the possibility of catching a truck from Limón to Sangrilaya then walking along the beach and wading across rivers for 1-2 days to get to Batalla. While this is possible it is not recommended because of the heat, bugs and general safety issues.

❶ Directory

Juticalpa *p106*
Banks HSNC (the only one that will change TCs), **Banco Atlántida**, **Banco de Occidente**. **Post** 2 blocks north from Parque Central, opposite Shell station. **Telephone** Hondutel on main street, 1 block from Parque Central.

Catacamas and around *p106*
Banks Banco Atlántida, Banco de Occidente, in Barrio El Centro. **Medical services** Dentist: Elvia Ayala Lobo, T2899-4129.

La Mosquitia *p107*
Medical services Hospitals: Alas de Socorro operates from Ahuas to collect sick people from villages to take them to Ahuas hospital. Contact the Moravian church (in Puerto Lempira Reverend Stanley Goff, otherwise local pastors will help).

Puerto Lempira *p110*
Banks Banco Atlántida.

Tegucigalpa to the Pacific

From the capital to the Golfo de Fonseca the route twists through mountain valleys down to the volcanic islands and Honduras' Pacific ports of San Lorenzo and Amapala. Near the coast the Pan-American Highway leads west to El Salvador and east though the hot plains of Choluteca to the quiet but popular beaches of Cedeña and Ratón and ultimately to Nicaragua. An alternative route to Nicaragua heads east, through the agricultural town of Danlí, to the border at Las Manos. Short detours from the highway lead to picturesque colonial villages and old mining centres in the hills.

Tegucigalpa to Goascarán

From the capital a paved road runs south through fine scenery. Beyond Sabanagrande (see page 23) is **Pespire**, a picturesque colonial village with the beautiful church of San Francisco, which has triple domes. Pespire produces small, delicious mangoes. At **Jícaro Galán** (92 km) the road joins the Pan-American Highway, which heads west through **Nacaome**, where there is a colonial church, to the border with El Salvador at **Goascarán**. At Jícaro Galán, Ticabus and other international buses from San Salvador, Tegucigalpa and Managua meet and exchange passengers.

San Lorenzo

The Pan-American Highway continues south from Jícaro Galán, to the Pacific coast (46 km) at San Lorenzo, a dirty town on the shores of the Gulf of Fonseca. The climate on the Pacific litoral is very hot.

Amapala

A 31-km road leaves the Pan-American Highway 2 km west of San Lorenzo, signed to Coyolito. It passes through scrub and mangrove swamps before crossing a causeway to a hilly island, around which it winds to the jetty at **Coyolito** (no *hospedajes* but a *comedor* and *refrescarías*).

The Pacific port of Amapala, on Isla del Tigre, has been replaced by Puerto de Henecán in San Lorenzo, and is reached by a road which leaves the Pan-American Highway at the eastern edge of San Lorenzo. The **Isla del Tigre** is yet another place reputed to be the site of hidden pirate treasure. In the 16th century it was visited by a number of pirates, including Sir Francis Drake. Amapala was capital of Honduras for a brief period in 1876 when Marco Aurelio Soto was president. Today, in addition to a naval base, Amapala is a charming, decaying backwater. The 783-m extinct Amapala volcano has a road to the summit where there is a US army unit and a DEA contingent. You can walk round the island in half a day. There is a ferry service from Coyolito, but fishermen will take you to San Lorenzo for a small fee, not by motor launch, and the trip takes half a day. The deep-sea fishing in the gulf is good. It is possible to charter boats to La Unión in El Salvador.

Choluteca and around → *For listings, see pages 116-118.*

Choluteca is expanding rapidly on the back of the local industries of coffee, cotton and cattle which flourish despite the hot climate. The town was one of the earliest settlements in Honduras (1535) and still has a colonial centre. The church of **La Merced** (1643) is being renovated. The **Casa de la Cultura** and **Biblioteca Municipal** are in the colonial house of José Cecilio del Valle on the corner of the Parque Central. The social centre of **San José Obrero** ① *3 Calle SO*, is where handicrafts, in particular carved wood and chairs, can be bought. The **Mercado Municipal** ① *7 Av SO, 3 Calle SO*, is on outskirts of town.

Cedeño beach, on the eastern side of the Gulf of Fonseca 40 km from Choluteca, is a lovely though primitive spot, with clean sand stretching for miles and often thundering surf. Avoid public holidays, weekend crowds and take a good insect repellent. Views and sunsets are spectacular. Hourly bus from Choluteca (US$0.60, 1½ hours). A turn-off leads from the Choluteca–Cedeño road to Ratón beach, more pleasant than Cedeño. Bus from Choluteca at 1130; returns next morning.

East of Tegucigalpa → *For listings, see pages 116-118.*

A good paved road runs east from Tegucigalpa through the hills to Danlí, 92 km away in the Department of El Paraíso. There are no signs when leaving Tegucigalpa so ask the way. Some 40 km along, in the Zambrano Valley (see page 53), is the Escuela Agrícola Panamericana, which is run for all students of the Americas with US help: it has a fine collection of tropical flowers (book visits in advance at the office in Tegucigalpa).

Yuscarán → *Altitude: 1070 m.*
At Km 47.5, a paved road branches south to Yuscarán, in rolling pineland country preserved by the **Reserva Biológica de Yuscarán**, which protects much of the land around Montserrat mountain. The climate here is semi-tropical. Yuscarán was an important mining centre in colonial days and is a picturesque village, with cobbled streets and houses on a steep hillside. Ask to see the museum near the town plaza; you have to ask around to find the person who has the key, antiques and photographs are displayed in a restored mansion which belonged to a mining family. There is a **Casa de Cultura** ① *in the former Casa Fortín, open Mon-Sat*. The Yuscarán **distilleries** ① *one in the centre, the other on the outskirts, tours possible*, are considered by many to produce the best *aguardiente* in Honduras. The Montserrat mountain that looms over Yuscarán is riddled with mines. The old **Guavias mine** is close to Yuscarán, some 4 km along the road to Agua Fría. About 10 km further along, a narrow, winding road climbs steeply through pine woods to the summit of **Pico Montserrat** (1891 m).

Danlí → *Altitude: 760 m.*
Danlí, 102 km from Tegucigalpa, is noted for sugar and coffee production, a large meat-packing company (Orinsa), and is a centre of the tobacco industry. There are four cigar factories. The **Honduras-América SA factory** ① *right-hand side of Cine Aladino, Mon-Fri 0800-1200, 1300-1700, Sat 0800-1200*, produces export-quality cigars at good prices. Also **Placencia Tabacos**, on the road to Tegucigalpa, where you can watch cigar-making. Better prices than at Santa Rosa. From Danlí to the north is **Cerro San Cristóbal** and the beautiful **Lago San Julián**.

Tegucigalpa to the Pacific listings

For Sleeping and Eating price codes and other relevant information, see pages 10-11.

🛏 Sleeping

Tegucigalpa to Goascarán *p114*
$$ Oasis Colonial, Jícaro Galán, T2881-2220. nice rooms, good restaurant and pool and an unnamed basic guesthouse.
$ Intercontinental, in centre, Jícaro Galán. Basic, tap and bucket shower, friendly.
$ Perpetuo Socorro, Barrio El Centro, Jícaro Galán, T2895-4453. A/c, TV.
$ Suyapa, Jícaro Galán. Basic, cheap.

San Lorenzo *p114*
$$ Miramar, Barrio Plaza Marina, T2781-2039. Has 26 rooms, 4 with a/c, good restaurant, overpriced, in rough dockside area, best not to walk there.
$ Perla del Pacífico, on main street, T2781-3025. Fan, bath, comfortable, clean, friendly, central, charming. Recommended.

Amapala *p114*
Ask for **Doña Marianita**, who rents the 1st floor of her house.
$$ Hotel Villas Playa Negra, Aldea Playa Negra, T2898-8534. 7 rooms with a/c, 7 with fan, pool, beach, restaurant, isolated, lovely setting.
$ Al Mar, above Playa Grande. Fan, scorpions, lovely view of mountains and sunset.
$ Pensión Internacional on the harbour. Very basic, otherwise only local accommodation of low standard.

Choluteca and around *p115*
$$ La Fuente, Carretera Panamericana, past bridge, T2782-0253. With bath, swimming pool, a/c, meals.
$ Brabazola, Barrio Cabañas, T2782-2534. A/c, comfy beds, TV, good.
$ Camino Real, road to Guasaule, T2882-0610. Swimming pool, good steaks in restaurant. Recommended.

$ Centroamérica, near La Fuente, T2882-3525. A/c, good restaurant, bar, pool, good value.
$ Escuela de Español Mina Clavo Rico, El Corpus, Choluteca 51103 (east of Choluteca), T2887-3501. Price per person, US$90 per week, full board, living with local families, language classes (US$4 per hr), riding, craft lessons, work on farms, number of excursions.
$ Hibueras, Av Bojórquez, Barrio El Centro, T2882-0512. With bath and fan, clean, purified water, *comedor* attached, good value.
$ Pacífico, near Mi Esperanza terminal, outside the city. Clean, cool rooms, fan, cable TV, hammocks, quiet, safe parking, fresh drinking water, breakfast US$1.50.
$ Pierre, Av Valle y Calle Williams, T2882-0676. With bath (ants in the taps), a/c or fan, TV, free protected parking, *cafetería* has good breakfasts, very central, credit cards accepted. Recommended.
$ San Carlos, Paz Barahona 757, Barrio El Centro. With shower, fan, very clean, pleasant.
$ Santa Rosa, 3 Calle NO, in the centre, just west of market, T2882-0355. Some with bath, pleasant patio, laundry facilities, clean, friendly.

East of Tegucigalpa *p115*
$$ Escuela Agrícola Panamericana. Rooms are available, but there is nowhere to eat after 1700.

Yuscarán *p115*
$ Hotel, T2892-7213. Owned by Dutch man Freek de Haan and his Honduran wife and daughter, private or dormitory rooms, beautiful views of Nicaraguan mountains in the distance.
$ Hotel Carol. 6 modern rooms with bath and hot water, annex to owner's fine colonial house, safe, family atmosphere, good value.

Danlí *p115*
$$-$ Gran Hotel Granada, T2883-2499. Bar, cable TV, accepts Visa. Restaurant and swimming pool, locals pay half price.

$ Apolo, El Canal, next to Shell station, T883-2177. With bath, clean, basic.
$ Danlí, El Canal, opposite **Apolo**. Without bath, good.
$ Eben Ezer, 3½ blocks north of Shell station, T2883-2655. Basic, hot showers.
$ Las Vegas, next to bus terminal. Noisy, restaurant, washing facilities, parking.
$ La Esperanza, Gabriela Mistral, next to Esso station, T2883-2106. Bath, hot water, fan (more expensive with a/c), TV, drinking water, friendly, parking.
$ Regis, 3 blocks north of Plaza Central. With bath, basic.

El Paraíso *p116*
$ 5a Av Hotel y Restaurant, 5 Av y 10 Calle, T2893-4298. Bath, hot water, restaurant specializes in Mexican-American food. Parking.
$ Lendy's, Barrio Nuevo Carmelo, by bus station, T2893-4461. Clean, prepares food.

❷ Eating

San Lorenzo *p114*
$$ Restaurant-Bar Henecán, on Parque Central. A/c, good food and service, not cheap but worth it.

Amapala *p114*
$ Mercado Municipal. Several clean *comedores*.
$ Restaurant-Bar Miramar by the harbour. Overlooking the sea, pleasant, very friendly, good meals, hamburgers and *boquitas*, and you can hang your hammock.

Choluteca and around *p115*
$$ Alondra, Parque Central. Old colonial house, open Fri-Sun only.
$ Comedor Central, Parque Central. *Comida corriente* daily specials, *licuados*, sandwiches, good for breakfast. Local specialities are the drinks *posole* and *horchata de morro*.
$ El Burrito, Blv Choluteca between 4 and 5 Av N. With good-value meals and fast service.

$ El Conquistador, on Pan-American, opposite **La Fuente**. Steaks, etc, outdoor seating but you have to eat inside, good but slow service. Will change money for customers.
$ Frosty, on main street. Owned by **Hotel Pierre**, good food and juices.
$ Tico Rico, Calle Vincente Williams. Has been highly recommended.

Yuscarán *p115*
$ Cafetería Colonial, opposite **Banco de Occidente**. Serves excellent *desayuno típico* and *comida corriente*.

Danlí *p115*
$ Comedor Claudio. Good *comida corriente*, good information from locals.
$ El Gaucho and **España**, town centre. Good.
$ El Paraíso de las Hamburguesas. Cheap, good, owner very friendly.
$ Pizzería Picolino, 2 blocks southwest of Parque Central. Good pizzas.
$ Rancho Típico, El Canal, near **Hotel Danlí**. Excellent.

El Paraíso *p116*
$ Comedor Edith, on a small square on main road, after Parque Central towards border. US$0.85 for a meal.

❸ Festivals and events

Choluteca and around *p115*
8 Dec The feast day of the **Virgen de la Concepción**, a week of festivities, followed by the **Festival del Sur**, 'Ferisur'.

Danlí *p115*
3rd week Aug Fiesta del Maíz lasts all week, with cultural and sporting events, all-night street party on the Sat; it gets very crowded with people from Tegucigalpa.

❹ Transport

San Lorenzo *p114*
Bus Frequent *busitos* from **Tegucigalpa** to San Lorenzo (US$1) and **Choluteca** (US$1.50).

Amapala p114
Boat Motorized *lanchas* run between **Coyolito** and Amapala, US$0.35 per person when launch is full (about 10 passengers), about US$4 to hire a launch (but you will probably have to pay for the return trip as well). 1st boat leaves Amapala at 0700 to connect with 1st Coyolito–San Lorenzo bus at 0800; next bus from Coyolito at 0900.

Choluteca and around p115
Bus To **El Espino** (Nicaraguan border) from Choluteca, US$1.15, 1 hr, 1st at 0700, last at 1400. Also frequent minibuses to **El Amatillo** (El Salvador border) via San Lorenzo, US$1, from bus stop at bridge. Buses to Choluteca from Tegucigalpa with **Mi Esperanza**, **Bonanza** and **El Dandy**; **Bonanza** continues to San Marcos and departs Tegucigalpa hourly from 0530, 4 hrs to Choluteca, US$1.90. The municipal bus terminal is about 10 blocks from the municipal market, about 8 blocks from cathedral/Parque Central; **Mi Esperanza** has its own terminal 1 block from municipal terminal.

Yuscarán p115
Bus Frequent buses to **Zamorano** and **Tegucigalpa**; from the capital buses leave from Mercado Jacaleapa. For information, ask anyone in the Parque Central in Yuscarán.

Danlí p115
Bus From **Tegucigalpa**, US$2, from Blv Miraflores near Mercado Jacaleapa (from left-hand side of market as you face it), Col Kennedy, Tegucigalpa, hourly, 2 hrs, arrive 1½ hrs before you want to leave, long queues for tickets (take 'Kennedy' bus from C La Isla near the football stadium in central Tegucigalpa, or taxi, US$1.20, to Mercado Jacaleapa). **Express** bus from Col Kennedy, 0830, 1230 and 1700, US$2. One road goes east from Danlí to **Santa María** (several buses daily), over a mountain range with great views.

El Paraíso p116
Bus Minibuses from **Danlí** terminal to El Paraíso, frequent (0600 to 1740), US$0.40, 30 mins, don't believe taxi drivers who say there are no minibuses. **Emtra Oriente**, Av 6, Calle 6-7, runs 4 times a day from **Tegucigalpa** to El Paraíso, 2½ hrs, US$1.50. Buses from El Paraíso to **Las Manos**, about every 1½ hrs, US$0.35, 30 mins, or taxi US$4, 15 mins.

⊙ Directory

San Lorenzo p114
Banks Bancahorro (changes US$ cash and TCs), **Banco Atlántida**, and **Banco de Occidente** (no exchange); Chinese grocery gives good rates for US$ cash.

Amapala p114
Banks Banco El Ahorro Hondureño.

Choluteca and around p115
Banks Of the many banks in town, **Banco Atlántida** has a Visa ATM, and only **Banco de Comercio** changes TCs. Can be difficult to exchange money in Choluteca.
Embassies and consulates El Salvador, to south of town, fast and friendly, daily 0800-1500. **Post** Mon-Fri 0800-1700, Sat 0800-1200, US$0.15 per letter for Poste Restante. **Telephone** Collect calls to Spain, Italy, USA only.

Danlí p115
Banks Banco Atlántida changes TCs without problems. Cash on Visa card, maximum US$50. Other banks as well.
Medical services Dentist: Dr Juan Castillo, Barrio El Centro, T2883-2083.

El Paraíso p116
Banks Several branches in town including **HSBC**.

Contents

Footnotes

Basic Spanish for travellers

Learning Spanish is a useful part of the preparation for a trip to Latin America and no volumes of dictionaries, phrase books or word lists will provide the same enjoyment as being able to communicate directly with the people of the country you are visiting. It is a good idea to make an effort to grasp the basics before you go. As you travel you will pick up more of the language and the more you know, the more you will benefit from your stay.

General pronunciation
Whether you have been taught the 'Castilian' pronunciation (z and c followed by i or e are pronounced as the th in think) or the 'American' pronunciation (they are pronounced as s), you will encounter little difficulty in understanding either. Regional accents and usages vary, but the basic language is essentially the same everywhere.

Vowels

a	as in English cat
e	as in English best
i	as the ee in English feet
o	as in English shop
u	as the oo in English food
ai	as the i in English ride
ei	as ey in English they
oi	as oy in English toy

Consonants

Most consonants can be pronounced more or less as they are in English. The exceptions are:

g	before e or i is the same as j
h	is always silent (except in ch as in chair)
j	as the ch in Scottish loch
ll	as the y in yellow
ñ	as the ni in English onion
rr	trilled much more than in English
x	depending on its location, pronounced x, s, sh or j

Spanish words and phrases

Greetings, courtesies

hello	hola	please	por favor
good morning	buenos días	thank you (very much)	(muchas) gracias
good afternoon/ evening/night	buenas tardes/noches	I don't speak Spanish	no hablo español
		do you speak English?	¿habla inglés?
goodbye	adiós/chao	I don't understand	no comprendo
pleased to meet you	mucho gusto	please speak slowly	hable despacio por favor
see you later	hasta luego		
how are you?	¿cómo está? ¿cómo estás?	I am very sorry	lo siento mucho
		what do you want?	¿qué quiere? ¿qué quieres?
I'm fine, thanks	estoy muy bien, gracias	I want	quiero
I'm called...	me llamo...	I don't want it	no lo quiero
what is your name?	¿cómo se llama? ¿cómo te llamas?	leave me alone	déjeme en paz/ no me moleste
yes/no	sí/no	good/bad	bueno/malo

Questions and requests

Have you got a room for two people?
¿Tiene una habitación para dos personas?
How do I get to_? *¿Cómo llego a_?*
How much does it cost?
¿Cuánto cuesta? ¿cuánto es?
I'd like to make a long-distance phone call
Quisiera hacer una llamada de larga distancia
Is service included? *¿Está incluido el servicio?*
Is tax included? *¿Están incluidos los impuestos?*

When does the bus leave (arrive)?
¿A qué hora sale (llega) el autobús?
When? *¿cuándo?*
Where is_? *¿dónde está_?*
Where can I buy tickets?
¿Dónde puedo comprar boletos?
Where is the nearest petrol station?
¿Dónde está la gasolinera más cercana?
Why? *¿por qué?*

Basics

bank	*el banco*	market	*el mercado*
bathroom/toilet	*el baño*	note/coin	*el billete/la moneda*
bill	*la factura/la cuenta*	police (policeman)	*la policía (el policía)*
cash	*el efectivo*	post office	*el correo*
cheap	*barato/a*	public telephone	*el teléfono público*
credit card	*la tarjeta de crédito*	supermarket	*el supermercado*
exchange house	*la casa de cambio*	ticket office	*la taquilla*
exchange rate	*el tipo de cambio*	traveller's cheques	*los cheques de*
expensive	*caro/a*		*viajero/los travelers*

Getting around

aeroplane	*el avión*	insured person	*el/la asegurado/a*
airport	*el aeropuerto*	to insure yourself against	*asegurarse contra*
arrival/departure	*la llegada/salida*	luggage	*el equipaje*
avenue	*la avenida*	motorway, freeway	*el autopista/la*
block	*la cuadra*		*carretera*
border	*la frontera*	north, south, west, east	*norte, sur,*
bus station	*la terminal de*		*oeste (occidente),*
	autobuses/camiones		*este (oriente)*
bus	*el bus/el autobús/*	oil	*el aceite*
	el camión	to park	*estacionarse*
collective/		passport	*el pasaporte*
fixed-route taxi	*el colectivo*	petrol/gasoline	*la gasolina*
corner	*la esquina*	puncture	*el pinchazo/*
customs	*la aduana*		*la ponchadura*
first/second class	*primera/segunda clase*	street	*la calle*
left/right	*izquierda/derecha*	that way	*por allí/por allá*
ticket	*el boleto*	this way	*por aquí/por acá*
empty/full	*vacío/lleno*	tourist card/visa	*la tarjeta de turista*
highway, main road	*la carretera*	tyre	*la llanta*
immigration	*la inmigración*	unleaded	*sin plomo*
insurance	*el seguro*	to walk	*caminar/andar*

Accommodation

air conditioning	el aire acondicionado	power cut	el apagón/corte
all-inclusive	todo incluido	restaurant	el restaurante
bathroom, private	el baño privado	room/bedroom	el cuarto/l
bed, double/single	la cama matrimonial/		a habitación
	sencilla	sheets	las sábanas
blankets	las cobijas/mantas	shower	la ducha/regadera
to clean	limpiar	soap	el jabón
dining room	el comedor	toilet	el sanitario/excusado
guesthouse	la casa de huéspedes	toilet paper	el papel higiénico
hotel	el hotel	towels, clean/dirty	las toallas limpias/
noisy	ruidoso		sucias
pillows	las almohadas	water, hot/cold	el agua caliente/fría

Health

aspirin	la aspirina	diarrhoea	la diarrea
blood	la sangre	doctor	el médico
chemist	la farmacia	fever/sweat	la fiebre/el sudor
condoms	los preservativos,	pain	el dolor
	los condones	head	la cabeza
contact lenses	los lentes de contacto	period/	la regla/
contraceptives	los anticonceptivos	sanitary towels	las toallas femeninas
contraceptive pill	la píldora anti-	stomach	el estómago
	conceptiva	altitude sickness	el soroche

Family

family	la familia	boyfriend/girlfriend	el novio/la novia
brother/sister	el hermano/la hermana	friend	el amigo/la amiga
daughter/son	la hija/el hijo	married	casado/a
father/mother	el padre/la madre	single/unmarried	soltero/a
husband/wife	el esposo (marido)/		
	la esposa		

Months, days and time

January	enero	November	noviembre
February	febrero	December	diciembre
March	marzo		
April	abril	Monday	lunes
May	mayo	Tuesday	martes
June	junio	Wednesday	miércoles
July	julio	Thursday	jueves
August	agosto	Friday	viernes
September	septiembre	Saturday	sábado
October	octubre	Sunday	domingo

at one o'clock	*a la una*	it's six twenty	*son las seis y veinte*
at half past two	*a las dos y media*	it's five to nine	*son las nueve menos*
at a quarter to three	*a cuarto para las tres/*		*cinco*
	a las tres menos quince	in ten minutes	*en diez minutos*
it's one o'clock	*es la una*	five hours	*cinco horas*
it's seven o'clock	*son las siete*	does it take long?	*¿tarda mucho?*

Numbers

one	*uno/una*	sixteen	*dieciséis*
two	*dos*	seventeen	*diecisiete*
three	*tres*	eighteen	*dieciocho*
four	*cuatro*	nineteen	*diecinueve*
five	*cinco*	twenty	*veinte*
six	*seis*	twenty-one	*veintiuno*
seven	*siete*	thirty	*treinta*
eight	*ocho*	forty	*cuarenta*
nine	*nueve*	fifty	*cincuenta*
ten	*diez*	sixty	*sesenta*
eleven	*once*	seventy	*setenta*
twelve	*doce*	eighty	*ochenta*
thirteen	*trece*	ninety	*noventa*
fourteen	*catorce*	hundred	*cien/ciento*
fifteen	*quince*	thousand	*mil*

Food

avocado	*el aguacate*	fish	*el pescado*
baked	*al horno*	fork	*el tenedor*
bakery	*la panadería*	fried	*frito*
banana	*el plátano*	garlic	*el ajo*
beans	*los frijoles/*	goat	*el chivo*
	las habichuelas	grapefruit	*la toronja/el pomelo*
beef	*la carne de res*	grill	*la parrilla*
beef steak or pork fillet	*el bistec*	grilled/griddled	*a la plancha*
boiled rice	*el arroz blanco*	guava	*la guayaba*
bread	*el pan*	ham	*el jamón*
breakfast	*el desayuno*	hamburger	*la hamburguesa*
butter	*la mantequilla*	hot, spicy	*picante*
cake	*el pastel*	ice cream	*el helado*
chewing gum	*el chicle*	jam	*la mermelada*
chicken	*el pollo*	knife	*el cuchillo*
chilli or green pepper	*el ají/pimiento*	lime	*el limón*
clear soup, stock	*el caldo*	lobster	*la langosta*
cooked	*cocido*	lunch	*el almuerzo/la comida*
dining room	*el comedor*	meal	*la comida*
egg	*el huevo*	meat	*la carne*

minced meat	*el picadillo*	sausage	*la longaniza/el chorizo*
onion	*la cebolla*	scrambled eggs	*los huevos revueltos*
orange	*la naranja*	seafood	*los mariscos*
pepper	*el pimiento*	soup	*la sopa*
pasty, turnover	*la empanada/*	spoon	*la cuchara*
	el pastelito	squash	*la calabaza*
pork	*el cerdo*	squid	*los calamares*
potato	*la papa*	supper	*la cena*
prawns	*los camarones*	sweet	*dulce*
raw	*crudo*	to eat	*comer*
restaurant	*el restaurante*	toasted	*tostado*
salad	*la ensalada*	turkey	*el pavo*
salt	*la sal*	vegetables	*los legumbres/vegetales*
sandwich	*el bocadillo*	without meat	*sin carne*
sauce	*la salsa*	yam	*el camote*

Drink

beer	*la cerveza*	ice/without ice	*el hielo/sin hielo*
boiled	*hervido/a*	juice	*el jugo*
bottled	*en botella*	lemonade	*la limonada*
camomile tea	*la manzanilla*	milk	*la leche*
canned	*en lata*	mint	*la menta*
coffee	*el café*	rum	*el ron*
coffee, white	*el café con leche*	soft drink	*el refresco*
cold	*frío*	sugar	*el azúcar*
cup	*la taza*	tea	*el té*
drink	*la bebida*	to drink	*beber/tomar*
drunk	*borracho/a*	water	*el agua*
firewater	*el aguardiente*	water, carbonated	*el agua mineral con gas*
fruit milkshake	*el batido/licuado*	water, still mineral	*el agua mineral sin gas*
glass	*el vaso*	wine, red	*el vino tinto*
hot	*caliente*	wine, white	*el vino blanco*

Key verbs

to go	**ir**
I go	*voy*
you go (familiar)	*vas*
he, she, it goes,	
you (formal) go	*va*
we go	*vamos*
they, you (plural) go	*van*

to have (possess)	**tener**
I have	*tengo*
you (familiar) have	*tienes*
he, she, it,	
you (formal) have	*tiene*
we have	*tenemos*
they, you (plural) have	*tienen*

there is/are	*hay*
there isn't/aren't	*no hay*

to be	**ser**	estar
I am	soy	estoy
you are	eres	estás
he, she, it is,		
you (formal) are	es	está
we are	somos	estamos
they, you (plural) are	son	están

This section has been assembled on the basis of glossaries compiled by André de Mendonça and David Gilmour of South American Experience, London, and the Latin American Travel Advisor, No 9, March 1996

Index

Titles available in the Footprint *Focus* range

Latin America	UK RRP	US RRP
Bahia & Salvador	£7.99	$11.95
Buenos Aires & Pampas	£7.99	$11.95
Costa Rica	£8.99	$12.95
Cuzco, La Paz & Lake Titicaca	£8.99	$12.95
El Salvador	£5.99	$8.95
Guadalajara & Pacific Coast	£6.99	$9.95
Guatemala	£8.99	$12.95
Guyana, Guyane & Suriname	£5.99	$8.95
Havana	£6.99	$9.95
Honduras	£7.99	$11.95
Nicaragua	£7.99	$11.95
Paraguay	£5.99	$8.95
Quito & Galápagos Islands	£7.99	$11.95
Recife & Northeast Brazil	£7.99	$11.95
Rio de Janeiro	£8.99	$12.95
São Paulo	£5.99	$8.95
Uruguay	£6.99	$9.95
Venezuela	£8.99	$12.95
Yucatán Peninsula	£6.99	$9.95

Asia	UK RRP	US RRP
Angkor Wat	£5.99	$8.95
Bali & Lombok	£8.99	$12.95
Chennai & Tamil Nadu	£8.99	$12.95
Chiang Mai & Northern Thailand	£7.99	$11.95
Goa	£6.99	$9.95
Hanoi & Northern Vietnam	£8.99	$12.95
Ho Chi Minh City & Mekong Delta	£7.99	$11.95
Java	£7.99	$11.95
Kerala	£7.99	$11.95
Kolkata & West Bengal	£5.99	$8.95
Mumbai & Gujarat	£8.99	$12.95

Africa & Middle East	UK RRP	US RRP
Beirut	£6.99	$9.95
Damascus	£5.99	$8.95
Durban & KwaZulu Natal	£8.99	$12.95
Fès & Northern Morocco	£8.99	$12.95
Jerusalem	£8.99	$12.95
Johannesburg & Kruger National Park	£7.99	$11.95
Kenya's beaches	£8.99	$12.95
Kilimanjaro & Northern Tanzania	£8.99	$12.95
Zanzibar & Pemba	£7.99	$11.95

Europe	UK RRP	US RRP
Bilbao & Basque Region	£6.99	$9.95
Granada & Sierra Nevada	£6.99	$9.95
Málaga	£5.99	$8.95
Orkney & Shetland Islands	£5.99	$8.95
Skye & Outer Hebrides	£6.99	$9.95

North America	UK RRP	US RRP
Vancouver & Rockies	£8.99	$12.95

Australasia	UK RRP	US RRP
Brisbane & Queensland	£8.99	$12.95
Perth	£7.99	$11.95

For the latest books, e-books and smart phone app releases, and a wealth of travel information, visit us at:
www.footprinttravelguides.com.

footprinttravelguides.com

Join us on facebook for the latest travel news, product releases, offers and amazing competitions: www.facebook.com/footprintbooks.com.